D0065369

Praise for
EVERYDAY HOCKEY HEROES

"In these moving, inspirational, and entertaining stories, Bob McKenzie, the 'Mr. Hockey' of insight and analysis, and sportscaster extraordinaire Jim Lang have found the pulse of Canada—and the beat is as strong and healthy as ever."

Roy MacGregor, bestselling author of
Wayne Gretzky's Ghost and *The Home Team*

"Inspiring. Truly hard to put down. Bob's and Jim's great storytelling abilities prove that hockey is so much more than just a game. Loved it!"

David Chilton, bestselling author of *The Wealthy Barber*

"Hockey never ceases to amaze me with the quality of the people in the game. This book is full of hockey champions who will inspire you and show you the true depth of the people in and around this game."

Brian Burke, former NHL executive

"These heartwarming stories illustrate the power hockey has to unite us and inspire us to be the best we can be."

James Duthie, TSN Hockey host

"My friends Bob McKenzie and Jim Lang have a lifetime of stories from covering the great game, and these pages are wonderful evidence of what they've collected over the years. You'll laugh at times, you'll be inspired at times, and you may even cry as well, but through it all you'll know that Canada is hockey and hockey is Canada. It really is *our* game."

Peter Mansbridge

"Compelling accounts of personal strength and the power of hope. *Everyday Hockey Heroes* gives a spotlight to important issues that people are dealing with and exhibits their ability to not only overcome these obstacles but, more important, to try to make positive change in the wake of them."

> Sheldon Kennedy, former NHL player and founder
> of the Sheldon Kennedy Child Advocacy Centre

"Bob and Jim shed some fantastic light on a coast-to-coast truth: there are hockey heroes in every rink in Canada. *Everyday Hockey Heroes* reminds us that you don't need to make a million to be a real hockey hero."

> Ken Reid, Sportsnet Central anchor and
> author of *Hockey Card Stories 2*

"By seeing hockey at the margins, Bob McKenzie and Jim Lang's work shines with a kind of log-cabin storytelling, illuminating the sport's humanity and showing that every path is crooked no matter where you end up in the game."

> Dave Bidini, author of *Keon and Me* and member of Rheostatics

"These heartwarming stories illustrate the power hockey has to unite us and inspire us to be the best we can be."

> James Duthie, TSN Hockey host

ALSO BY BOB McKENZIE AND JIM LANG

Everyday Hockey Heroes

EVERYDAY HOCKEY HEROES

VOLUME II

MORE INSPIRING STORIES ABOUT OUR GREAT GAME

BOB McKENZIE
& JIM LANG

Published by Simon & Schuster
NEW YORK   LONDON   TORONTO   SYDNEY   NEW DELHI

SIMON &
SCHUSTER
CANADA

Simon & Schuster Canada
A Division of Simon & Schuster, Inc.
166 King Street East, Suite 300
Toronto, Ontario M5A 1J3

This Simon & Schuster Canada edition November 2020

SIMON & SCHUSTER CANADA and colophon are trademarks of Simon & Schuster, Inc.

For information about special discounts for bulk purchases,
please contact Simon & Schuster Special Sales at 1-800-268-3216
or CustomerService@simonandschuster.ca.

Manufactured in the United States of America

1   3   5   7   9   10   8   6   4   2

Library and Archives Canada Cataloguing in Publication
Title: Everyday hockey heroes 2 : more inspiring stories about our great game
/ Bob McKenzie with Jim Lang.
Other titles: Everyday hockey heroes two
Names: McKenzie, Bob, author. | Lang, Jim, 1965– author.
Description: Simon & Schuster Canada edition
Identifiers: Canadiana (print) 20200206494 | Canadiana (print) 20200206508 |
Canadiana (ebook)
20200206508 | ISBN 9781982132705 (hardcover) | ISBN 9781982132712 (ebook)
Subjects: LCSH: Hockey—Canada—Biography. | LCSH: Hockey—Canada.
Classification: LCC GV848.5.A1 M2953 2020 | DDC 796.962092/2—dc23

ISBN 978-1-9821-3270-5
ISBN 978-1-9821-3271-2 (ebook)

*To all the frontline workers who put themselves in harm's way
for the greater good in the fight against Covid-19.*

Contents

Introduction

Out of darkness comes light; out of despair comes hope.

That's how I felt in the spring of 2018, when I was writing the introduction for the first volume in this series. That's how I feel again in the spring of 2020 as I write this now for *Everyday Hockey Heroes, Volume II*. Two years ago, it was the Humboldt Broncos' horrific bus tragedy that caused so much darkness and despair, but how so many responded to it brought so much light and hope. Now it's the Covid-19 crisis.

It's not easy to find a silver lining to a pandemic that has afflicted millions and killed hundreds of thousands while crippling the global economy and our very way of life. Yet here we are, lauding the determination, sacrifice, and sheer courage of frontline workers who put themselves in harm's way around the clock in order to serve the community.

The virus is highly contagious. But so is the human spirit. It's incredible how many earnest people, in the face of a life-and-death struggle, find a way to help make things better. And it never ceases to amaze me how hockey ends up being woven into the very fabric of those ties that bind and, of course, inspire us.

Take Sulemaan Ahmed. Sulemaan is a first-generation Canadian. His father, Saleem, came to Canada from Pakistan to study in 1963 and married Tahira when she emigrated nine years later. Saleem got a job at CBC; Tahira is a medical doctor. But to say that the Ahmed family is crazy about hockey, most notably the Montreal Canadiens, well, no words do justice.

"My mother arrived in Canada in the 1970s and immediately fell in love with hockey," Sulemaan said. "Her favourite player was Guy Lafleur. She loved the Canadiens."

She still does. Dr. Tahira Ahmed has a Guy Lafleur–autographed photo in her medical office.

One of the most well-told family stories goes something like this. The Ahmed home was bustling with preparations for a big traditional wedding celebration and was being used to rehearse an elaborate Bollywood-level dance production. The music was playing and a large gathering of the wedding party was there dancing up a storm when Sulemaan's mother rolled in.

Tahira pulled the plug on the music, quite literally, and turned on the television. "It's the playoffs, Boston-Montreal, the game is on," she said. And that was it, end of discussion, end of dance rehearsal.

Sulemaan inherited his mother's unbridled passion for the *bleu, blanc, et rouge* and devoured all things hockey, including a subscription to *The Hockey News*. And he's still a die-hard Habs fan today.

Sulemaan and his wife, Khadija Cajee, now live with their three children in Markham, Ontario, where they run a business that trains senior executives to use digital and social media effectively. When the coronavirus pandemic hit Canada hard in March of 2020—knowing so many people in the medical community, including Sulemaan's mother—they had to do something to help.

So they launched Conquer Covid-19, a grassroots initiative that started with just the two of them. The mission was to get much-needed but difficult-to-obtain personal protective equipment (PPE) to Canadian frontline workers, quickly and efficiently. They created a website, took to social media, created a profile for their new organization, and then assembled their starting lineup—the core group that shared their vision and values.

"You start with six, just like in hockey," Sulemaan said. "A goalie, two defencemen, three forwards. Then you build it from there."

Within two weeks, Hockey Hall of Fame player Hayley Wickenheiser—who simultaneously works as assistant director of player development with the Toronto Maple Leafs and is a medical student in residency at a Toronto hospital where she is an aspiring emergency room physician—had teamed up with Conquer Covid-19, greatly raising its public profile. Hollywood actor Ryan Reynolds, a Vancouver native, jumped on board, too. Conquer Covid-19 had star power plus smart, committed, and passionate leadership. It took off. It went viral, so to speak.

In less than two months, it raised millions of dollars, mobilized community support across Canada on PPE drives, and recruited a fully volunteer base of one-hundred-plus who worked around the clock for weeks to help keep frontline workers all across the country safe.

Heroes.

Sulemaan bristled at the mere hint of any personal recognition for himself. His mantra, the essence of the organization, was and is: it's all about the frontline workers. The leadership of Conquer Covid-19 is as selfless as it is smart; they're willing to do whatever it takes to get the job done.

Even if it means Habs fan Sulemaan being photographed in a Toronto Maple Leaf jersey when Maple Leaf alumni Wendel Clark showed up at a Conquer Covid-19 PPE drive in Toronto. It was good-natured payback for the many Leaf fans in his group going the extra mile and it is, as Sulemaan is fond of saying, doing whatever it takes to "lift each other up."

Which brings us to this book in your hand. I believe these stories will lift you up, too. I know they did me.

Let's be candid, before the pandemic put everything on hold in mid-March, the 2019–20 NHL season was less than ideal for a number of reasons.

In November, Don Cherry was dismissed by Rogers from his iconic *Hockey Night in Canada Coach's Corner* platform for making on-air remarks that implied Toronto's immigrant population was in some way responsible for the dearth of people not wearing poppies for Remembrance Day. The intense fallout from that further contributed to the toxicity of the remarks.

That same month, Calgary Flames head coach Bill Peters was effectively forced to resign because of revelations he used racial slurs—involving a Black player, Akim Aliu—a decade earlier in the American Hockey League. It was subsequently revealed and confirmed that Peters had also struck a player on the bench during an NHL regular-season game when he was head coach of the Carolina Hurricanes.

In the aftermath of that, barely a week would seem to go by without another revelation of a hockey coach who had said or done something hurtful and unacceptable. It felt like professional hockey was experiencing an epidemic of sorts—before an actual epidemic shut things down in March. Hockey culture was taking a beating; it was under fire, and understandably so.

But here's the funny thing about hockey culture. Or any culture, for that matter. It's a double-edged sword. Can it be racist, homophobic, sexist, misogynistic, and toxic? Oh, yes, it can, it is, and, unfortunately, it will be. At times. There are stories on these pages that do not sugar-coat that.

But in many of these stories, there are also shining examples of how harmonious, tolerant, encouraging, welcoming, and inspiring hockey culture has been, can be, and will be.

NHL player Andrew Cogliano's story of dedication, sacrifice, and commitment to be an NHL iron man is at the very core of hockey culture. As is former pro player Joey Hishon's difficult battle to come back from the deep darkness and despair of a traumatic brain injury. So, too, is Jack Jablonski's heroic quest to courageously find purpose and joy after he was tragically paralyzed in a Minnesota high school hockey game. And the best of hockey culture is fully on display in the embodiment of #NoBadDays, a movement born out of the love of a father, NHL scout Rob Facca, for his amazing young son Louis, who was diagnosed with Duchenne muscular dystrophy.

Joey Gale's story of being in the closet and leaving hockey because of the toxicity and homophobia is heartbreaking. Yet it becomes so uplifting when something as seemingly simple as rainbow-coloured Pride Tape allowed him to express his true self and, ultimately, return to the game. The companion piece to that, on Jeff McLean and Dean Petruk, the founders of Pride Tape, is an absolute joy to behold. And I don't think I've ever read anything that so clearly illuminated and crystallized to me what it's like for young transgender hockey players who are trapped in a body they don't identify with than Jessica Platt's story, which shows just how much courage and determination it took for Jessica to transition and come back to hockey.

This book is also a soaring tribute to women in hockey and their ongoing efforts to keep breaking down barriers in a male-dominated sport that has come a long way but still has so far to go: Danièle Sauvageau, a former Olympic coach paving the way for a woman to one day become an NHL head coach. Alexandra Mandrycky, who with no real background in hockey rose to become a key NHL executive analyst and is part of the burgeoning cohort of women in the front offices of the NHL. Katie Guay, a pioneer not only in women's hockey officiating but someone who may very well have planted the seeds for a woman to referee an NHL regular-season game. Emilie Castonguay, a former player breaking into the male-dominated world of player agents and doing it with the number one prospect, Alexis Lafrenière, in the 2020 NHL draft.

At its best, Canadian hockey culture has always been about community and service. Nothing says community service quite like the stories of Danielle Grundy from British Columbia, Jeremy Rupke from Ontario, and Christian Gaudet from New Brunswick. These are amazing people who have done amazing things to lift others up.

I do hope you will like the first chapter in the book, about a journey back to my childhood, to compare and contrast my minor hockey life experiences with two Black players who grew up in what was then quite-white Scarborough, Ontario, a community that is now second to none in producing Black NHL players. Terry Mercury and Lindbergh Gonsalves never made it to pro hockey, but they have stories to tell, and we have lessons to learn.

Thanks to them, and all who allowed their stories to be told on these pages.

Hockey is for everyone, the slogan says. That's certainly the goal, an admirable one, and we must always strive to uphold it and give the words true meaning. Hockey culture is like any culture, really—there's good and there's bad. It's simply the way of our world. We must learn from the bad, continue to push for the good, celebrate it, and let it guide us.

Out of our worst always comes our best—the everyday hockey heroes of volume II.

Bob McKenzie

EVERYDAY HOCKEY HEROES

VOLUME II

Black and White

Bob McKenzie

I'm from Scarborough, Ontario. I consider it my hometown since my parents moved there when I was only three years old in 1959. It was home for the next twenty years. The only thing that has changed about Scarborough since then is everything.

Well, almost everything. The boundaries—Lake Ontario on the south, Steeles Avenue on the north, Victoria Park Avenue on the west, the Rouge River and its valley on the east—are still the same.

I grew up in a Scarborough that was quite white. It was first settled in 1799 by Scottish stonemason and farmer David Thomson and his wife Mary. As a young boy in the sixties, I briefly went to Sunday school at St. Andrew's Presbyterian Church, which was built on the Thomsons' land and includes a graveyard where they're buried. You could say Scarborough was the very picture of White Anglo-Saxon Protestant life, though WASP didn't necessarily mean affluent. Scarborough was far more middle class than upper crust. As near as I could tell, it was more blue collar, working class—a lot of young families of whom both parents needed to work to afford their first-time homes.

Today, the quite-white Scarborough of my youth has become one of the most ethnically and racially diverse communities in all of Canada. In the 2016 federal census, 67 percent of its population were visible minorities. Of the more than 630,000 people who called Scarborough home, 25 percent were from South Asia, 19 percent from China, and almost 11 percent were Black. Drive any thoroughfare and its multiculturalism is ubiquitous, from the faces of the people walking its streets to the cornucopia of international cuisines available to the strip mall signs in many languages.

Scarborough has earned national, at times international, recognition for its citizenry—comedian/actor Mike Myers (you didn't really think *Wayne's World* was set in Aurora, Illinois, did you?); The Barenaked Ladies; race car driver Paul Tracy; marathon swimmer Cindy Nicholas; Abel Makkonen Tesfaye, better known as the Grammy Award–winning singer/songwriter/producer The Weeknd; Olympic sprinter Ben Johnson, and countless pro athletes in the NHL, NBA, CFL, and NFL.

But in such a richly diverse Canadian community, it should come as no surprise that Scarborough is second to none in putting Black hockey players in the NHL.

While the first Black man to break the NHL colour barrier was from Fredericton, New Brunswick—Willie O'Ree in 1957—the next Black player to do so was from Scarborough. Mike Marson was the nineteenth overall selection in the 1974 NHL draft and played 196 games over six NHL seasons, surpassing O'Ree's 45 over two seasons. Marson was the first of many more from Scarborough to make the NHL.

Anson Carter played 698 NHL games between 1996 and 2007; his neighbourhood friend, goalie Kevin Weekes, played 357 games in a pro career between 1995 and 2009; Joel Ward played 809 NHL games in a thirteen-year career spanning 2005 to 2018. The Stewart brothers—Anthony and Chris, the latter of whom played part of the 2019–20 season with the Philadelphia Flyers—combined for 969 NHL games starting in 2005; Wayne Simmonds finished the 2019–20 season with the Buffalo Sabres, 953 NHL games and still counting in a career that started in 2008; Devante Smith-Pelly had 446 NHL games from 2011 to 2018, including playing a key role in the Washington Capitals' winning the Stanley Cup in 2018.

Nathan Robinson played seven NHL games in a pro career that spanned sixteen seasons, and goaltender Chris Beckford-Tseu saw action in part of one NHL game during his seven-year career, but they nevertheless helped swell the ranks of Black kids from Scarborough who can say they made it to the NHL.

That's ten in total and number eleven isn't far off.

Scarborough's next Black NHL standard-bearer will almost certainly be Akil Thomas, the Los Angeles Kings' second-round pick in 2018, who's expected to start his pro career in the 2020–21 season. Thomas scored the game-winning goal for Team Canada at the 2020 World Junior Hockey Championship.

Quantity and quality of Black NHL players; Scarborough has it all.

On a day when I was taking note of how many Black NHL players have come from my hometown, I started thinking about when I was a kid playing minor hockey. Mike Marson was born in 1955, the year before me, but I never saw him play minor hockey or even knew of him until he went on to the OHA Junior A Sudbury Wolves and then the NHL Washington Capitals. From 1964 to 1975, I had a Black teammate on only two occasions, but I do recall playing *against* a few players of colour in that eleven-year span. Two in particular stand out. Vividly. Even now I still remember them—one was tall and gangly; the other was shorter but strong and powerful—and how they played. There's no doubt they stood out to me because they were Black. To suggest otherwise would be silly. But these guys also stood out because they were good players, better than average in our age group and far better than me, though that was a pretty low bar.

There was a third reason I remember them so well—they had memorable names.

Terry Mercury.

Lindbergh Gonsalves.

I got to wondering what it might have been like for them—Black kids playing an almost all-white sport in an almost all-white community in the 1960s and 1970s—and it struck me that Terry Mercury and Lindbergh Gonsalves were pioneers of sorts. All these years later, they must have some stories to tell. Wouldn't it be interesting, I thought, to track them down and have a conversation.

And that's exactly what I did.

•   •   •

Terry Mercury's family tree could be featured as part of Black History Month. His father, David Austin Mercury Sr., was born and raised in Toronto, but Terry's paternal grandfather, Reverend George Luther Mercury, was born in St. Vincent and the Grenadines. When George Mercury couldn't get into divinity schools in Canada, he opted to go to the Tuskegee Institute in Alabama, which was headed up by Booker T. Washington, and later became Tuskegee University. In fact, Booker T. Washington was one of George Mercury's professors.

"When I heard that, I thought, 'Oh, someone is blowing smoke' until my cousin showed me the photograph," Terry said. "I was like, 'Holeeeeee, there's my grandfather in this classroom and there's Booker T. Washington at the front of the class.'"

Terry's paternal grandmother, Gladys Smith, was from the tiny St. Mary Parish in Jamaica, just miles away from where Bob Marley would later grow up.

Terry's mom, Barbara Thompson, has roots that date back to 1800s Virginia. "My mom's family came to Canada via the Underground Railroad," Terry told me. "That makes me a sixth-generation Canadian on my mom's side of the family."

Terry's parents met in Toronto. His dad attended Harbord Collegiate and his mom went to Central Tech, two high schools separated by less than a kilometre in Toronto's west end. Terry was born December 14, 1956, at Toronto General Hospital, the fourth of six Mercury children, three boys and three girls. Of the six, three were adopted.

His dad worked as a real estate agent, mostly for RE/MAX, while his mom was an operator for Bell Canada. When Terry was four, his parents—like many young couples living in the city at the time—wanted a new home in wider, more open spaces and found just that in the Midland-Eglinton area of Scarborough. Terry and his siblings went to nearby Lord Roberts Public School. They weren't the only Black family in the new neighbourhood, but the fact Terry can remember the name of the only other one—the Berrys—paints the picture pretty well.

What Terry quickly realized is that he loved hockey.

"I played it all the time," he said. "I played street hockey with my friends until the streetlights came on. Then I'd go downstairs into the rec room and play with the net that my dad got me for Christmas. But I remember being scared to skate because I didn't want my friends to see me fall down." Terry, who would grow up to be six-foot-three, was always a tall kid, much taller and more gangly than other kids his age. "I was all arms and legs," he said with a laugh. "I didn't want them to find out I couldn't skate."

Terry's father had none of that. For the 1964–65 season, he registered Terry for Cedar Hill House League, which played their games at McGregor Park Arena, a two-pad outdoor rink that was just a couple of miles from their home.

"I'll never forget it," Terry said of his first time on skates. "My dad pushed me out on the ice and I couldn't skate. I wanted to get off, but he said, 'No, you've been bugging me about buying you hockey sticks and a net. Just get out there and learn to skate.' He wouldn't let me off the ice. And by the end of the season, I could skate."

Those two years playing house league for Cedar Hill were pretty idyllic for Terry, who was eight and nine at the time.

"Kids that age just want to play hockey and have fun," Terry said. "It was completely innocent. I was a member of the Paul Willison Valiants. All of my teammates were white and I was Black and it didn't matter to them or me. I was just one of the guys. We'd sit in the dressing room and laugh and have fun and I'd have other fathers on the team come up to me, pat me on the shoulder, 'You go get 'em out there, Terry,' and they would sit with my dad and drink hot coffee to stay warm. My dad had helped some of the other fathers buy houses and they appreciated that. I was accepted, my dad was accepted. You know how they talk about 'hockey being for everyone'? Well, I look back on that time period and that's when I felt hockey really was everyone's game."

The innocence and joy of those early years would soon be gone. It started in Terry's third year of hockey when he moved up to a more competitive level of play, with the West Hill Rangers minor atom team that played in the Metro Toronto Hockey League (MTHL).

Terry started on defence, was more or less happy just to be there. Fairly early in the season, though, he recalled a game in which he saw an opening and took off with the puck and made a play. The coach was surprised at how well he could skate and encouraged him to keep taking off with the puck anytime the opportunity presented itself. So he did. He had the puck more and was having more of an impact on the games. His confidence grew, but so did resentment from some teammates and their parents.

"A couple of the guys wanted to be the stars, and all of a sudden I was being talked about," Terry recalled. "People would say, 'Look at

Terry at eleven years old on the ice with the Scarboro Olympics in his major atom year. Even then, he was all arms and legs as evidenced by the short sleeves of his jersey.

number six, look at him fly.' It was just normal jealousy that happens in hockey sometimes. I don't believe it started out as racist, but I think it became that after parents started complaining to the coach. They would say, 'Not him,' and my father would respond, 'What do you mean, not him?' That's when I would hear my mom and dad talking in hushed tones in the kitchen, and when I'd walk in, the conversation would stop. I'd ask them what they were talking about and they'd say, 'Nothing you need to know. Just go play hockey and have fun.'"

Some teammates, who had seemed to embrace him at the beginning of the season, stopped talking to him, but there were others who remained his friends all season long. Terry said he was, at times, subjected to racial epithets from opposing players—including the N-word among other assorted slurs—but he'd also known he was going to get it because he was emerging as a pretty good player. If he hadn't had the puck so much, he probably would have been insulted less.

There was more change coming for Terry. A couple of years before high school, his family moved farther east to a neighbourhood on the shores of Lake Ontario called Guildwood. Now, Guildwood would never be confused with, say, Rosedale, Toronto's bastion of great wealth and status. But the Guildwood subdivision, including its landmark centrepiece, the storied Guild Inn, was widely recognized in Scarborough circles as a prestigious address.

Terry described living there as akin to "all this white paper and a couple of black dots." The houses on either side of the Mercurys' new home were a microcosm of the whole neighbourhood. The Mercurys lived at number 23. The Zimmermans were at number 21. Mrs. Zimmerman and Terry's mom became best of friends. The family at number 25?

"Didn't know them," Terry said. "Never spoke to them, they never spoke to us. They wanted nothing to do with us. That's just the way it was in that neighbourhood. Half spoke to us; half didn't."

In fact, a couple of weeks after the move, a neighbour showed Terry's dad a scribbled note from a group of other neighbours who had discussed buying the Mercurys' house so they wouldn't have a Black family living on the street. The man said it was wrong and he wasn't part of it, but he wanted my parents to be aware of what was going on. Terry's dad explained to the kids that, "Some people, well, some people are like that."

As Terry grew older, he started to be warier of his surroundings and was careful to keep his guard up. His father had a thick skin, but his mother was much more sensitive. Which is to say his dad was more likely not to be rattled by someone's ignorance or respond to it; his mom was more likely to make an issue if she felt someone was out of line. Terry tended to lean more toward his mother's temperament, but his dad would tell him, "Terry, it's like getting mixed up with barbed wire, when you say something back to them, it only makes it worse; it gets them angrier."

Once Terry got to his teen years, he knew himself that the social scene would present new complications. And his father sat him down and said, "Look, with parties and everything, it's probably not for you." Fortunately, he was more interested in sports than girls or parties and would often spend Saturday nights at Heron Park Arena playing pickup hockey. Terry knew he was also potentially saving himself from being in difficult spots, where racism was more likely to boil over than simmer, but with all that testosterone kicking in for him and his teammates, hockey wasn't a total escape.

It was, as they say, the best of times and the worst of times. Mostly the worst, though. That was the story of Terry's major bantam season, 1970–71, with West Hill in the MTHL.

He was playing centre now, not defence, and was the tallest player on the ice. He was also named the team captain. The coach began the season by telling him: "You're the leader on this team. This team is going to go as far as you can take them."

Statistically, it was quite likely his best season ever. In every other respect, it was misery.

"My happiest point of the year was when we were eliminated from the playoffs and it was over," he said. "I was happy because I knew I would never have to go back into that dressing room again. It should

*Terry, middle second row, with the West Hill
hockey team in his minor bantam year.*

have been a happy time for me. The *Toronto Telegram* named them city all-stars and I remember seeing my name in the paper. My parents were so proud. But I just remember thinking, 'I can't wait for this to be over. This is really terrible.'"

The problem started with one teammate, whose father was a member of the right-wing John Birch Society, but it spread to others, creating a divided team. Terry was ostracized. Some teammates wouldn't talk to him. If they did, it was to taunt him or antagonize him. Other players on the team were fine with Terry, but he never felt like they truly understood what he was going through. It wasn't just that some of his teammates were making his life miserable, it was that he felt there were no consequences for the perpetrators. Instead, he was being portrayed as sullen and withdrawn, a kid with a chip on his shoulder, as if somehow *he* was the problem. That was particularly true of his coaches.

"Here I am, I'm thirteen, just turning fourteen, a young teenage kid. And I'm being told, 'Oh, just get over it.' At thirteen or fourteen, are you capable of showing that kind of maturity to just 'get over it'?

You don't have the articulation skills to tell people, 'Look, this is what's going on. This is what's bugging me. This is what I hate.' I couldn't explain the frustration and the resentment I was feeling when other people got angry with me for being good."

Or being Black.

Terry never felt as alone on a team as he did when that troublesome teammate taunted him with the N-word. "No teammate would tell the player, 'No, you can't say that.' They would just stand there. And some of them enjoyed the conflict; I think they liked seeing me upset." In a game in Leaside, even the referee called him the N-word. He came back to the bench extremely agitated and upset and explained to his coaches what was said. His winger on the ice backed him up, but his coaches told him to just let it go.

"That was such a bad year for me," Terry said. "It really coloured my view of the hockey culture for a long time. But it never coloured my view of the game. Hockey is the best game in the world, but it bothered me that so many people—coaches and players—would stand around and let that happen. I mean, do they not see what's wrong with this? I wasn't asking them to be my best friend, I was just asking them to be my teammates."

There was one ray of light that season and it came in the most surprising form: a tournament in Deerfield, Illinois, a well-to-do suburb just north of Chicago. The players on Terry's team were going to be billeted with local families. Terry's mom had grave concerns about letting Terry go—until she got a phone call ahead of time from Terry's billet family in Deerfield.

"The family's name was Boden," Terry recalled. "Mrs. Boden called my mom and said: 'I know your fears. I understand them. I get them. Terry will be safe with us. We will make sure that nothing happens to him.'"

The trip to Deerfield couldn't have gone any better, on and off the ice. Terry scored four goals in the first game and was amazed when the opposing players sought him out to tell him what a great game he had played. Mrs. Boden was true to her word: Terry found a warm and welcoming family who treated him, and his dad, like royalty. Terry even went to a party with the Boden kids.

"There wasn't one negative, not one," Terry said of the trip. "I'll never forget that."

Terry went on to play four more years of organized hockey after his ill-fated major Bantam season, but that one year took its toll. When his next season ended with the Dorset Park Bruins, he was called up to play a few playoff games with the Pickering Panthers of the Metro Toronto Junior B Hockey League. He did well enough, but he knew he was losing interest in hockey.

Terry's final year of high school at Sir Wilfrid Laurier Collegiate Institute was his final year playing hockey. It was his second season in the juvenile age group, a far cry from having the *Toronto Telegram* honouring him as a city all-star in Bantam. Juvenile hockey was a fine enough place for seventeen- and eighteen-year olds to continue playing hockey for fun, but for any teenager with aspirations to playing at a higher level, well, juvenile is where hockey dreams go to die.

Terry at sixteen in his school photo from
Sir Wilfrid Laurier Collegiate Institute.

The next year, Terry was off to carve out a career in broadcasting at Scarborough's Centennial College, where he also played on the varsity basketball team. He was asked to come out and play for the varsity hockey team, the Colts, but he declined. As did one of his classmates, a young man by the name of Paul Smithers.

Smithers is Black; biracial, actually. Just three years earlier on February 18, 1973, a racially charged on-ice dispute with a white player, Barry Cobby—Smithers was repeatedly being called the N-word by Cobby and opposing players and fans—had spilled over into the parking lot of Dixie Arena in Mississauga after the game. In the parking-lot fight, reportedly initiated by the sixteen-year-old Smithers, Cobby choked on his own vomit and died.

Smithers was found guilty of manslaughter, in a trial that got international attention, and was sentenced to six months in the minimum-security Brampton Adult Training Centre. It was reported that Smithers was the only Black player in the Mississauga midget league at the time; it was also reported that he was the best player in that league.

In 1976, Smithers was at Centennial College with Terry Mercury.

"The Colts wanted me to play hockey," Terry said. "And they wanted Paul to play, too. Paul told me, 'I don't play hockey anymore, I don't even play floor hockey. I just stay away from the game altogether.' Paul and I sat down and had a couple of long talks. I could understand where he was coming from."

• • •

Lindbergh Gonsalves's hockey journey began at eight or nine years old when he went pleasure skating on the then-brand-new outdoor rink at Nathan Phillips Square in the forecourt of City Hall. For a young kid from Antigua, it was a very Canadian thing to do—no, check that, a very Toronto thing to do.

"I didn't know much about hockey," Lin recalled. "I just saw the kids skating at the playground in the wintertime. I wanted to try that. So my dad got me brand-new skates. I would skate at the park, at the school, and I would venture out to other places, like City Hall. Everyone wanted to go skating at City Hall."

As Lin was zigzagging through all the people at the rink, he was approached by a man named Mr. Mills.

"Do you play hockey?" he asked Lin.

"No," Lin replied.

"Would you like to?"

"Yeah, yeah."

He took Lin's number and got in touch with his dad, and that's how Lin started playing hockey with the Toronto Olympics house league out of St. Mike's Arena.

None of that would have happened without Lin's maternal grandmother, Melanie Charles, who was responsible for bringing the Gonsalves family to Toronto in 1958. Melanie emigrated to Canada earlier in the 1950s and arranged for her daughter Naomi and son-in-law Alphonso to follow her. Lin was just two years old. He and his younger brother Bert were born in Antigua; his sister Debbie and brother Greg were born in Toronto, where his father worked as a longshoreman at the Toronto docks, and his mother got a job at Bell Canada.

They first moved into an apartment above Sherman's Hardware on Queen West, just a few blocks from City Hall. Lin doesn't remember feeling particularly singled out for being Black or an immigrant.

"I don't recall any kids of colour at my school then," Lin said. "There were one or two Chinese kids I can remember. I never had any problems there. We were all so small, right? Little kids, little kids that age, they don't know hatred."

Partway through Lin's elementary school years, the family moved east to Regent Park, the large public housing development in the three-city-block square east of Parliament Street and north of Queen. As early as the 1900s, when Regent Park was populated by mostly English and Irish immigrants, it was known as a poor, tough, and hardscrabble area of the city. In the 1960s, when the Gonsalves family arrived, there was a huge influx of visible minorities; it was one of the few spots in the city with affordable housing.

*Lin (left) and his brother, Bert (right), dressed
and ready to go down to St. Mike's Arena
for their house league games.*

"There were a lot of Black people, so there were no issues with racism," he said, chuckling. "But we weren't there long, maybe a year and a half. My grandmother and mother, they were the ambitious type. They wanted to get out of there."

And they did. The Gonsalves family was off to quite-white Scarborough.

Moving onto Packard Boulevard, Lin wasn't the only Black kid at St. Andrew's Public School. There was Dan Thompson (Terry Mercury's cousin), Brian Bush, and Phil Knight, but he still had to fight, literally, to stake out his new territory.

"It was just about all white," Lin said of his grade-five and grade-six school years at St. Andrew's. "When I went to St. Andrew's, the first guy I had a problem with was Dwight Foster. He was bugging my younger brother because they were in the same grade. My brother told me, 'This guy named Dee-wight, he keeps bugging me, man.' So, you know, I had to pay a visit to Dee-wight. I just, kind of like, told him to leave my brother alone. And, yeah, we had a scuffle." At that point, Lin paused to have a really good, long laugh. "Oh, yeah, we had a scuffle, for sure. You know what? That's what it takes sometimes to make friends. Yeah, I truly believe that's what it takes to make friends."

Dwight Foster and Lin did become friends. Fifty years later, they're still friends and they see each other once or twice a year along with some other St. Andrew's classmates.

For 1956-born hockey players from Scarborough, Dwight Foster was a very big deal. Which is kind of funny, because Foster was actually born in 1957, but he always played up a year against those born in '56. He was that good. Foster was a big-time player for the Toronto Red Wings of the MTHL. He was the man—fast, strong, powerful, and skilled. He was the guy everyone else used as a measuring stick, a rival, someone to do battle with, as Lin did in the schoolyard and on the ice.

The kicker, of course, is that Foster went on to play in the NHL. He played four years with the OHA Junior A Kitchener Rangers and remains the franchise's leading scorer of all time. He was selected in the first round, sixteenth overall, by the Boston Bruins in the 1977 NHL amateur draft. He went on to play more than five hundred NHL games with Boston, Colorado, New Jersey, and Detroit.

Foster wasn't the only guy Lin got into it with. Far from it. There were a lot of beefs, a lot of scores to be settled.

"Kids are insensitive. They say stupid stuff sometimes. I won't lie, yes, yes, I was in a lot of fights," he said, punctuating his words with a hearty laugh. "Sure, some kids would use the N-word or stuff like that. They would try to intimidate us because we were different. They would say, 'What are you doing here?' Because some of them had never seen Black guys before. So, yeah, I got into my fair share of scraps at school."

Though Lin never grew to be any taller than five-foot-seven and weigh more than 165 pounds, as a kid who was entering his teens, he was fearsomely powerful, strong, and well built. He was a physical specimen, far more athletic and physically mature than most of the kids his age. And, as evidenced by his fight card, competitive and fearless, too.

Small wonder then that he quickly developed as a hockey player, rocketing past the other kids in the Toronto Olympics house league program. He and his parents were a little miffed that Lin didn't get elevated to play rep hockey for the Olympics, but in Pee Wee, at age twelve, he did get to play for an Olympics all-star entry in the season-ending King Clancy tournament.

Lin's team lost in overtime against a much more highly regarded MTHL team, the Agincourt Canadians, sponsored by Horton's Spice Mills and coached by Tom Horton Sr., but Lin made an impression on Horton. Immediately following that season, Horton showed up at the Toronto docks to convince Alphonso Gonsalves that his son should play with the Horton's Spice Mills Canadians in the coming minor Bantam season.

"I don't know how he found my dad but he must have scoured the city," Lin said. "He told my dad, 'I want your son on my team.'" It was a seminal moment for Lin Gonsalves. "For me, Tom Horton was the greatest coach in the world. He was so good to me. My dad was working a lot and my mom didn't drive, so Tom drove me to nine out of every ten games and practices. I loved that guy."

After minor Bantam, Tom Horton moved his sponsorship over to the Toronto Red Wings and Lin went right along with him for the following seasons. Lin was playing with and against the top players in the city, doing well, having fun, and completely supported by the head coach. It was joy to play on those Horton-coached teams because there was never any issue with any teammates. Lin was just one of the guys, fully embraced and accepted. But he did get a rough ride from opposing players and teams. Was it because he was Black? Or because he was a better-than-average player?

"Let's say it was both," Lin said. "Sometimes I would look across the ice to the other bench and I'd see the coaches telling their guys, 'You gotta get that guy,' because maybe I just finished scoring a goal. But things were said, too. All the usual stuff about being Black. It wasn't always easy for me. But my team was great. We stuck together, we helped one another. Tom would see the stuff happening and notice I was down a bit and he'd say, 'C'mon, no problem, don't worry.' He picked me back up. Such a great guy, a great motivator. He had my back all the time."

Lin wasn't just a very good hockey player; he was a very good multi-sport athlete. He played baseball for Scarborough Village and soccer for the Scarborough Spurs; he ran track and did pole vault at school; he loved football and excelled at it, too.

Meanwhile, he was progressing up the ranks in hockey. He didn't grow as tall or big as others, but he was still very athletic. He played for the Toronto Red Wings Butter Beeps midgets and then the Red Wings Metro Junior B team, but hockey took a decided turn for the worse once he got to Junior B, at age sixteen and seventeen.

"It was harder for me," Lin said. "The guys on the team, they had already been there for a while. I was a rookie coming in. It was a whole new game. I just never felt comfortable either because I wasn't as welcome as I had been on my other teams." It wasn't necessarily overt racism, Lin said. Call it whatever you want, but he wasn't well accepted by his own teammates. "The guys on that team weren't very receptive to me. I guess it was because I was the only Black guy there and they didn't know me at all. I lost that feeling of being on a team. Then I lost my drive. That junior team took all the wind out of my sails. Hockey wasn't the same for me after that."

Lin still played some juvenile hockey, as well as soccer and junior football, first with the Woburn Wildcats and then as a running back for the Oshawa Hawkeyes in the high-level (under twenty-three) Ontario Junior Football League. He said he was on the verge of getting a tryout with the CFL Toronto Argonauts but a badly dislocated shoulder snuffed that out. He still managed to find some bright spots in hockey as a teenager, including a team trip to Newfoundland that he'll never forget.

"I loved Newfoundland," he said. "I love those Newfies. They welcomed us into their homes. They are the greatest, friendliest people on earth. No racism. None. That was one of the best experiences I ever had playing hockey. I'll never forget it."

Once Lin graduated high school and got into his twenties—his shoulder issue ended his competitive football days—he quickly settled into a workingman's life. His job was in production at an automotive parts company, one he would hold for thirty-three years before retiring. While he was working, he was still playing a lot of sports, including the weekend-warrior competitive Metro (Toronto) Touch Football League. He still played some men's league hockey, too. He was one of the better players. Which meant, men's hockey being men's hockey, it would sometimes get a little stupid.

"Some idiot ran me into the boards and screwed up my back," Lin recalled. "I had to miss a month of work. My boss, Randy, called me into the office and told me, 'You gotta quit playing hockey. You should referee hockey.' Randy was a ref. He said, 'Trust me, you'll make some nice money, you'll stay involved in the game, and you won't miss work because you're injured.'"

Lin hated the idea. Randy kept pestering him. Finally, Lin succumbed, took the certification course, and was assigned a little kids' game. He loathed every minute of it. One of the coaches never stopped yelling at him. Did he think it might have been racially motivated?

"Who knows?" he said, laughing. "Probably was, but all referees get yelled at, right?"

As he was taking off his skates, fully intending to never officiate another game, the referee supervisor for the league came in, Norm Belyea. Lin told him he was quitting. "I was so pissed. But Norm, who was a great guy, talked me through it. If it wasn't for Norm, I would have never refereed another game."

Instead, Lin went on to officiate hundreds if not thousands of minor hockey games. He did little kids to high-end AAA minor midget games in the MTHL. He got to see and officiate games involving many future NHLers, including some of the young Black players

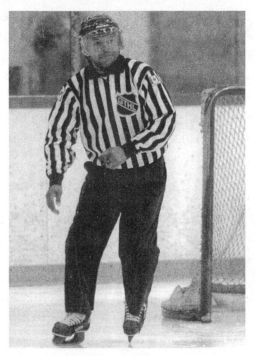

*Lin on the ice once more as a referee for
the Greater Toronto Hockey League.*

currently starring in pro hockey. He recalled one game in particular, the finals of the Toronto Marlies Christmas tourney, when he called a penalty shot in the final minute and the resulting goal gave P. K. Subban's team a win over John Tavares's Marlie team.

Lin had rediscovered his passion for hockey, this time in the black-and-white world of an on-ice official.

He got used to the verbal abuse, didn't overly concern himself about whether it was racially motivated or just the normal by-product of the job and/or the idiocy of minor hockey coaches and parents. But that isn't to say racism didn't rear its ugly head.

Lin was asked to fill in as a last-minute replacement linesman for a Junior A game at Herb Carnegie North York Centennial Arena. The other linesman he would be working with hadn't been told about the switch until Lin showed up. It was clear to Lin that he didn't like that, or him. The rest of the officiating crew that day, which included venerable veteran ref Ralph Sparks, something of an amateur zebra legend, welcomed Lin with open arms. But not this one fellow linesman. Lin has no doubt the issue was racial.

"Some people—not all of them, not many of them, really—are just like that," Lin said. "When you grow up with it, you just learn how to deflect it and move on."

◆　　◆　　◆

Being the same age and growing up at the same time in Scarborough, I can identify with many things in the lives of Terry Mercury and Lindbergh Gonsalves.

Terry moved to Scarborough at age four; I moved there at three. Lindbergh's house was less than two kilometres from mine; his school, St. Andrew's, was barely a ten-minute walk from my home. Lindbergh and his friends played in the same open fields and forest on the north side of Ellesmere Avenue, now home to the Scarborough Town Centre, as I did with my friends.

Our parents all held down jobs: Terry's dad in real estate, his mom at Bell; Lindbergh's dad as a stevedore, his mom also at Bell; my dad, Bob Sr., on the production line at de Havilland Aircraft, my mom, Maureen, in the service department of Golden Mile Chevrolet. They all had dreamed of buying their first homes, which they did in Scarborough.

And of course, the three of us had hockey in common. We all spent every waking moment of our childhoods skating and playing the game. Terry's first two years of minor hockey, with Cedar Hill, were played at McGregor Park Arena. My first two years, with Dorset Park, were also played there. Terry, Lindbergh, and I played games against each other.

Dwight Foster, to varying degrees, was a presence in all our lives. Foster was a hockey rival to Terry; he was at first a schoolyard foe, then a schoolyard friend/rival/teammate to Lindbergh. I got to know Dwight, if only superficially, because my good pal Ron Walker played on the Red Wings with him, and Dwight would come over to Ron's house on occasion and we would horse around together.

Yet, for all those shared experiences, there were two things I'd never be able to relate to. One, they were better-than-average hockey players; I was not. Two, they were Black; I was not.

The former caused me what little angst I would experience in minor hockey; the latter meant the vast majority of my minor hockey experiences were positive, if not idyllic, unlike Terry and Lindbergh's.

After two years in the Dorset Park House League, I moved up and played two more with the Agincourt Lions in the SHA. Both experiences were great. In Pee Wee, I played for the Scarborough Lions in a four-team division of the MTHL. It wasn't the highest calibre—my team didn't play against Dwight Foster's Red Wings, for example—but it was a big step up for me.

On the way to Pee Wee tryouts, my dad would often have to pull the car over to the side of the road so I could throw up. I was worried sick that I wasn't good enough; I was also concerned that Pee Wee hockey was getting a lot more physical. Let's just say I wasn't a naturally aggressive or confident kid.

I got by. And it was, all things considered, a pretty good year. My coach was Bob Park, the father of Hall of Fame defenceman Brad Park, who was just breaking into the NHL then. Brad would come out to tryouts and practices when he could. That was cool. We got to go to the 1969 Quebec International Peewee tournament. That was *very* cool.

Given my lack of confidence at these higher levels and my timidity, I'm not sure what possessed me to try out for the Agincourt Canadians, a team that did play at the top level, but I did. I made the team. It was coached and sponsored by Tom Horton Sr.

Lindbergh Gonsalves and I were teammates.

"We were teammates?" Lindbergh said with a cackle when I told him. "I didn't know that. Small world."

The reason Lindbergh didn't remember me was that we were only teammates for a few weeks. I was in over my head. I lacked confidence.

I was playing soft. Tom Horton called my parents to tell them I was being released.

I was devastated. Hurt, embarrassed, you name it. But *this* was as much hardship as I would ever face in minor hockey.

The long and short of it is that I went all the way back to the Cedar Hill House League for a couple of years, where I was one of the best players. My confidence soared at the lower level. When one of my friends' dads was entering a team into the MTHL minor midget division, and a bunch of my pals were playing on it, I made my rep hockey comeback. There was a moment of truth in an early season game when my old "friend," fear, returned. I decided that I either had to quit competitive hockey that night or go back out on the ice and overcome my fears. Inexplicably, a switch went off. I never took another backward step.

My yips were gone. I hit; I got hit. I fought and lost a lot, but I showed up. I went on to enjoy a great six-year run: two years in midget; two years in juvenile; and even two years in intermediate—you really had to love hockey to play intermediate. As far as juvenile hockey goes, I found my niche as a pretty good late bloomer and those years were the most fun I ever had playing the game.

My journey was the very opposite of that of Terry Mercury and Lindbergh Gonsalves, who played out the string in juvenile, robbed of their passion for the game. The difference could not have been more black-and-white.

◆　◆　◆

Five decades later, it wasn't difficult to find Terry Mercury and Lin Gonsalves.

If you listen to Sirius/XM satellite radio in Canada, you have probably heard the dulcet tones of Mercury, doing sports updates, among other assignments, on multiple sports and information channels there. He's been a sports or business broadcaster for much of his life, with stops in Cambridge, Kitchener, and Toronto.

Terry now lives with his wife, Esther, in the Don Mills area of

North York. He has one daughter, Samantha, from a previous marriage. His minor hockey teammates who may have found him quiet and withdrawn as a kid might be surprised at how warm, open, and naturally conversational he is now. He's a big man, six-foot-three, thicker now than the towering beanpole I remember, though he could say the same about me and my five-foot-nine frame.

As for Lin, it was probably twenty years ago, while at a minor hockey tournament of my son's in Toronto, that I saw a referee with GONSALVES on his nameplate. A Black referee. It had to be the same Lindbergh Gonsalves I remembered as a kid, and, of course, it was. Armed with that recollection, after I'd reached out to the Greater Toronto Hockey League office, it was easy to find Lin in 2020.

Lin now lives in the Morningside-Sheppard area of Scarborough, with his wife, Elizabeth, and their son, Leondre. Lin also has a daughter, Lisa, from his first marriage. He's been retired from his automotive parts company job for five years. Now he drives a school bus—Leondre is one of his passengers each day—and he stays extremely busy refereeing a lot of boys' and girls' hockey.

Lin is easygoing, quick to smile, prone to long, loud laughs, and, at his current height and weight of five-foot-seven and 165 pounds, he seems much smaller and slighter than I remember him, but he still gives off a lean athletic vibe, very much unlike his inquisitor.

Terry and Lin couldn't have been more open to taking this trip down memory lane, relating their childhood experiences in detail—painful as some of them were—and offering some adult perspective on them. As they shared their stories, it was obvious that, out of everything they went through, the racism and exclusion they experienced at the hands of their own teammates scarred them the most, and the fact that it went unacknowledged hurt—it still hurts.

"Even now," Terry said. "I'll come across someone I played with and they'll say, 'I remember playing with you, you didn't talk to anyone.' How could you not know? Could you not see the look on my face? How could you not hear those words? That's what makes me angry now. They said I had a chip on my shoulder. Teachers at school even said that about me. Could they all not see what was being said to me, how I was being treated? I went from being exasperated to upset to angry. It took time but I got better at articulating what my anger was about. It's one thing if you're my teammate and you see what's going on and take the path of least resistance, you *choose* to not stand up and say something. I get that. Not everyone will put themselves out there. But when you tell me it's not happening or it didn't happen? That's when I get really angry."

It's hard not to look back and think about how things might have been. Both Terry and Lin wonder how far they might have gone in hockey if they hadn't lost their passion for the game.

"Could I have had a career in hockey?" Terry wondered. "Could I have had a shot? I remember playing against Dwight Foster. I had people tell me I was better than him. Was I? I don't know, but I never gave it a shot. That's the one thing I regret. I might not have been good enough, but I would have liked to find out, you know, rather than walk away. Now? I look back and see how silly it was to be resentful. I chose to walk away from hockey. They didn't chase me out. I chose to go. That's on me. That's one of the reasons I admire people like Tony McKegney or Jarome Iginla or Wayne Simmonds [Terry's second cousin]. They pushed through. Wayne had something that I maybe didn't have enough of—fire in the gut."

Lin echoed that sentiment: "I'll tell you, man, I'm not going to lie. If it wasn't for the year in Junior B, I don't know where I might have ended up with hockey. Those guys killed me. Yeah, man, they really killed me. Hockey was never the same for me after that . . . If I had to do it all over again, I would have stuck with it, tried to make it to the pros. You know why? Dwight Foster, because of my pal Dwight. He sticks in my mind because I was as good or better than him. He kept going. I didn't. Trust me, if you're a white guy, you're going to have it easier than a Black guy. Back then anyway. But I will say this: Dwight was really dedicated to hockey. The Red Wings had a summer camp up north. Dwight went to that all the time. I was asked to go. I didn't go. I was playing too many other sports, soccer and football. I wasn't

24/7 hockey, like Dwight was, like kids are today. When I went to junior, you had to be disciplined, you had to do things exactly this way for the coach, turn this way or do that. It was a big jump for me, a big change from playing for Tom Horton, who was really laid-back. I didn't like it. I wasn't disciplined. You know, I was on my own. I had no one to tell me. No one to blame, but I wish I knew then what I know now. Because I was better than Dwight."

And with that, Lin let out a good, long laugh, something the old St. Andrew's classmates can talk about when they next cruise the Toronto harbour on their annual summer reunion.

Lin, third from the right, and Dwight, second from the right, with the St. Andrew's crew on their annual boat cruise on Lake Ontario.

•　　•　　•

When I was growing up in Scarborough, Ontario, my family was working class, same as everyone else. My family life, though, was by no means easy, so I can honestly say I never felt privileged. But I like to think that over the course of my life, I've been able to figure out the difference between not growing up "privileged" but still growing up with "white privilege."

I was an only child, but that was because my mom was afflicted with severe rheumatoid arthritis when I was one. Having any more children for her was out of the question. Rheumatoid arthritis is a cruel, vicious, debilitating, crippling disease that attacks the joints and causes swelling, intense pain, and often disfigurement. This was especially true back in the 1950s and 1960s. My mom had surgery on at least fifteen to twenty occasions and pretty much every joint in her body was red, swollen, and/or severely disfigured. She was, every minute of every day I knew her, racked with pain. Yet for a good many years, she still managed to drive herself to the car dealership where she worked full-time. She eventually ended up in a wheelchair for the last fourteen years of her life and, quite suddenly really, died of complications from this dreaded disease at the age of fifty-nine in 1992.

That made my dad's life very tough, too. In addition to working his job and taking care of me when my mom was working nights, he had to be a caregiver to her. When she had to quit her job because of her arthritis, he had to take on a second job. In those fourteen years my mom was in a wheelchair, my dad's job as a caregiver was as full-time as his job at de Havilland. It was not an easy or joyous life for him. Or her.

In spite of the hand my parents were dealt, I grew up in a loving, caring family. My parents went out of their way to support me in all my endeavours, but especially, as a kid, playing minor hockey. They showed me the way—work ethic, sacrifice, commitment, and love. No time for pity parties. Everyone has a sad story. Onward and upward. No surrender.

That's how I was raised. And it was anything but privileged. But there's obviously a huge difference between my childhood and Terry's and Lin's. And that's white privilege.

White privilege isn't so much about what things in life you had to overcome as much as it is all the things you *didn't* have to overcome, simply because you are white in a predominantly white community. I never had to fight because of the colour of my skin. I was never harassed or excluded by my teammates because I was white. Outside of some confidence issues I had, minor hockey was mostly fun and welcoming for me. I was never ever made to feel like an outsider. Because I was white.

The very first time I had any inkling of white privilege was back in 1967, when I was eleven years old, in grade six at Bendale Public School. Our class that year read *Black Like Me* by John Howard Griffin, published in 1961 and later made into a movie. It was the story of a white American journalist from Texas who temporarily altered the pigment of his skin to effectively become a Black man and travelled through the Deep South—Louisiana, Mississippi, Alabama, Arkansas, and Georgia—in 1959. A jarring social science experiment, that book left a lasting impression on me at such a young age simply because of the virulence of the racism it described.

When I was talking to Terry Mercury and Lin Gonsalves about what it was like for them as Black children playing hockey and living in Scarborough in the 1960s, I couldn't help but think back to *Black Like Me*; I couldn't help but confront my own white privilege.

When Terry and Lin say they think they maybe could have played pro hockey, that they felt they were as good if not better than Dwight Foster, I could easily lapse into my job as a hockey analyst. I could be the utter pragmatist, maybe even cynically tell them, "Take a number; the road is littered with guys who coulda, woulda, shoulda played pro hockey if not for this or that." I could tell them that Dwight Foster was a year younger than them; that he *always* played at the highest competitive level and they didn't; that he was more disciplined than Lin, bigger than Lin, and more consistent than Terry; and that there's probably a trail of 1956-born white hockey players telling their friends they were as good or better than Dwight Foster, too. "That's hockey."

I could say all that, and I obviously considered some of those thoughts, because that's how I'm wired to do my job, to break things down. But you know what? I wouldn't tell them that. It's not my place to do so. Because for me, as a white man, it's utterly incomprehensible to *feel* what it's like to have your passion and love of the game stripped bare from you for no other reason than the colour of your skin. That's *not* hockey. Or at least it shouldn't have been, though it was for them.

Maybe Terry and Lin are right. Maybe under different circumstances, they could have played pro. Who am I to say? Who is anyone to say? It's their story to tell; it's their truth. I'm sure as hell not the guy to try to take that away from them, not after they had so much stolen from them as teenagers.

It's an incredible testament to both men that they have handled everything as well as they have. That qualifies them as everyday hockey heroes. They are indeed pioneers who helped pave the way for future generations of young Black kids from Scarborough to overcome their own experiences with racism. Some of them even made it to the NHL.

A favourite saying of mine over the years is: *never judge a man until you've walked a mile in his shoes.* I feel that's especially fitting as it relates to Terry Mercury and Lindbergh Gonsalves, even if I didn't take that walk, so to speak, until some fifty years after the fact.

Terry Mercury is a broadcaster on Sirius/XM Canada satellite radio. He lives in North York, Ontario, with his wife, Esther.

Lindbergh Gonsalves is a retired automotive parts worker, who currently referees and drives a school bus. He lives in Scarborough, Ontario, with his wife, Elizabeth, and their son, Leondre.

The Comeback Kid

Joey Hishon

I remember that day so clearly. I had been sitting on my bed, feeling sorry for myself and wondering if I would ever don my skates again, when my girlfriend, Dori, came up to me.

"Joey, there are people that don't think you can come back," she said.

I perked up. "What do you mean?"

"They don't believe that you want to get better. But I know you can."

Her words snapped me out of my funk. They made me realize that I was hurting myself more than helping myself. "You're right."

That night, I headed to the Rotary Arena and laced up my skates for the first time in fourteen months.

When I was growing up in Stratford, Ontario, the thought that someday I'd be working to make a comeback in hockey never crossed my mind. I was a classic Canadian kid who ate, slept, and breathed hockey, and I dreamed of playing in the NHL one day.

I was a bit of a rink rat. My dad worked at the Rotary Arena, right across the street from my school. Thanks to him, I skated countless hours. Every day at noon, I'd spring out of class to the arena and skate for at least forty minutes before sprinting back to school for the rest of my classes. On the weekends, my mom would drop me off at the arena and I'd stay there all day long with my dad. I thought I was helping him out, but I don't know if he saw it that way.

During the Christmas and March breaks, whenever there was an opening in the arena schedule, I'd get a call at home. "Hey, Joey, the ice is open." We lived only a short walk from the arena, so I would run to the rink and skate as long as I could.

When I wasn't at the arena, I was on the homemade rink my dad built in our backyard. Almost every day, whether it was late at night or early in the morning, my dad and my mom would be out there flooding the rink so it was always ready for me to skate on. They never pressured me to play—and I'll always respect them for that—it was just that I loved the game.

My parents have a video of me skating around the rink and my dad asking me, "How many goals are you going to score for the Leafs?"

I answered right away. "Seventy-one!"

I was always a bit smaller than the other kids on my team, but I was never afraid of getting hurt on the ice, and I wasn't. If anything, being small made me work harder on the ice to make sure I could keep up with my teammates.

Hockey was always where I made some of my best friends. Like

Practicing my shot on my backyard rink.

Ryan O'Reilly. I actually first met Ryan at a volleyball tournament, but we knew of each other through hockey, and by the next year we were playing spring hockey for the same team. Our games and practices were two hours away in Toronto, so we would carpool together. After that, we became good friends.

When I was fifteen, I made the Stratford Warriors Midget AA team. Going into that season, I wasn't thinking about the OHL draft; I was thinking about eventually playing for my favourite junior team, the Stratford Cullitons. But that season was my strongest yet and I was putting up good numbers each game. When OHL and NCAA teams and agents started to contact me, I realized I could do something with hockey, and I started to train harder to get to the next level.

In school, teachers would ask me what my backup plan was. I'd reply, "I don't need one." As I look back now, it would have been nice to have a better plan in life than that. But at the time, I saw hockey as a potential career.

By the end of that season, I'd played 50 games that year and finished the season with 44 goals and 42 assists. The day of the 2007 OHL draft, I was selected eighth overall by the Owen Sound Attack. It had always been my dream to play in the NHL, but until I was actually drafted, I never believed that my dream could become a reality.

Going into the draft, I only really knew of the London Knights and the Kitchener Rangers, and so I naturally was interested in playing for them. But as soon as I got up to Owen Sound, I knew it was where I belonged. It's such a small tight-knit community of hockey fans, and no matter where you go, there's someone who knows who you are.

I'll never forget my first road trip to the United States with the Attack. They had two busloads of fans—the Attack Pack—follow us to our games. They would drive to Plymouth and Saginaw, Michigan, and Erie, Pennsylvania. Seeing them in the seats at those road games was incredible for us players. And after we played, we'd go to their bus to thank them for their support and they would make us chocolate chip cookies and other snacks. Everywhere we went in Ontario and in the United States, they came along and cheered us on.

My good buddy Ryan was drafted by the Erie Otters, and every now and then, we faced off against each other when the Attack played the Otters. One night we were in Erie, set to take on the Otters. As Ryan was skating off the ice, I gave him a little whack on the back of his legs as a joke. Ryan didn't even react—he has ice water in his veins—but the next thing I knew, his teammates were coming at me.

The Otters were one of the toughest OHL teams, and Ryan's year boasted monsters like Mike Liambas, Luke Gazdic, and Anthony Peluso, and they had a lot of respect for Ryan and would do anything to protect him. Those guys chased me around the ice for the rest of the game. The whole time, I tried to plead my case. "He's my friend! He's my friend!" But they didn't care.

I made sure I never gave Ryan any "love taps" after that.

That first season with the Attack was so much fun. I finished the season with 20 goals and 27 assists in 63 games, which, as the youngest player on the team, was an impressive showing. I was lucky to have the perfect coach in Mark Reeds. He was ahead of his time. A lot of coaches back then yelled a lot more than they do now, but Mark never would. He was an unbelievable communicator and got us players to buy into what was best for the team in a way that also allowed each of us to pursue our own personal success. And if there was an issue, we'd have a conversation, man-to-man, and hash things out. That went a long way with me—he was a coach that treated us as people, not just players.

That summer, I moved in with Ryan for six weeks to train. Ryan's dad, Brian, is a life coach but he also ran a high-performance hockey boot camp every summer. He was a phenomenal trainer and can bring out the best in anybody. A lot of trainers talk about motivation, but the truth is that you can only motivate yourself. Brian taught me to evaluate my own work ethic so when he wasn't there, I could still keep pushing on. Something I would need to fall back on later in my life.

Over the next two seasons with the Attack, I came into my own, and each summer I would train with Ryan. Despite missing some games in the 2009–10 season because of a broken foot and slightly torn MCL, I was awarded the Attack's Harold Sutherland Cup for top draft prospect, making me eligible for the 2010 NHL entry draft.

I was told that I should expect to be drafted, but I had no idea who would select me. I had some good conversations with different teams. Both Montreal and Buffalo told me that they were picking later on in the first round, and if I was still there, I wouldn't get past their pick.

The day of the draft, I nervously awaited my fate with my mom and dad, and Joe Vanni, my roommate from Owen Sound.

Edmonton was picking first that year and they selected Taylor Hall first overall. Boston was up next, and on and on it went. As the Colorado Avalanche management walked up to the podium, I turned to Joe and said, "How cool would it be if the Avs took me?" They had taken Ryan in the second round the year before.

"That'd be awesome." Joe grinned.

The next thing I heard was "from the Owen Sound Attack." I looked up at the stage, my eyes bugging out. "Wait, really?" Then I heard my name.

I was in shock. I had just been drafted in the first round, seventeen overall. I was the Avs' first pick. After dealing with my injuries the past year, I was blown away by the confidence they had in me. I hugged my family and Joe, just ecstatic at the news. It was the most incredible feeling. Then I called Ryan to tell him.

That summer, I attended the Avalanche's rookie camp, and then I went to their main training camp, eager to play at the next level. Right away, I realized these were the smartest players I'd ever played with. We saw the ice and the game in the same way.

Speed and size were a different matter. I was drafted at the beginning of the hockey era in which first-round picks would make the team straightaway, and it hit me how much harder it was to get around the ice at the NHL level. It was tough to win a puck battle. These guys were older than me, in their twenties and thirties, and they made their living out of battling for the puck. Fortunately, I tended to play a pretty intense game. Being only five ten, I had a bit of chip on my shoulder, so the physicality of the Avs camp didn't bother me too much.

That said, I learned quickly that in the NHL, you have to stay close to the boards when you're in the offensive zone. During one of my first intra-squad games with the Avs, I went into the corner with veteran defenceman Adam Foote. It was a bit of a race to the puck and I got there first. Adam basically decided, "No, not today, kid." He grabbed me by the scruff of my neck and tossed me aside like he was throwing away an empty chip bag.

Adam was naturally strong; it wouldn't have mattered how much time I spent in a gym before the start of camp. Whatever Adam Foote wanted to do to me in that corner, he could. It was a learning experience I will never forget.

As I headed back to Owen Sound for one more year, I had a lot more confidence, and it showed. My game had clicked somehow, and with Mark's coaching, our team gelled on the ice. Garrett Wilson, who's now with the Toronto Maple Leafs organization, was a staple on my left wing the entire season and we worked really well together. In 50 games, I put up 87 points and was named OHL first-team all-star. I had been focused on team success, so to get that recognition was a huge honour.

In 2011, we rolled through the playoffs. We were the underdogs, but we came out on top, beating the Mississauga St. Michael's Majors in seven games to win the J. Ross Robertson Trophy and become OHL champions.

We were off to the Memorial Cup in Mississauga to compete for the title of junior ice hockey champions of the entire CHL.

Our first game of the round robin was against the Kootenay Ice. We were on the board with a goal late in the first period and followed up early in the second with another. Halfway through the third, we got another in. After that, I guess the Kootenay Ice were smarting from being behind because they started playing rough. At one point, this guy came at me after the whistle and we ended up trading a few blows, which got us both sent to the box for a roughing penalty.

After two minutes, I strode out of the box, eager to get back in the game. I remember trying to move the puck deep into the zone and scoot off the ice before the Ice defence cornered me. I was so focused I didn't even see Brayden McNabb barreling toward me. At the last second, I caught him out of the corner of my eye and tried to get away, but I was too late. McNabb's elbow collided with my head, snapping it sideways.

I didn't go down right away. It was like a fog fell over me. I turned away, thinking, *I've got to get to the bench.* But I only took a few strides before I fell, and then there was blood on the ice beneath me. The next thing I knew, our trainer, Andy Brown, came rushing out to take care of me. I had a cut above my eye and a broken nose and a pounding in my head.

Uh-oh, I thought as I lay there. *This is not good. I don't feel good at all.*

Two of my teammates helped me off the ice and into the dressing room. There were only about five minutes left in the game, so I stayed where I was as Andy did a brief evaluation. Meanwhile, on the ice, we scored two more goals, closing the game 5–0.

I felt fine after a few minutes, as fine as you can feel with a broken nose, I guess, so when I was told I was being named the third star of the game and asked if I wanted to go out on the ice, I said sure. When they announced the third star of the game and said my name, I went out, raised my stick in the air to acknowledge the crowd, then headed back to the dressing room.

That night, I stayed with the team in Mississauga and they monitored me closely, waking me up frequently. The next morning, the guys said, "You look like you went five rounds in the UFC."

I certainly felt like I had. One eye was swollen shut, the other was black, and my nose was so broken it looked like it was pointing sideways. My head was killing me.

I met with the training staff, who put me through the ImPACT testing to assess me for a concussion. Even though I felt like crap, I ended up passing. On paper, my cognitive functioning was fine and I was clear to play, but I knew something was wrong. The fog hadn't lifted. I had some sort of concussion.

I didn't want to let my team down. I was close with all the guys and we'd been battling hard all season to get to the Memorial Cup. But I knew I should sit out. It was a difficult decision—especially when on paper I had been cleared—but in the end, it was the right call. I was too sick to even attend that night's game.

I made it to the arena for the second game, still struggling with a raging headache. It was so frustrating to sit on the sidelines and watch the boys give it their all on the ice. We were losing and there was nothing I could do about it. The Memorial Cup slipped through our fingers.

Garrett worked hard to lift my spirits. He had suffered a concussion the game after I was injured, and while it wasn't as serious as mine, we supported each other.

After the tournament, I travelled with the team back to Owen Sound, but the season was over, so I went to my billet house, packed up my stuff, and I headed home to Stratford. From there, I was under the care of the Colorado Avalanche.

That first month, I continued to have severe headaches and neck pain, and I knew it was going to take a while to get healthy again. I spent a lot of time on the phone with doctors, going over all of my symptoms. I definitely had a concussion. They told me to take it easy and rest, which, after a long season, wasn't hard to do. I couldn't physically bring myself to do anything anyway. I just lay in my bedroom with the lights off.

After a couple of weeks, though, I had the urge to get going again. I'm a pretty active guy, and in the summer, I always enjoyed golfing, but if I felt up to going for a walk or doing some light exercise, I paid for it afterwards. I was plagued by constant headaches, my neck was in pain, and every once in a while I'd be hit with an unexpected bout of dizziness, which was especially frightening.

The Avs flew me to Colorado to get evaluated by a neurologist. He told me that my recovery would be a slow process and advised me to limit my physical activity as well as my screen time and my reading time like I had been doing. Day after day, I sat and did nothing as I allowed my brain to heal, which took its toll on me mentally, and I fell into a depression.

I was only nineteen years old. I had been planning on enjoying the summer and getting ready for my first NHL season with Ryan. I knew that was out of the question now. In the blink of an eye, it had been taken away from me.

This went on for a long time and I wasn't getting any better, but the doctors kept telling me, "Let's give it more time."

I began to wonder if I would ever return to the ice, and then if I would have a normal life at all. I wanted to have a family someday and be able to play with my kids. Had my injury taken away that future? I didn't have a ton of hope.

That year was the toughest in my life, but I wasn't alone. I had my parents, my girlfriend Dori, and Brian O'Reilly. They were my pillars.

Dori was beside me every step of the way. We had met way back in grade seven and had always gotten along really well. She was extremely athletic and incredibly attractive, but we were just good friends. We went on a few dates in grade twelve and then I asked her to prom. We'd been together ever since.

When I got hurt, she made it her mission to keep me thinking positive. She knew how much hockey meant to me and did everything she could to help me. Looking back, I'm blown away at her unfailing support. But at the time I'd gotten to the point where I didn't want any help. I just wanted to be miserable. I spent every day thinking about what I couldn't do anymore, not just on the ice, but off, too. I couldn't go out to the movies or to parties with Dori and my other friends. Deep down, I was scared and anxious about what would happen if I tried to skate again or if I went and worked out.

It was Dori's words that got me out of my funk. "You know, there are some people who don't think you'll make a comeback. But I know you can do this. You can move forward. All you have to do is take the first step, even if that's just getting out of your room."

She made me realize my dream wasn't over unless I let it be. It was the man in the mirror that was my greatest enemy in all of this. That night—over a year after my injury—I went to my dad's arena and skated for the first time. It felt like coming home.

From there, I started my physical recovery. It was actually Bob McKenzie who got the ball rolling on that front. He had heard about my story and reached out to connect me with Dr. Mark Lindsay. Dr. Lindsay travels all over the world working with high-profile athletes, but his right-hand man, Dr. Daniel Gallucci, was in Toronto. I was put into Dr. Gallucci's care right away. That's when things started to turn around for me.

After a few sessions, he recommended I see Dr. Frederick Carrick in Atlanta, Georgia. "He's the best of the best at treating concussions."

So, I went with my dad to Atlanta. After examining me, Dr. Carrick told me that he thought my lingering neck pain was what was causing my headaches, my main symptom. He began treating my neck, and within two or three days, I felt better.

I remember saying to my dad, "I feel normal again. This is unbelievable."

It was a mental shift as much as a physical one. After that, my recovery was day by day and I was gradually able to push the envelope a little more. Some days I would skate and feel fine, but there were other times when I would get a headache. Every time, it was like Russian roulette; I never knew how I would feel physically, but the important thing was that mentally I felt like a hockey player again. Slowly my depression was beginning to lift.

I called up Ryan's dad, Brian, and asked him if he would help me overcome this hurdle in my life. While the doctors helped me get to where I needed to be physically, Brian helped me mentally. If it wasn't for him, I don't know where I would be today. He got me to start to trust myself again, that I would be okay, that my life was good, no matter how things played out. I still get a little speechless thinking about everything he did for me.

The whole time, the Avs checked up on me. While I had missed the 2011–12 season, I was, at last, recovering. By the beginning of the

2012–13 season, the Avs had put me on the roster for their AHL team, the Lake Erie Monsters, as a black ace, or extra player.

I wasn't yet cleared for full-contact practice or games, and so I spent the year in Cleveland, watching games from the stands. Every day I would go to the rink and get treatment on my neck or talk to the team doctors. After, I'd hang out with Stefan Elliott, Tyson Barrie, and the other guys on the team. Everyone was supportive. They knew my situation and had all seen the hit many times on YouTube.

By Christmas, I decided that I was ready to give hockey a go again. The doctors agreed and cleared me for noncontact practice. At first, I spent two days practicing with the team, then I took two days off, just making sure I didn't push myself too hard. I kept chipping away until I could do just about anything without any symptoms returning.

Almost two years after my injury, I was given the green light to play, and on March 19, 2013, I suited up with the Monsters and faced off against the Toronto Marlies. My parents came down from Stratford to watch. I was glad to have their support in the arena because leading up to the game, I was nervous and anxious. But after that first shift on the ice, all I felt was happiness and pure joy.

I ended up playing nine games that year, and in my fifth game back, I even scored a goal and an assist. I started to feel good about myself again, both as a hockey player and as a person.

There were still some setbacks along the way. In the first shift of my ninth game, I got hit from behind and suffered a mild concussion. While the symptoms were minor, it was scary to go through another injury like this—to have those same headaches, to have to rest. By now, I knew the importance of taking it easy, and so I sat out the last two games of the season and spent the summer training.

By the start of the 2013–14 season, I felt stronger and faster and ready to take on whatever came next. I got a lot of ice time with the Monsters that year, playing a total of fifty games. There were still good days and bad days, both mentally and physically, as there are with everything else in life. But I felt my confidence returning. It was more than just playing the game. It was about being an athlete and a part of a team again after sitting on the sidelines so long. That was more important to me than anything else. It wasn't just about being on the ice. It was about the hours my team members and I spent together on our bus, road-tripping to away games and chirping one another the whole time. That camaraderie worked wonders on my health.

And then something unexpected happened. One day I was getting undressed after practice when I was told the coaches wanted to see me. I thought that was odd, but I finished changing and headed to the office. I was passing the trainers' room when Dusty Hallstead, our trainer, popped his head out and said, "You're going to play in the NHL!"

I shook it off. "Yeah, right. There's no way I'm going to play in the NHL." The Avs were in the first round of the playoffs and had a great forward lineup—there's no way they needed me.

According to my coach, Dusty was right. Tyson Barrie, who had moved up earlier that year, had been kneed by Minnesota Wild winger Matt Cooke and was too injured to play. The Avs were calling me up to play.

I freaked out when they told me. I immediately texted Dori with the news, and then I called my parents. I couldn't believe it—I thought playing the NHL was a bygone dream, but here I was about to catch a flight to Minnesota to skate in the Stanley Cup playoffs.

As soon as I landed, I went to see Ryan. He was still with the Avs and we were pretty excited to be playing together. The Avs were right in the middle of their first-round playoff series and they had a 2–1 lead, which added another level of drama to the situation. It was a little surreal.

The first thing I noticed when I walked into the Avs dressing room was the name "Hishon" on the back of my sweater. That was cool, but the "Oh my God" moment happened when I stepped on the ice and heard the Minnesota Wild fans. Even in the warm-ups, they were loud.

My parents had made the trip to see me. It was at least a sixteen-hour drive from Stratford and they basically hadn't slept, but it meant so much to me that they were there. At one point during warm-up, I looked over and saw my dad standing there with a big smile on his face. I'll never forget that.

When we got back to the dressing room to get ready for the game, Ryan and I looked at each other and smiled, then started laughing a bit. We didn't need to say anything: we both knew how special this night was.

The game was definitely a lot faster and more physical than I was used to, but I felt good about my performance. I participated in the power play, so I got offensive opportunities, and I touched the puck in key moments. Unfortunately, the Wild beat us 2–1 to tie the series.

We went on to win game 5, but lost the next game, which I sat out. Everything would be decided in game 7. We battled as hard as we could, and I even picked up an assist, but the Wild beat us 5–4 in tough overtime to win the series.

Even though we lost, I had enjoyed every minute because I was an NHL hockey player. And after that playoff run, I was so excited to train and get ready for camp.

In the fall of 2014, I started the season with the Monsters once more, but by March, I was called back up to rejoin the Avs. This time around, I wanted to prove that I could stay up with the big team and play in the NHL on a regular basis. When you get called up, you never know how long it is going to last. But as the season went on, I held my ground.

In April, my parents and Dori flew out to Colorado to watch me play. It was the first regular NHL season in which they would see me play live.

We faced off against the Nashville Predators that night and they came out strong in the first period with a goal by Ryan Ellis, but late in the second period, Jarome Iginla and Ryan O'Reilly scored within nine seconds of each other to put us in lead. Ellis came out of the third period swinging and tied us up. The pressure was on and the clock was running out.

And then I had the puck, and I was making my way to the net as fast as I could. Adrenaline was running through my veins. Ahead of me, two defencemen were closing in, but I saw an opening and flicked my wrist. And it went in!

I had scored my first NHL goal! And man, was it sweet.

The guys crowded around me on the ice, tapping me on the head, and then I skated back to the bench, where Ryan was one of the first guys to give me props. We had been through so much together—it meant a lot to see him right away. All the guys were so happy for me. Gabriel Landeskog, or Landy, as we called him, even did me the honour of splashing water in my face. Jarome Iginla put his arm around me and smiled, "So you danced Shea Weber, you toe-dragged Roman Josi, and then you fired it by Pekka Rinne. That one is going to be pretty fun to tell your buddies!" The entire bench started to howl.

The Predators tried their best to tie us up again, but they couldn't get anything by our goalie and the buzzer sounded. We had won 3–2. It had been three years since my injury, and I had just scored a game-winning goal in the NHL. I felt like a million bucks.

The cherry on the cake was that Dori and my parents were there, cheering me on. I must have been saving my big goal for when they

Moments after I scored, I skated back to the bench to see these happy faces on my teammates. From left to right, Ryan O'Reilly, John Mitchell, Matt Duchene, Jarome Iginla, Gabriel Landeskog (getting his water ready), and Alex Tanguay.

were there because I had tried to score a few nights earlier against the Canucks, but had hit the post on an empty net. Alex Tanguay had skated up to me and said, "That one was too easy. You didn't want that one. Your first goal will be nicer than that." All the great veterans on that team were supportive like that.

That season, I lasted with the Avs until there were no more games left to play, which was a big achievement for me.

By then, the Avs had signed a new agreement, making the San Antonio Rampage their AHL affiliate team, and the Columbus Blue Jackets took over the Lake Erie Monsters, and so I moved to Texas to play for the Rampage for the 2015–16 season. I had a good year with them, but unfortunately wasn't called up to the NHL.

Dori and I had talked a lot about where I might play next, and I had received a good offer from Jokerit, a Kontinental Hockey League (KHL) team in Helsinki, Finland. Since my comeback, I had been fairly healthy—just a few little bumps and bruises here and there, but nothing major. The AHL was a good league, but I found there were more dirty hits in it because a lot of players are trying to get noticed by the NHL. Dori and I both wanted to avoid any injury, so we decided to make a change.

The KHL was an extremely skilled league that prioritized defensive playing. I found that the neutral zone was always clogged with bodies, which made it hard to even get a shot on goal. Power plays were the only opportunity to play offensively, but getting that time was a challenge as there were so many skilled players. I could still be an effective player, but I did miss flexing my offensive muscles and producing the numbers.

Off the ice, it was an incredible experience for me and Dori to live in Helsinki. We met so many nice people and were treated like we were part of an NHL team. Helsinki itself was a beautiful city and we had a gorgeous apartment close to downtown. The best part was that since Jokerit was based in Finland, our main sponsor was Finnair and they had a charter plane for road trips and travel.

After that season, I got an offer from Luleå Hockeyförening of the

Swedish Hockey League (SHL), and since the Jokerit didn't re-sign me, Dori and I decided to say yes.

Luleå was the complete opposite of Helsinki. It's a small city in northern Sweden, close to the Arctic Circle, but it was by far the coolest place that I ever lived. During the winter months, there is almost no daylight. We lived on a lake that froze over and we would go skating on it whenever we wanted—it reminded me of Stratford.

Unfortunately, I only played twenty-two games of a possible fifty-eight that year because of a concussion I got early on in October. It was my third official concussion, but truthfully, I probably had more than that. I knew my body, more specifically my brain, just couldn't take any more damage.

I said to Dori, "I'll finish out the year and do everything I can to help the organization, but I don't think I will play after this."

We both knew it was the right decision. I knew I could find happiness and success in a different career. It was time to say goodbye. I had dragged Dori all over Finland and Sweden and now it was time for me to support her. We both wanted to settle down back in Stratford, Ontario, and get married, which we did on June 8, 2018.

I knew I wasn't ready to leave the game altogether. The year before I went to play in Sweden, Dale DeGray, the GM of the Owen Sound Attack, who had been my GM when I was on the team, had called to ask me if I was going to play again.

"I've signed up with the SHL," I had replied. "Why?"

"I've got an opening on the team for an assistant coach and was wondering if you were interested."

I was flattered and told him so. I'd always had a soft spot for the Attack, the team that had molded me in so many ways. And while I turned the job down then, the thought stayed with me.

Back at home in 2018, I called Dale up again to ask if he had anything available.

"I'm sorry, Joey," he said. "We've already filled the coaching position. But we really want you to be part of the team. I'll find a way to bring you on board. Let me get back to you."

Soon after that call, he got in touch to ask if I wanted to be the Attack's skills development coach and scout for them as well.

I jumped at the opportunity. While Stratford is my home, Owen Sound has always been a close second. It was where I billeted for four years and came into my own as a player. As a scout, in finding the best players for the team, I found a sense of competition that I had been missing. As a coach, I wanted to help other players have the same experience as I'd had. And as a player, I had always played the best for coaches who saw me as more than just a player, who connected with me on a personal level, and that's what I determined to bring to my new job.

The thing that hit me the most when I started coaching with the Attack organization was just how young the kids were. A decade ago, I was them, moving away from home to live with a new family and play junior hockey; at the time, I didn't realize what big step that is. As a coach, I make it my priority to foster a good relationship with the players so they feel comfortable coming to me, especially during that first year away from home, with any issue—hockey related or not.

The OHL has changed a lot since I played. It's such a fast game now and the players are much more skilled than they used to be—even the fourth line of these teams boasts majorly talented players. The rule changes have helped. The OHL has a zero tolerance for head shots, and after three fights, players get suspended. As someone who suffered a career-altering injury, I'm happy that the OHL has taken these steps to make the game safer. The game is less about hits and more about technique, which makes for quality hockey.

My new dream is to work my way up the hockey ladder in some capacity. A year into my job, I was named the assistant coach and the assistant GM for the team, which has given me the opportunity to find what career path appeals most to me—coaching or management. I'm still learning the Xs and Os, but when I'm standing behind the bench as the anthem comes to an end and the game is about to begin, I still get the rush that I felt as a player.

And I remember that I wouldn't be standing where I am without

*My second act with hockey is behind the bench
with the Owen Sound Attack. As you can see,
I'm just as focused on the on-ice action.*

the support of all the all-stars in my life. My parents, for the countless hours skating—and love and encouragement. Brian, who was instrumental in my mental recovery. Ryan, my buddy on and off the ice.

Ryan is one of those guys who will be a friend for life. Ever since we were kids, he's been one of the hardest-working players I've known. He was traded to the St. Louis Blues in 2018, and when they made their run for the Stanley Cup in 2019, I felt like I was with him every step of the way. I don't think anyone else deserved to win the Cup as much as he did.

And without Dori, I don't know where I would be right now. When I was at my lowest, she inspired me to pick myself up and soldier on. We were just two nineteen-year-old kids, but she stuck by me. And when my on-ice relationship with hockey ended, my relationship with Dori got even stronger than it was before. She's a huge a part of why I am here today.

When I was a kid, I dreamed about seventy-one NHL goals. I'm not going to complain about my one. After all the challenges I faced, it was a wish come true. Now I'm thankful for my health, my family, and that I can still be a part of hockey and help others achieve their goals, no matter what obstacles are in their way.

Joey Hishon is a former NHL player for the Colorado Avalanche, who chose him as their first-round pick in 2010. He is the current assistant coach, assistant general manager, and scout for the Owen Sound Attack OHL team, and during his downtime, he works as a high-performance development coach for Hishon Skills Corp., his skills development business. He lives in Stratford with his wife, Dori, and their border collie, Abby. An avid golfer, Joey plays to a one handicap.

 *@skills_corp*

@HishonJoey

Behind the Bench

Danièle Sauvageau

The crowd in the E Center arena in Salt Lake City, Utah, was electric. It was the 2002 Winter Olympics and this was the gold medal game for women's hockey between Team Canada and our long-time rivals, the United States. I had been coaching for over eighteen years, but this was the biggest game of my career. I stood behind the bench, watching our starting lineup getting ready for the opening face-off.

We had Kim St-Pierre in net, Cheryl Pounder and Becky Kellar on defence, and Vicky Sunohara, Laura Dupuis, and Jayna Hefford up front. That was our best two-way line. All three of those forwards could score, but they were there to shut down the other team's number one line. They were the best in the world at doing that.

We wanted that gold medal more than anything. This was familiar ground. We had faced off against Team USA in the 1998 Games in Nagano, Japan—the first time women's hockey had been played at the Olympics—and we had gone home with silver. That had stung, and we were determined to change things this time around. Unfortunately, we were still smarting from being defeated by Team USA in the eight games leading up to the 2002 Olympics. It didn't help that we'd be playing on their home turf.

But my mind was calm. I had done everything I knew to prepare the team for this moment. It was their turn now.

No matter what the outcome, I had to believe this is what I was born to do.

◆   ◆   ◆

The road that led me to this moment in Salt Lake City began thirty-nine years earlier, in Deux-Montagnes, Quebec, just outside of Montreal.

I grew up playing hockey on the outdoor rink in a park just two houses down from my home. Our small town didn't have an indoor rink, but that didn't matter. Every spare moment, I was out on the ice with my younger brothers, Michele and Sylvain, and the other neighbourhood kids. We would make up our own teams and play hockey for hours until we were yelled at to stop playing and get home for dinner. After we'd eaten, we'd be right back out and playing till the lights went off. When I think about those days, the first word that comes to mind is "freedom."

When I was old enough, my parents decided to register me and my brothers in organized hockey in the neighbouring town of Saint-Eustache. *They* had an indoor rink. I was so excited to play in a real league, but when I went to sign up, the organizer pointed to my brothers and said, "They can play, but you can't because you're a girl."

This was the first time I heard: girls don't play hockey. In my heart, I couldn't understand why. I played with my brothers all the time at the park and I was just as good as them. It was my dream to play hockey, but in the 1970s, there were very few organized girls' hockey leagues. When it came down to it, I just wanted to be involved in the game.

"Can I help?" I asked.

He studied me for a minute. "Uh, yeah. We have water bottles you can fill. You could hang around."

I didn't need to hear more. My parents weren't surprised by my response. If someone told me no, I always wedged my foot in the door and tried to open it a bit more. And from that day on, I was always at the rink. I did everything I could to help out. I filled water bottles; I opened and closed the gate as the players came off the ice. I was at the rink so much that I was part of the scenery. I think the staff eventually felt sorry for me because they had told me no, but I hadn't listened. When some of the coaches noticed my passion for hockey, they let me help out as a coach.

Since I couldn't play hockey, I started playing broom ball. Broom ball is similar to hockey, except instead of playing with hockey sticks, a puck, and skates, players use sticks with a rubber triangular head similar to a broom and a small round ball, and they wear special rubber-soled shoes. Broom ball is now an established international sport with its own world championships, but back then, the important thing about the sport was that there were women's and men's leagues and so women like me who wanted to play hockey, but couldn't because there was no league available, ended up playing broom ball.

I played broom ball all through high school and then at Cégep de Saint-Jérôme, a vocational college where I was the captain of my team. On the side, I was also coaching boys' A-level hockey. As I was heading off to university, the coach of Saint-Jérôme's men's and women's broom ball team left the school, and so they reached out to ask if I would consider coaching the women's team.

"Why only the women's team?" I asked.

"Oh, we never thought about offering you a chance to coach both teams."

Here I am at age seventeen playing broom ball at Cégep de Saint-Jérôme.

"The previous guy was coaching women. If you want me to coach, I'm going to coach both teams. If not, I'm not coaching."

They agreed and gave me the job.

Coaching is coaching, whether it's broom ball or hockey, and being a coach means supporting the players and giving them a chance to go from point A to point B, and that was something I always enjoyed. The whole time I was coaching broom ball, I was learning what it took to be a hockey coach and working on getting my hockey coach qualifications.

In 1984, I was making my way up the ranks coaching women's hockey in Quebec when I caught a break. I was supporting the Ferland Quatre Glaces of the Regional League of Women's Hockey in Quebec and one of the coaches was suspended after getting into an argument with the referee.

They turned to me and said, "Danièle, could you help us?"

Since that day at Saint-Eustache, I've been eager to help—it's always my first word. Helping whenever you can, will open doors down the road.

"Sure, why not?" I replied, and with that I became the new coach. I was only twenty years old.

Around this time, I was also asked to coach the Quebec men's provincial broom ball team. That was the moment that I realized I had the potential to be a coach because I was being asked to coach male players who were much older than me—most of the players were in their thirties.

The problem was, coaching didn't pay the bills. For that, I had to look elsewhere.

My desire to be of service to others had led me to study social work at the University of Montreal. (Unfortunately, the school didn't have a women's hockey program then, which was another reason coaching continued to draw me in. It was a way to stay involved in the sport.) After I graduated, I was on call for various social work organizations and would work eight hours here and eight hours there, sometimes with kids with drug problems and sometimes with kids with disabilities. I was working all the time, trying to get as much experience as I could.

Then, in 1985, I saw an ad in the newspaper. The RCMP were looking for people who had an interest in law, psychology, and social work. I decided to apply. They told me it was a two-year process before I would even start my training and there were a lot of people ahead of me on the list who were trying to get hired, so I didn't bother telling my parents right away.

Less than six months later, I came home to find my parents waiting for me.

"You didn't feel like talking to us about going into the RCMP?" my dad asked.

Turns out, the RCMP had started calling that list of people and many had changed their minds. While I had been out, a black car had pulled up to our house and two officers came in to interview my parents and make sure I would be a good candidate.

When I joined the RCMP, I was in demand because I was bilingual and a woman. While the training was brutal, I graduated in the top five of my class and was handpicked with a few others to work in Powell River, BC. Powell River is a pretty isolated place with a population of just over thirteen thousand people, and the first few months out there were hard. I was a long way from home, working in English, and working alone. I had to respond to calls by myself, calling for another officer only if I needed backup.

After two and a half years, I got an opportunity to join the Montreal police force—I couldn't pass up the chance to come home.

At that time, there were about 112 women on the Montreal police force; now there are close to 1,500. But because I had thirty months of RCMP work under my belt and was trained by the RCMP, I believe that most of the men respected me. I had my fair share of challenges, though. I came into the force wanting to make a name for myself, which meant I was singled out by a lot of the veterans who didn't like how much I was trying to do or change. It wasn't because I was a woman, but because I was so driven. At times, I would feel alone, but what saved me was having great partners to guide me early in my career.

I learned many lessons from my job on the force that affected my approach to coaching, which I had taken up again. Both careers are about developing people skills and team chemistry, discipline, and commitment. Personally, I've learned how to control my emotions in high-pressure situations. Throughout my career, I've been involved in hundreds of drug busts. When I was headed to a raid with the SWAT team, my sidearm out and at the ready, my heart would beat so fast I could barely breathe. Once I had experienced that, the stress of sports didn't seem so bad. My family jokes that I don't know what the word "panic" means. I'm even-keeled. When people ask me how I am doing, I am not one to say, "Fantastic." To me, "fantastic" is a big word.

The other thing I learned was the importance of paying attention to detail. When you're investigating a crime, you have to ask questions and dig for the answers before you can confidently say whether someone is guilty or innocent. The same mind-set can be applied to hockey. As a coach, I learned to look at every strength and weakness of a player. They might be physically strong, but are they mentally tough or technically skilled? I would look at my players' varying strengths and put together lines that complemented one another to ensure the best possible team performance on the ice. I became a better coach because of my job, and better at my job because of coaching.

By the time I moved back to Montreal, there had been a change in women's hockey. A national women's team had been formed, and in 1990, the first women's world championship was held in Ottawa. In 1992, the International Olympic Committee announced that women's hockey would be an Olympic event and it was scheduled to appear in the 1998 Games in Nagano, Japan. For women, this was a huge milestone. Now there was a future for them in the sport beyond the provincial level.

And I was about to be a part of it.

I had my Level 2 hockey coaching qualifications, which meant I was qualified to coach AAA and other elite levels of hockey. Back then, there weren't a lot of coaches at that level, so I moved up the ranks of coaching women's hockey in Quebec fairly easily. I was lucky to work with such talented players as Danielle Goyette, France Saint-Louis, and Denise Caron. Danielle was the kind of player who always fought right to the end. She was capable of scoring a goal with one second left on the clock.

Off the ice, it was a struggle. We had very little support from Hockey Quebec or anyone at the national level. We were not being paid to coach and the players were paying to be part of the league. Players would tell me, "Coach, I can't play. I don't have any more sticks."

We had to build everything from the ground up. I remember going to D&R, the company that makes hockey gloves and goalie pads, to ask them for ten pairs of gloves for the team.

The person looked at me like I was crazy. "What are you talking about—ten pairs of gloves? You need to have more than that for all your players!"

They supplied gloves for each player, and we were the first team in the league to play with the same colour gloves. Eventually, we all had the same colour helmets, too.

In an effort to gain support for our team, I sent letters to the national team with names of players whom I felt deserved to compete at the international level. Even with our limited resources, we were having great success and people were taking notice. That's how, in 1993, I got scouted by Hockey Canada to work with the women's national hockey team as an evaluator. I also asked Tom Renney, head coach of the national men's hockey team, if I could work with him, and he agreed.

In May 1995, Hockey Canada founded Canada's first junior women's team, the Canadian Under 19 (now the U-18s), for players under nineteen years old, and to my great joy, I was made the head coach.

The junior team was a crucial step in building the foundation for women's hockey in Canada. By the 1998 Olympics, the average age of the women's team would be thirty, so I was already thinking about building the next generation of players who would represent Canada at the Olympics.

Then, in 1996, Shannon Miller, the first female head coach of Team Canada, asked me if I would move to Calgary and help her build a program at the Olympic Oval and work with the 1998 Olympic team as an assistant coach. I immediately said yes. Shannon was instrumental in making me part of the national team.

When I arrived in Calgary and walked into my office, which was in the Father Bauer Arena, I started to believe that maybe my life was predetermined.

A decade earlier, when I was working for the RCMP, I was assigned to go to the 1988 Calgary Games and run security. The first thing I saw when I got there was the Father Bauer Arena and the Olympic Park. Now, ten years later, the national team was training at Father Bauer Arena and we were announcing the women's team in that same Olympic Park.

We put together a strong team: Jennifer Botterill, Thérèse Brisson, Cassie Campbell, Lori Dupuis, Danielle Goyette, Geraldine Heaney, Jayna Hefford, Becky Kellar, Vicky Sunohara, and the one and only Hayley Wickenheiser. There were so many great leaders who were a big part of building women's hockey in Canada. No one had endorsements or big contracts—they all had jobs on the side to help pay the bills. They were playing for the love of the game. They were pure hockey.

Our program was still young and new. And we had so much to prove in this, the first Olympic Games with women's hockey. In the lead-up to the Games, we beat the United States in every competition and were favoured to come out on top. But we left some stones unturned.

Which is why the defeat by Team USA in the gold medal game at the 1998 Games was such a bitter pill to swallow. After the buzzer, we were on the ice for so long while Team USA went back to their dressing room. Then they came back out to receive their gold medal and we stood around, waiting to receive our silver medals. When we finally made it back to the dressing room, it was filled with media. There wasn't much to say at that point; we were all feeling the pain of the loss.

After the Games, Hockey Canada, under Bob Nicholson, named

me the new head coach of the national team and general manager of the women's hockey program. My new job was to build a structure that would foster talent for our national team. The first thing that I did was build an evaluation process to find our best players. I wanted to know who the best fifty players across the country were. Before 1998, we didn't have anything like that.

At first, Hockey Canada didn't agree with my evaluation process; they felt it was going to take too long.

"It's okay," I told them. "You're not doing the job. I am."

I was still working full-time as a police officer and building and coaching the national team at least six to eight weeks a year. I couldn't be everywhere at once, so I set up different hubs with doctors, sports psychologists, and trainers in Toronto, Montreal, and Calgary. I also leaned on two successful coaches from Ontario, Karen Hughes and Ken Dufton, to help me find talent. At one point, Karen Hughes told me, "We have this player here in Ontario. She needs to be invited to the next camp."

I had never seen this woman play before, but I trusted Karen. That player was Jayna Hefford. Once I saw Jayna in action, I knew my plan was working because I had built the necessary structure to find players like her.

What I was looking for was the best team, not the best athletes. I could pick the best athletes, but at the end of the day, it was the team that was going to work together to win, and that meant seeing what natural strengths the players had because that's what was going to surface when they were under pressure. I looked at our roster and developed an individual plan for each player that would challenge them to be the best they could be. I wanted each one to be able to play on a penalty kill, meaning when the team was down a player, the ones on the ice had the skills to cover what the missing player had brought to the table. We identified players we could push out of their comfort zones. I wanted the best to become better.

This was the way that I asked Cassie to play forward for me. In the 1998 Olympics, Cassie was a defenceman, but I saw her as a very defensive forward, who was secure and dependable. She was the kind of player you wanted on the ice at the end the period if you were trying to hang on to a one-goal lead. I told her that if she wanted to continue on the team, she needed to be a forward.

"By playing forward, you'll become one of the best two-way players on the team. On defence, it can be risky, but you bring a lot of leadership to the team."

I guess she trusted me, or perhaps felt she had no choice, and she agreed. Cassie worked hard. She was not an up-and-down player, and I always knew what to expect from her every game. Every coach needs someone on the team like that. She later became captain and was invaluable to the entire coaching staff. I knew if a player was having a difficult time, I could go through Cassie to find a way to help that player. We always communicated well.

I was building a system, a set of tactics, that I thought would make the difference at this Olympics. We had one simple rule: In the offensive zone, players could pretty much do whatever they wanted, but when they had to come back to our zone, they were coming "home" and everyone needed to be on defence. This was my team rule, everyone defends first, then they could break out and go back on the offence.

When building a system, many coaches start by perfecting the breakout—moving the puck from the defensive to the neutral zone. But I wanted to start by strengthening our forecheck—being in the offensive zone and applying pressure to get the puck. I felt if we were good on the forecheck, we wouldn't give up a lot of 3-on-2s and 2-on-1s like we did in 1998. That was another big change for our team.

We had a number of great players already, but in 1999, we added eleven new players. That's unheard of now. We had the youngest team Canada had yet going into Worlds—we still ended up winning gold. Within a year, I had built a structure, evaluation process, three training hubs across the country, and brought back gold to Canada.

But after, Hockey Canada wanted to evaluate other coaches and Melody Davidson was brought back to the program after being released in 1997, and she took over the team. I knew Melody—she was a good coach—but I didn't understand why I was being replaced. The press tried to make it about a French-English divide within the organization, but I immediately put a stop to that and told reporters, "I'm not going there."

That's another thing I've learned during my career as a police officer—when you have an obstacle in front of you, it's more effective to find a solution than to talk about it. As a cop, there are scenarios in which you don't even have time to think about your actions, you just must act on what you know and rely on your gut instinct. Hockey Canada had made a decision and the only thing I could do was make sure I was in a position to go back to the national team if and when they asked me.

That's when I got an unusual phone call from Serge Savard, the former Montreal Canadiens defenceman. I had met him several times at different functions and we knew each other, but he had never called me before.

He said hello, and then he got straight to the point. "Would you be interested in coaching the Quebec Major Junior Hockey League?"

I paused. "I'm going to call you back," I said. I was suspicious that this wasn't the real Serge Savard and that someone was trying to trick me. When had a men's junior league ever asked a woman to coach?

After he hung up, I called someone else and I asked to confirm Serge Savard's phone number. They did, and I quickly called him back.

"I know that you need a place to coach," he said, unfazed by the fact that I'd asked him to wait. "I'm putting a new franchise together for the QMJHL—the Montreal Rockets. We need coaches, and we would like to have you on the team."

"I would like that," I replied eagerly. This was an incredible opportunity—never had a woman coached in QMJHL history.

The job was to be an assistant coach and technical adviser, but as the only female coach on staff, I wasn't taken seriously at first by the other coaches or the players.

Being teenage boys, the players would play tricks on me and put pucks in my skates to test me. I started by working with players who were not in the lineup, to make sure they were doing extra work after practice. The head coach, Gaston Therrien, was better at telling them what they weren't good at. I was better at telling them what they were good at. When they realized that I was an Olympic-level hockey coach and I knew what I was talking about, they began to respect me. In the lead-up to the league playoffs, the players would come off the ice after a shift and ask me about face-offs, in front of the other coaches on the bench next to me. I believe the boys were on my side before the rest of the coaching staff.

One day, I worked out an in-depth ranking of all the players with combinations of which players would fit best together—it was something I had done before on other teams I had coached. I dropped it on Gaston's desk. "Have you ever seen something like this?"

He looked at the report. "Oh, yeah, yeah, for sure."

But I could tell he hadn't. Soon after, the rest of the staff completely accepted my input and came to me for advice on the technical aspects of the game, and I'm still friends with them to this day.

For a first-year team, we did very well. We made it to the league playoffs, and though we ended up losing in double overtime in the opening round, we had gone much further than people expected.

By that time, Hockey Canada had come calling again. We were two years away from the next Winter Olympics, but I was torn. I just wanted to coach players on a daily basis. I asked a few other coaches if I should stay in the QMJHL or go back to the national women's team, and they all told me, "Danièle, the Olympics is the summit of hockey; it's the pinnacle of sports. You can't turn that down. You could come back after you're done."

I took their advice. Gaston was upset that I was leaving the team. "When you started with us, we knew who you were, but we came to recognize what you can do. And now, everyone else in the hockey world knows, too."

That was a big compliment for me.

I didn't have much time to dwell on my decision—I had twenty-four months before the 2001–02 season began. Team USA was the

In the 2000–01 season, I coached the Montreal Rockets
of the QMJHL, the first woman to do so. In this photo,
you can see me on the left, behind the bench.

same tight-knit unit from the 1998 Games. The core of our team was the same as it was in Nagano—Jennifer, Thérèse, Cassie, Lori, Danielle, Geraldine, Jayna, Becky, Vicky, and Hayley—but half of our team would be first-time Olympians, including Caroline Ouellette, who I had coached in the Canadian Under 19, and Kim St-Pierre, our goaltender and the top rookie for her university women's team.

In January 2001, we played two games against Team USA in Denver, and it was clear we were way behind them on the physical side of the game. Our director of sport physiology and strategic planning, Dr. Steve Norris, confirmed it: if we didn't start preparing a new program right then and there, I knew we wouldn't catch up to Team USA in time for the Olympics.

I went to Bob Nicholson and told him we needed to push the players harder. That meant they would be overtrained and tired for Worlds and we might lose, but it was worth it for the big picture: winning the Olympics.

Bob agreed, but just as I was leaving his office, he said, "By the way, Coach, you still need to win the world championship!"

We did end up winning Worlds, in large part because of our goalie, Kim St-Pierre, who was unbelievable. We were outshot by Team USA and we still beat them in the final game by a score of 3–2. Some stars were born, including Gina Kingsbury, who is now the head of the national program.

After the game, Bob came up to me and said, "See? I told you that you were capable of winning."

We had started out strong, but as the season went on, it was clear that we had room to improve. We needed to be better physically, mentally, and technically. In June 2001, we went to a military camp for three weeks in Valcartier, Quebec, to train. The players hated me for taking them there—it was so demanding—but I trusted the experts who told me that if we wanted to be physically ready for 2002, we needed to put in the work. I was the first person to introduce these types of training camps to the program, probably because of my RCMP background, but the players rose to the challenge and the camps proved to be effective. Today the Canadian women's hockey program still runs them.

Why else did I take the team to a military base? Because of the cost. Three weeks at the base was the same price as one week in a hotel training at a nice facility, but Hockey Canada and I didn't always see eye to eye on money and I thought they'd still say no, so I put in a request to the federal government. Denis Coderre, who was the secretary of sport at the time, was a huge help.

Around this time, Dan O'Neill, the president of Molson, saw an interview about what we were trying to do with the women's team and asked me to meet with him. He said he wanted to give an incentive if we won the gold medal, but I told him that we didn't need money after the Olympics, we needed money before.

That's when he asked, "How much do you need to help this team win?"

I talked to him about meal cards, so the players would eat properly;

about phone cards, so they could call their family; about paying for parents to come to Salt Lake City to watch their daughters in the semifinal and final games; about a dedicated goalie coach; about extra computers. The list of requests came to well over $250,000.

After I sent him a detailed plan, I received an e-mail, "Okay, I agree."

My first thought was, *Damn, I didn't ask for enough money!*

I never told Bob about my meeting with Dan. When he found out, he was upset and said that we should have talked about it first. I just asked, "What do you want me to do, return the money?"

Even with all this support, Team USA beat us eight games in a row in the lead-up to the Olympics. They were playing some of their best hockey ever.

It was hard not to be a little rattled, but my training as a police officer kicked in. With every loss, I told the team, "Yes, we are losing now, but that's okay. What are we doing today to get better?"

We had a team meeting in which we looked at Team USA's power plays because they were winning a lot of games based on them.

At one point, Hayley Wickenheiser stood up. "We are so much better than this, but we need to be consistent on details."

It was true. We were already so much better than we had been at the beginning, and I reminded the team that we needed to focus, not on winning, but on becoming better players and developing properly as a team so we could be real contenders in February when the Olympics started. That was the game that mattered most.

I couldn't let myself focus on the stakes. But they were high. We were playing for Canada's honour. Canada hadn't even won a gold medal in men's hockey in the prior fifty years.

Finally, the Olympics arrived. During the open ceremonies, some members of Team USA's "Miracle on Ice" 1980 men's team and Cammi Granato passed by me to the lighting of the Olympic flame. I remember saying: "It will be us this time."

We then rolled through the preliminary rounds, easily beating out Kazakhstan, Russia, Sweden, and Finland on our way to the gold medal game. At each step, I was taking in information as if this was an investigation. Every night before I went to bed, I could see myself coaching in that final game. And then, before I knew it, it was there.

The tension in the arena was palpable, with the majority of the onlookers rooting for our opponents, who were on a thirty-five-game win streak, but I remembered to stay calm and to stay in the present moment. Before the game, I told the players, "I'm not asking you to do anything you haven't done before. But now you all have to play as one."

Early in the first period, the ref made a call against us. And then another, and another. Some said it was because the ref was an American, but I couldn't afford to start worrying about how many penalties we were getting. All we could do was make sure we didn't open ourselves up on the penalty kills. With less than two minutes left in the first, Caroline picked up an errant puck and dunked it in the net to score our first goal and her first Olympic goal.

Having the lead early in the game helped. Now they had to catch

At the 2002 Olympic Games in Salt Lake City,
imparting some important advice to the team.

us. After their fourth power play, I saw a big attitude change on their bench because they realized things were not going the way they thought. They retaliated with a goal, but by the end of the second period, we had come back with two more, one a joint effort by Hayley and Danielle with four minutes left and the second when Jayna got a breakaway and slipped one in the net with one second left in the period. We were up 3–1 and we felt in charge of the game and in charge of the moment.

Still, never in my wildest dreams did I imagine they would give us eight penalties in a row. We were shorthanded twenty-six minutes that game and we needed five players in every zone. All night, I had to readjust based on who had the penalty and what I had to work with on the bench. At one point, I sent Danielle over the boards to kill a penalty and she said, "I don't want to go."

I looked at her. "You're always complaining about your ice time. Let's go with a smile!"

I knew that Team USA would possibly come at us with a play we called "The Torpedo." It was a special breakout they would use to get the puck out of their end. When they tried it during the game, we had our forecheck system in place and our second defenceman came in close to centre ice. No matter what they threw at us or how many penalties went against us, we stayed focused and readjusted as the game went on.

Kim held us together in the third as the United States amped up their offence. The clock was counting down. At 3:33, they managed one goal, and then pulled their goalie for the final minute, but even with six attackers, our line, and Kim, held. The seconds melted off the clock and then the buzzer went off. We had won! Our team poured out onto the ice, throwing their sticks and gloves, and collapsed in a pile on top of Kim at the net.

That was one of my happiest moments—not just because we had won gold—but because the team had performed at their highest level. With all those penalties, with playing shorthanded, they had been resilient.

I couldn't stop smiling all night. That win—now, that's what I call fantastic!

After we won the gold medal, Dan O'Neill walked into our dressing room and said, "When I first met Danièle, it was to give you money if you won the gold medal. She refused. Well, now that you won the gold and the game is over, I can do whatever I want. So, I am giving you guys a half a million dollars."

Celebrating our gold medal win. Left to right: (front row) Sami Jo Small, me, Kim St-Pierre; (second row) Hayley Wickenheiser, Tammy Lee Shewchuk, Jennifer Botterill, Isabelle Chartrand, Vicky Sunohara, Lori Dupuis in her hat, Jayna Hefford, Cherie Piper, Becky Kellar, Danielle Goyette, Kelly Bechard just below; (third row) Robin McDonald, Cheryl Pounder, Colleen Sostorics, Charline Labonté, Thérèse Brisson, Geraldine Heany, Kimberly Amirault leaning forward, Dana Antal, Mavis Wahl-LeBlanc also leaning forward, Cassie Campbell; (fourth row) Bob Nicholson, Gaetan Robitaille, André Brin, Karen Hughes, Caroline Ouellette, Denis Haineault, Ryan Jankowski, Doug Stacey, and David Jamieson.
(Adrian Dennis/AFP via Getty Images)

All of a sudden we had $500,000 to distribute among the players. Because I had said no at first, we ended up getting more.

As a coach, I was demanding, maybe too much so, but I had bet on these women and their abilities, and winning that bet—there was no greater feeling. I was humbled by the recognition that followed, but that win belonged to those women, who worked so hard for that medal and changed the landscape of women's hockey in Canada—that was something bigger than all of us. It brought women's hockey to the next level.

But for me, that gold medal game was a pinnacle in a journey that started as a young woman in a rink in Saint-Eustache.

◆　◆　◆

Following the Olympics, Hockey Canada asked me if I wanted to oversee women's hockey as general manager. The salary was around half of what I was making as a police officer in Montreal, and I would have to move to Calgary, where their head office was. While I wanted the job, I couldn't make the move to Calgary and give up almost twenty years of service as a police officer. I asked if I could stay based in Montreal, but it was a no-go.

I still remember the day in the Father Bauer Arena in Calgary when I looked at Bob Nicholson and told him, "I can't stay."

I went back to my office and began packing up my things.

Bob walked in. "Coach, could we go for lunch?"

"Sure."

We went out for Chinese food, and I told him I was a little burnt out. Between coaching and my job, I was probably sleeping three hours a night. On top of that, after our win, I'd been busy speaking at banquets and conferences and it was all getting to be a bit much. I was stepping down as coach. Bob understood.

While I said no to moving to Calgary, I ended up saying yes to several different ventures and opportunities that I would never even have been considered for before. Later that year, the Canadian government asked me to be a part of a five-member panel to review the sports system in the country. Given that this was a request from the federal government, it was considered an official secondment and I was able to give my full attention to the panel without jeopardizing my career. The panel evolved into Own the Podium, a not-for-profit organization to help Canadian athletes medal in the Olympics by ensuring they had access to top technology and development and providing them with the funding they needed to compete on the international stage.

Through that, I was asked to build a development program for the women's water polo team for the 2004 Summer Games in Athens. From there, I joined the Canadian Olympic Committee and went to the 2008 Summer Games in Beijing as a mentor and a high-performance coach for the team sports. I had the same role at the 2010 Winter Games in Vancouver, where I ended up being involved in fourteen different sports in varying capacities.

After I came home from the Vancouver Winter Games, the University of Montreal, my alma mater, asked me to start and coach a new women's hockey program, the Montreal Carabins. I was delighted they were finally investing in a women's hockey team. I was honoured, but wasn't sure if I could invest the time needed.

There was a pause on the line. "Well, could you just build the program?"

It was like they said a magic word. "Build." I immediately said yes, and I went to work building what I felt the program needed and mentoring a young coach, Isabelle Leclair. After another year, we had a new dressing room and a team on the ice. Ten years later, the program has done well, ranking among the top women's university hockey programs in Canada from 2015 to 2020.

Ask Cassie Campbell and Jayna Hefford and they will tell you, "Danièle is a builder."

But my work isn't over yet; there is still so much to build in women's hockey. When I left the national team in 2004, the mandate was to develop women's hockey in Canada. The problem is that we're still talking about trying to do that today.

In 2018, at the Pyeongchang Winter Olympics, I was in the rink with Cassie Campbell when Team USA beat Team Canada in the gold medal game. At first, neither one of us could talk, it was too painful.

Then I turned to Cassie. "I believe we handed this gold medal to the United States by not developing the structure that we need to grow women's hockey in Canada."

That's where I'm putting my energy today. I want to make sure that women's hockey in Canada has the same financial investment as men's hockey so that women can have the same opportunities—the same equipment and working environment—to prove themselves. My next goal is to establish a high-performance centre for women's hockey in Quebec, but we're facing the same barriers as we faced decades ago.

For instance, I was talking about this new venture and someone said, "What about the guys?"

"What about the guys?" I replied. "They have it all already, so don't talk to me about that."

The inequality is still there, not just in playing the game, but in coaching as well. In non-Olympic years, I made $5,000 coaching the women's team while the men's team had a full-time coach and team. It's not just the money, it's the opportunities. I have worked in almost every level of hockey open to female coaches, and even coached in the men's major junior league. I've had offers to go to the United States to coach. I always refused because I wanted to build women's hockey here in Canada, but there's a pretty firm ceiling still in place.

At one time, I honestly thought that my love of hockey was going to take me to the NHL one day. Nearly every man who was involved in the women's Olympic hockey team is in the NHL in some capacity. Rob Cookson, our video coach from the 1998 team, became an NHL coach. Ryan Jankowski, our video coach from 2002, went on to be an NHL scout and then a GM. I thought that since I was the head coach of the gold-medal-winning team, one day I would end up in the NHL, too, but when I tried to knock on that door, I was told, "You didn't play the game." If you can't play in the NHL, you can't coach in the NHL. That sets women up for failure.

For me, coaching has been a labour of love. And every time that

I felt like I was carrying a load uphill, I always had a champion supporting me—people like Serge Savard, Dan O'Neill, Bob Nicholson, and Geoff Molson. Today, when I see people like Bob Nicholson or Tom Renney, I feel the respect. When I see players whom I know I was tough on, we laugh about it now. I love when a parent comes up to me and says, "You talked to my daughter and it meant everything to her."

If I could do it all over, I don't know what I would change. Hockey has helped shape me and challenge me to be the person that I am today. In my life, I was told no so many times, but each obstacle along the way has taught me to work harder. Winning without adversity is no fun. I love the game—that's why I am always at the rink, always watching games. I still have an important part to play.

The other day, I found myself back in Deux-Montagnes, Quebec, driving past the new indoor rink, remembering when there was only the outdoor one down from my house. And I smiled. The arena is called Danièle Sauvageau, in honour of my path from this little town to the Olympic stage.

Danièle Sauvageau is a Canadian ice hockey executive and a former coach and as such has worked in nearly every level of women's hockey, including the Quebec provincial team, the first junior team, and the national team, which she led to gold in the 2002 Olympic Games, Canada's first Olympic gold medal in hockey in fifty years. She became the first female coach in QMJHL history when she joined the Montreal Rockets in 1999 and the first female NHL Saturday Night Hockey TV analyst for Canada's French station, Télévision de Radio-Canada. In 2013, she was named an officer of the order of Canada for her work in women's hockey. During the 2016–18 seasons, she mentored Les Canadiennes of Montreal of the Canadian Women's Hockey League and coached the team in 2019–20. She was a member of the RCMP and the Service de police de la Ville de Montréal for thirty-three years, serving several years in the narcotics division. In the spring of 2020, Danièle volunteered with the Health and Security Committee in Montreal, delivering meals and supplies to the elderly and the disabled during the Covid-19 crisis. She lives in Montreal, Quebec.

 @coachDaniele

How to Hockey

Jeremy Rupke

Hockey has been a part of my life since I was three years old. As soon as I could walk, I wanted to get out on the ice. I grew up on a farm in Beaverton, Ontario, and we only had three channels on our TV, so I spent most of my time playing outside, either in the fields or on the frozen pond in our bush. When I was little, my parents would shovel the snow off our pond, and we'd go out for a skate. My mom was a hockey player, so she'd be down there, and we'd shoot the puck around.

Playing hockey on the pond was always a highlight for me, whether I was with my friends or my family. Scoring a goal never ceased to be a thrill, but even as a little kid, I loved the challenge of learning a new skill and practicing until I perfected it. Sometimes the ice was rough, but when it was nice and clear, there was nothing better and I would stay out there until it got dark. My toes would nearly freeze from the cold, and my dad would have to take my skates off and rub my feet to warm them up.

When I was five, my parents signed me up for minor hockey and I joined a tyke team called the Beaverton Blades. I was one of the smallest kids on the team, but I absorbed all the knowledge I could from our coaches. One drill I still remember because our coach, Paul, acted it out so well. He skated down the ice with two hands on his stick, throwing the stick wildly from side to side.

"That's the pitchfork," he said. "Don't do that." He showed us how to skate with more rhythm by holding the stick with one hand and pumping our arms vertically to match our legs. When he did it, it looked so easy, but for some reason I couldn't quite get the hang of skating by pushing off with two feet. My dad noticed, too.

"Do you like to skate fast?" he asked.

I answered right away. "Yeah, I like to skate fast!"

"If you push with both feet, you can go twice as fast."

It was like in the cartoons—a lightbulb went off over my head. "Oh, I get it!"

That was one of the best pieces of advice I ever received. My coaches had been trying to get me to push with two feet, but it was my dad who knew how to break it down so I could understand.

I loved hanging out with a few friends on the pond—it was more personal—but the structure of playing on a team with ten to fifteen kids who all loved hockey, and with coaches and parents teaching me, helped me become a better player. I loved the drills we were being taught and practiced them endlessly. I guess that was the work ethic my parents instilled in me from a young age. I remember just being a little kid when my dad taught me how to drive a tractor.

"Don't knock over the corn rows," he'd say, putting the tractor into gear. He told me what speed to keep it at and what gauge to watch. All I had to do was hold on to the steering wheel and keep the tractor between the rows. I would putter down the length of the row, and when I got to the end, my dad would hop on and turn it around, and then it was up to me to keep it straight all the way back.

My life on the farm—and on the ice—changed when my parents divorced. At the time, I was seven years old and my brother, Ryan, was nine years old and my sister, Sherry, was ten. When they told me they were splitting up, I cried, but I didn't really understand what was going on. My first thought was about what would happen next. I just wanted to figure that out.

During the divorce, which would end up taking four years, there was a lot of conflict and uncertainty about which one of our parents would live on the farm and have primary custody of us kids. The farm went back and forth between my parents. At one point, we were living

Here I am at age two with my brother, Ryan,
age three, helping my opa build a deck.

with my mom and her boyfriend on the farm, but that didn't end up being a good situation, and so for a while we went to live with my grandparents. The farm flipped back to my dad. After a year with my grandparents, my mom got a trailer, which she parked on their lawn, and we lived with her for a summer while we all worked on the farm to make money. Eventually, all four of us moved into a one-bedroom apartment with my mom and she worked three jobs until finally she was given the farm in the divorce and we moved back here. My dad moved into a basement apartment and we would spend weekends with him. Both my parents loved us unconditionally, and I'm thankful for that, but it was hard going back and forth between them.

Money was one of the issues that came up often. Even at seven, I knew hockey was expensive, so I told my parents that I didn't really want to play anymore. The truth was that I really *did* want to play, but with all the arguments about the cost, I told them that I didn't, just to make things easier. If I was lucky, I would play a little on the weekends, but nothing organized. I remember the Saturdays we spent with my dad, we would go upstairs to his neighbour's place and watch *Hockey Night in Canada* together, and it was during those moments with my dad, my siblings, and a couple of neighbours that I felt like I was part of a hockey family again.

Hockey really became my therapy. Despite my not being in a league, the whole experience made me turn to the game even more. Whether it was out on the pond or at the rink with my friends, playing hockey was a great release for me. No matter what was happening off the ice, I could count on hockey to be there for me. On the ice, all my troubles disappeared and nothing else mattered but playing the game.

Every day after school, my brother and I would invite our friends over to the pond to play for the hour and a half before it got too dark. On the weekends, I'd spend the whole day out on the pond, practicing my stick handling and skating.

When I first signed up for hockey I couldn't decide if I wanted to be a goalie or a player. I eventually decided I liked scoring goals more than I liked stopping them.

It was me and my brother's job to shovel the rink, and sometimes we missed a few days of shoveling and the amount of snow that built up on the pond was a little hairy. When that happened, I tried to recruit my friends to help.

"Oh, yeah, we'll meet you there right after school," they'd say.

At three thirty in the afternoon, I'd go down to the pond and start shoveling, then, over an hour later, my buddies would show up, just as it was almost cleared.

"Gee, thanks, guys," I'd say, looking at the darkening sky. Sometimes there was only ten minutes of daylight left, but we'd still end up playing until the sun went down.

When I was able to join a team again, I joined the local B team, one level down from the A team, but I didn't really understand the difference at the time. I could have tried out for the A level I guess, but all my friends were on the B team, so that's why I decided to join it. To be honest, for me there wasn't that much of a difference between the A and B teams in Beaverton—sure, they were a little more skilled and the A team had matching socks, but I just wanted to hang out with my friends and play the game.

Fortunately, I had gotten some coaching from an entirely different and unexpected source. One Christmas, when I was eight years old, my mom gave me a VHS tape of Don Cherry's *Rock 'Em, Sock 'Em, Volume 5*. I was ecstatic. The next day, I popped that VHS into the player, and until the end of the video, I was mesmerized by the incredible goals and plays unfolding on the ice with Grapes's classic commentary on the soundtrack. As soon as it was over, I rewound the tape and played it again, and then again. On New Year's Eve, I watched the tape over and over, trying to stay up until midnight. After a while I had my favourite plays and goals and would fast-forward the tape to those moments, studying the moves.

Every Christmas after that I got the latest edition of Don Cherry's *Rock 'Em, Sock 'Em* series. I could hardly wait for Christmas morning because I knew the next installment would be waiting for me under the tree. Those tapes were instrumental in improving my game. I loved seeing what the top pros could do, and eventually, I decided to try out some of their techniques myself.

On one of the tapes, I noticed that Pavel Bure didn't break his stride before he shot the puck. He would be skating at top speed and then, all of a sudden, the puck would be off his stick and in the net. That really stood out to me because I always had to stop or slow down before winding up my stick.

I went out to the pond to see if I could do it. At first, every time I tried to keep skating as I took a shot, I broke my stride, but then, after some practice, I did it. After that, whenever I was in a game, I had that new skill in my toolbox that I could use.

In another video, Patrik Eliáš went behind the net, and as he did, the opposing goalie and defenceman both went to the other side of the net, anticipating that he would bring the puck around, but he didn't. As he was moving, he switched the puck to his backhand, popped it out behind him, and passed it out in front, where his teammate tapped it into the opening left by the goalie. Once my brother and I saw that, we went straight out to the pond and practiced the move over and over again until we got to the point where we could use it in a game.

When I was fifteen, I saved up and bought a VHS tape set by Sean Skinner called *Stickhandling Beyond Belief*. I remember watching the video and thinking, *How come I don't know all this stuff? I've been coached for years, and I don't know how to do that.*

The more I watched the tapes, the more tricks I picked up on to try out myself. I think I almost wore out that VHS with all the replays.

As much as the tapes helped me learn skills, when I did finally make an A team, it was in part because there weren't that many players to choose from when I showed up at tryouts. I also finally had a growth spurt and caught up to my teammates after being the shortest kid on every team for so long.

Money was still an issue, of course. So in the summers, I was busy helping my mom out on the farm. I'd always done odd jobs around the place like picking berries, but as I got older, I started doing harder work, like picking rocks from the fields and throwing hay. We grew crops like sweet corn and we had pick-your-own strawberry and raspberry fields and a petting zoo, too, which drew people from the surrounding communities. Corn season for us started at the end of July. As a teenager, I spent a lot of time selling corn on the side of the road. It was a lot like the show *Letterkenny*. There I would be. Sitting in a chair. Working the corn stand. Twice a year, we brought in the hay, which lasted a couple of weeks, and I helped out with that, too. I also got a part-time job at a golf course to help out with our bills. I ended up doing a lot of odd jobs to make money to pay for my equipment and fees. Everything I did went back to hockey.

While I did find time to play video games and ball hockey with my friends, training on the ice and working on the farm gave me some good life lessons about the value of hard work. My parents always taught me that it was important to work hard to make a life for myself, but a lot of my work ethic came from my mom. When we were poor and living in a trailer or small apartment, she never complained, she never looked for an easy way out; she just worked. She didn't earn much, but she always found a way to make things work for us. One Christmas, she very reluctantly got a few gifts for us from a toy drive. She had wanted to earn everything herself, but knew there wouldn't be a Christmas for us if it weren't for the toy drive donations. Living with my mom through those hard times and how she dealt with adversity taught me a lot about what I would need to be successful or even just get by in life.

Just as I was turning sixteen—my final year of minor hockey—I began to flourish as a player. I never really thought about making it to the NHL, but I did want to play at a higher level of hockey that wasn't necessarily available in Beaverton. I had applied and been accepted to Georgian College to study police foundations and thought I could play for the college team and see if I could become a late bloomer. I also contacted the Little Britain Merchants, a Junior C team in the OHA, about attending a tryout.

But the summer before college, something happened to throw me off course.

I had the day off and was riding my bike to a friend's place in Beaverton to play some video games when I was hit by a pickup truck. I don't remember how it happened. Just that everything went black.

The next thing I remember is waking up in an ambulance to see paramedics attending to me.

"Sorry," I muttered. In my stupor, I felt like I was troubling all these people taking care of me.

The next time I opened my eyes, I saw the ceiling of the hospital, and then suddenly I was in a different room. I don't remember much from that day.

I was told later that my friend's neighbour had found me on the road and called an ambulance, but my injuries were so severe that they had to transport me to another hospital. My parents were distraught when they saw me in the hospital, and to this day, my mom is still scarred from the whole ordeal. I didn't look too good. My shoulder was broken in two places, but of deeper concern was my brain injury. I hadn't been wearing a helmet and had split my head open. My doctor said I had almost died from all the bleeding inside my brain.

One of the doctors tried to assess my injuries by asking me a list of questions, but I could barely form a sentence. I couldn't tell time and I couldn't remember my dad's name. I was having problems recalling other words, too.

The doctor pulled out a pen. "What's this?"

"Watch," I answered. I knew it was a pen, but when I tried to say that word, "watch" would come out of my mouth.

The swelling on my brain was causing my speech problems. I'll never forget the first time I looked at myself in the mirror. My head was twice its normal size. I had this bubble on the top of my head from the fluid that was collecting on my brain after the accident. It was eerie to see.

I was in the hospital for the next two weeks as the doctors monitored my recovery. The swelling began to go down and my ability to recall words came back, but during one examination, one of the doctors said that there was a good chance that I would never be the same again. When I told him I was a hockey player, he said I couldn't play contact hockey anymore. My brain was just too fragile. And he doubted that I would play at all again. Just like that, all my hockey plans had ended.

But I wasn't ready to give up, so as the doctor was giving me his prognosis, I just told myself, *I'm not going to give up. I'm going to get through this.*

The doctors could say whatever they wanted. I wasn't going to believe any of it until it was actually real. Five years later, the gravity of my injury really hit me, but in that moment, I refused to accept it.

After I was released from the hospital, I went home to recover. I had a series of exercises to do to strengthen my shoulder and I made sure that I stayed active. But my mental rehabilitation was just as important as my physical rehab. I was still a little cross-eyed at first and my vision was blurry, so my mom went out and bought me an Xbox to help me train my eyes. I would spend an hour every day trying to follow objects on the screen while I played video games. I read books, I wrote, and I did everything they told me to in order to make a full recovery.

But I was still having trouble with my speech, and so a speech pathologist came to visit me once a week at my home. I explained that I wanted to take the rest of the summer to recover and then attend Georgian College that fall.

"You probably shouldn't go to college just yet," she said.

"No," I replied. "I'm going to make a full recovery." I didn't want to take the easy way out and pushed myself to make sure I was ready for school in time.

I continued to challenge myself to do even simple things. And there were signs of hope. On one test to gauge my IQ, I scored very high on problem solving, which is something that I always enjoyed. Each day, I got a little better and a littler stronger. After a few weeks, my vision cleared up, which was a big relief and I felt a lot more like my old self.

By the time September rolled around, I no longer needed to see my physiotherapist and I was on my way to Georgian College. My doctor was very clear that I couldn't play contact hockey, but he didn't say anything about non-contact hockey. Since I couldn't try out for any high-level teams like the Merchants, I signed up for intramural hockey at the college, which started in October. Not playing hockey was never an option for me, so when I stepped back out on the ice that first time, it seemed ordinary. I was back doing what I loved, playing hockey. To me, hockey season had started, and it was time to play. That season I didn't have my best showing, but considering how bad an accident I was involved in, I did okay. I was just glad to be on the ice again, playing the game I loved.

My buddy Ken and I continued to toss around the puck on my pond. One time, we had the day off from school and so I suggested we go out to the pond. We began shoveling it off and had it all cleared around noon. We started playing and didn't stop for close to four hours. Then we looked at each other. "Let's just keep going," I said. Ken nodded.

We ended up skating for over six hours straight, just the two of us, and by the time we finally stopped, we were absolutely exhausted. It was a pond hockey record. After we wrapped up, we went into town and grabbed some chicken and pasta and had a feast.

I was back to my normal self again. The only lingering effect was that I couldn't hold my own in a snowball fight anymore because of my shoulder injury. I could only throw four or five before my shoulder tired out. But that was okay—I could play hockey.

After college, I went on to Western University in London to study psychology and I continued to play hockey while I was there. I had an idea to be a police officer, but then I kind of fell into making websites and decided to go to Fanshawe College to study website development.

I had always been pretty tech-savvy. When I was eight or so, my dad brought home a laptop from his work. It was like a briefcase in size. All on my own, I started teaching myself how to navigate through the computer. It was an MS-DOS operating system, and as I typed different commands in the computer's director, I figured out how it worked. After that, I was always drawn to technology. Whether it was my first cellphone or the computers at school, I taught myself the ins and outs of how they worked.

So it wasn't unusual for me to create websites. I started with one for my mom's dog-breeding business, and then I made some for myself. I was always coming up with various business ideas, including one that involved selling toilet paper with people's faces on it. Little did I know that my coaching and my websites were about to collide.

I had begun coaching rep hockey. I was inspired by how Don Cherry had always given back to young players by teaching them simple lessons that could make a big difference in a game, and I wanted to do the same. At first, I thought it would be pretty easy. If I could play hockey, I could coach, right? Wrong. When I got out there on the ice with the kids, I couldn't remember any of the drills I used to do. That's when it hit me that coaching wasn't going to be as easy as I thought. Even after watching all those *Rock 'Em, Sock 'Em* videos, I still had to learn how to coach. I learn best from watching others, so I turned to the Internet, where a plethora of hockey videos lived.

And that's what I was doing one day in 2009 when I was mesmerized by a video of an elite player showcasing some spectacular stick handling. A kernel of an idea began to take shape in my mind. What if I created a hockey website with some tips and tricks to pass along what I'd learned? I'd cover the basics: how to skate, how to shoot, how to stick-handle, and other skills. I wouldn't put ads on the website. I wasn't interested in making money off it—I could do that on my other sites—instead, this would be a labour of love.

My first step was to see what else was already out there. I found the odd decent article, but a lot of stuff was out of date. While there were some bits and pieces scattered around the web, there wasn't one central online destination that people could turn to for substantial hockey tips.

I was surprised. "How is there not a website about hockey development in Canada?"

I wrote some initial articles, but I was having trouble finding good videos to accompany the pieces. One video about how to take a slap shot was awful. I cringed as the guy compared taking one to swinging a golf club or a baseball bat. I just couldn't take watching any more incorrect how-to hockey videos. That was my aha moment. I knew I could make a better video than what was out there. I was working at Deerhurst Resort in Huntsville, Ontario, as a security guard at the time, and they had a nice pond that I could use for free.

I thought of everything I didn't like in YouTube hockey videos—bad lighting and rambling commentary—and made sure not to do what they did. I asked Ken to help me shoot, and we went out on the pond with a handheld video camera and made about five or six videos.

I put them up on the website and that's how howtohockey.com was born. I didn't really think much of it until the comments started coming in.

I started reading through them. Some people were thanking us for the videos and said they were a big help. Others said they tried one of the skills and it worked for them. And still others asked for more.

"What about a backhand?" someone commented after I posted about how to take a wrist shot.

I know how to do that, I said to myself. *I can make a video.*

And I did.

"I've been struggling on my backwards crossovers. Can you do a video on that next?" another would say.

Each time a request came in, I grabbed Ken and we went out to shoot it.

Then I started receiving requests for skills that I had never thought of—the finer points of hockey and skating, like edge work. It hit me that I better make sure that I was on top of my own game. I searched out power-skating classes that were taking place in my area and called the coaches. I explained that I was also a coach and asked if I could come and help them out on the ice. That's how I met elite-level coaches Scott Grover, Jim Vitale, and others. They welcomed me to the ice. At Jim's camp, I learned key skating drills that would help me

use my inside and outside edges to improve my usual forward stride. Scott ran drills with up to thirty kids with military precision and infectious energy, something I wanted to replicate in my own coaching and communicate through my videos.

I learned a lot of valuable lessons from these guys that I translated to the website. But as I watched more and more coaches, I also discovered that there are different ways to do everything in hockey.

Shooting the puck is a prime example. Kids are taught to shoot off their outside leg, but pros can shoot off their inside or outside leg. I heard coaches teach players the same way to shoot the puck year after year. Then I watched YouTube videos of the pros, and I saw that sometimes they did the complete opposite with way better results. I watched videos of fifty different goals in the NHL in one year, and by my estimate, of the fifty, only five of the players had perfect technique. There are times in the NHL when the puck comes your way and you just have to rip it. What I realized through all my research is that there are dozens of different ways to shoot the puck.

When I made my videos, I was very careful not to say, "This is the only way." Hockey is so dynamic, there are many ways to do the same thing effectively. Take acceleration. During the fastest skater competition in the NHL All-Star Game, Connor McDavid started with a crossover. Meanwhile Dylan Larkin from the Detroit Red Wings started with an open hip. Which is the best? They are both effective and they each work for that individual player. If you watch Darryl Belfry from belfryhockey, you'll see that he likes to teach crossovers through the neutral zone to gain speed and be deceptive. When I started playing hockey, I only knew about using crossovers to pick up speed behind the net or around circles in drills. When you watch the pros, if they're carrying the puck through the neutral zone, they don't use the forward stride that often.

Another key lesson I've learned is that you don't always need two hands on the stick. Most coaches are always yelling at kids in practice, "Two hands on the stick!" Two hands on the stick allows for better

control with the puck, but if you watch Sidney Crosby, he will switch from two hands to one on the stick. If he has one or two guys on him, he'll keep one hand on the stick and use the other to push the guys off him. Skating with one hand on the stick also helps generate speed; then, when you want to make a move, you switch to two hands on the stick. It's important for players to be able to play either way and to understand when it is the right time to switch from two hands to one. A player should do one rep in practice with one hand on the stick, then another with two hands on the stick.

Whenever I saw a coach teaching a given skill, I always tested it out before making a video. If it improved my skills, I embraced it and continued working on it until I made it my own. Then I shot a video. If it didn't work, I found a different way. Sometimes I'd watch thirty different drills and use only three in a video. The more videos I made, the more I was becoming a better hockey player and a better coach. I felt like I had found my calling.

About once a month, I posted a video to my YouTube channel and embedded it into the articles on my website. And then more people started to tune in and check out the videos, and each one began to receive more and more views. I expected to hear mostly from people in Canada, and maybe a few in the United States, but I was receiving e-mails from people in Spain and Australia who didn't have as many resources or as much access to hockey as we do in North America. Some said that they always wanted to learn these skills, and because of the videos, they now can. Others told me that they learned so much from the videos, they're now passing the skills along as a coach. I get a lot of messages from kids who tell me they are only on the ice once a week, but they're watching my videos to help improve. Another kid said that he made an AAA team thanks to my videos.

It's messages like these that show me the power of the videos—and the transformational power of hockey. I got an e-mail from someone who weighed over 400 pounds, and he told me that he lost close to 250 pounds through hockey and skating. One seventy-three-year-old

gentleman in California decided he wanted to start playing hockey. He said my videos helped him learn how to play. The best feedback I got was from a dad who told me he watched the videos so he could learn how to play hockey with his son.

Close to a year after the YouTube channel was up and running, HockeyShot.com caught my eye. While I originally didn't want to put any ads on my website, HockeyShot had products like targets, nets, and radar guns that I could use to make better videos. I reached out to them and proposed that they send me some of their products to review on my website. They thought it was a great idea. From there, I developed a solid partnership with HockeyShot.

Not long after that, YouTube started allowing content creators to monetize their videos. At first, I said no. I had started the whole enterprise for the love of the game, but when the website's following reached two hundred thousand, the requests became almost over-whelming, and I had to re-evaluate. The paid ads and sponsorships of the videos would help fund the videos and allow me to make them accessible to a wider audience.

The important thing was that the website would still be free. My goal had been to help players learn all the skills they need for free so that no kid had to borrow his dad's credit card to buy a Don Cherry tape. So that the mom or dad who has no clue how to coach but signed up to coach a team to spend time with their hockey-obsessed kid has a place to learn about hockey. So that beginners, whether they're three or thirty years old, can improve their game. We often think coaching is just for kids, but hockey doesn't have an age limit. After five years, I decided to make howtohockey.com my full-time job and stopped working on my other websites so I could devote 100 per-cent of my energy to hockey and becoming a better coach and content creator.

Hockey is my job now. I'm lucky that my wife, Sammy, is a fan, too. Like me, she grew up playing hockey, but she quit when she entered high school after she got injured during a game. She likes to play hockey, but she also encourages me to get engaged in non-hockey events.

When we decided to start a family, I was excited for the day when I could bring our kids out on the ice and teach them to skate like my parents had taught me. Mason, our firstborn, arrived in January 2015. I envisioned him being obsessed with hockey and me teaching him everything I know.

When he was two and a half years old, I took him to the Summit Centre in Huntsville and laced up his skates, but when we got out on the ice, he just started crying. Like most hockey dads, I thought he would be the next phenom and envisioned taking videos of him ripping around the ice and doing crossovers! Of course, that wasn't realistic. Mason crying—that was realistic. He was just a little kid and had about a one-minute attention span, so I honestly didn't expect him to take to hockey immediately.

The next time we went, he had more fun. He giggled as I guided him along the ice. Over the next year or so, he got more comfortable on the ice and started to like skating and hockey, but after a few minutes, he would inevitably be ready to leave. Every time I tried to convince him to stay a little longer. One day I brought his toy robot and his toy sword onto the ice. This made him think we were not doing hockey drills, we were out there having fun and playing. When he got tired, I'd bribe him with Timbits if he did one more lap around the rink.

When Mason was four, I signed him up for hockey even though I knew he was just going to go out there and goof around. The most important thing for me was that he was on a team and having fun. We tried to teach him to skate with both feet instead of just one, but most often, he would push with one foot, try a bit, then quit. That was okay. All I wanted was for him to have fun, and he did. Each practice, I'd watch from the sidelines as he skated up to a teammate or a coach and said something then skated away laughing. What the heck was he saying that he found so funny? Then I thought, *I have a ton of video equipment—why don't I mic him up one day?*

The next practice, I did just that. I set him up with the mic and then filmed him doing his usual thing around the rink. After, I watched the video and I realized that Mason was chattering nonstop the entire practice!

"One-two, one-two, one-two," he said as he skated. He was practicing skating with both feet as I'd taught him. Then he turned to me in the crowd. "I'm doing it, Dad! I'm doing it!"

That brought the biggest smile to my face. He was so proud that he was skating properly, and I realized that he really did care about hockey and that he was listening to his coaches and me. I would never have heard that had I not put the microphone on him.

Then, of course, there was the funny stuff.

When he got tired of skating and just lay on the ice: "I need a nap. My legs are tired." A half-dozen times, he mentioned going to "Ba-Donald's," his way of saying "McDonald's," sometimes to a friend,

*I always try to make going to the rink fun
for Mason. Here we are on the way to practice
during his first year of Timbits hockey.*

sometimes to no one in particular. And once to the coach, who encouraged him to get off the ice where he was lying down for the last minute of practice.

When I posted the video, I had modest expectations. Of course, I think my own kid is hilarious, but I figured the audience for this particular brand of humour was small. Boy, was I wrong. Suddenly other Instagram accounts were taking the video and posting it on their sites, and then popular sites like Bar Down, Spittin' Chiclets, TSN, Sportsnet, and ESPN reached out to ask if they could post the video. Then it hit the front page of Reddit. Once that happened, the numbers exploded. In one day, it reached one million views, and the day after that it was all over the news.

To put this into context, it typically takes about a year for a video to hit one million views, but Mason captured people's hearts within a day.

The response was mostly good. However, I was shocked when my friend Steve Dangle sent me a link to a tweet from Eric Trump, who had used a photo of Mason.

"I assume you have seen this?" Steve said.

I was taken aback. I reached out to Eric and politely asked him not to use a photo of my kid for his political agenda, and he took it down the next day.

Despite the overwhelming response to the video, the whole experience gave me a much better understanding of my son and what was going through his mind during practice. I was just a dad at that moment, connecting with his kid through hockey, like my dad had done with me.

If Mason wants to go out on the ice and play, I ask him, "Hey, do you want me to teach you something?"

Usually he says no and asks to do something else, but I always throw it out there. One time I asked him, "Do you want to do crossovers?"

He looked at me. "Okay."

I got so excited. We went to the goal line and I showed him how to put one skate over the other. He got it on his first try! He did a few more crossovers, then got bored. "Okay, Dad, let's play tag now."

One night, when I was tucking him in bed and reading him a book, I told him that I was proud of him. "You're becoming a really good hockey player."

"Yeah, because you taught me! Dad, can you teach me some more?"

That was a very proud dad moment for me. Now I have a daughter, Olivia, as well. I love teaching both her and Mason how to play hockey. Anytime they ask me to show them something on the ice—even if it's only for a few minutes—I enjoy every second of it.

One of our favourite spots to visit during the winter is Ottawa. We always go for a skate on the Rideau Canal.

To me, that's what hockey's all about—the people it brings together. When I was twelve and finally able to join a hockey team, I noticed a kid on the team who had just moved to Beaverton and didn't know anyone. We were at our first practice and I thought to myself how tough it must be to be new. I decided right there that I was going to be his friend.

I sat down next to him in the dressing room. "Hey, my name's Jeremy. How's it going?"

"Good, I guess," he replied. "My name's Randy."

I ended up sitting next to Randy for every practice and we became good friends. To this day, we remain close. Randy lives in Alberta now, and once a year he'll travel to Ontario to hang out with me, or I'll go out west to see him. And that all happened because of hockey.

What began as a side project almost a decade ago has given me so many incredible opportunities within the hockey world. I've been fortunate to work with CCM, Bauer, and many other top hockey companies, film a video with Mark Messier, go to the 2018 NHL draft in Dallas, Texas, meet with Jack Eichel of the Buffalo Sabres, and speak to Carolina Hurricanes coach Rod Brind'Amour, who is incredibly insightful. I've played hockey on top of mountains, skyscrapers, and in caves. But regardless of whatever opportunities and partnerships that come my way, my goal is always to help others through hockey because the game is about so much more than being a good player or making it to the NHL; it's about the lessons that we learn.

One of the biggest lessons hockey has taught me was not about success, but rather about how to respond to failure. When you're faced with a setback, there's always a way to overcome it and it's that journey that's important. The training, the practice, the discipline. Getting better doesn't happen overnight, but when we put in the work each day to improve, we're not just bettering ourselves, we're bettering an entire team. We lay a foundation to build upon. It's a habit I've tried to put into place off the ice, too, so I can be a better husband, a better dad, and a better coach.

*A product of the ponds and rinks of small-town Ontario, **Jeremy Rupke** turned a lifelong passion for hockey into the most popular hockey channel on YouTube, with more than 340,000 subscribers. Although he never played hockey at a high level, Jeremy's videos are the by-product of his personal philosophy: getting better every day. When Jeremy isn't playing hockey or making how-to videos, he spends time with his wife, son, and daughter.*

For Jeremy's hockey tips and lessons, go to howtohockey.com, or connect with him on his YouTube channel @CoachJeremy.

 *@howtohockey*

Shift by Shift, Game by Game

Andrew Cogliano

When my dad wasn't working, he was often at the rink, watching me play hockey. After every game, we'd get something to eat on the way home and talk about the game and how I did. During minor hockey, I put up good numbers, but if I had a bad game, it was usually a quiet drive home. Even then, my dad always saw the good in me and pointed out the positives. No matter how late we came home from a game, he would be ready to go to work and drive me to school the next morning. He didn't have to say anything to me; I just knew that if he was going to be ready, then I was going to be ready, too. That was the way to get ahead in life.

Hard work was something my parents inspired in me from a young age. My dad, Carm, worked for the City of Toronto's Parks and Recreation Department and managed different parks, arenas, and recreational facilities, and my mom, Teri, had a few jobs. She was a preschool teacher and a fitness instructor. Because of them, I was fortunate enough to go to St. Michael's College School. Back then, it was a lot of money to go to St. Mike's, but my parents wanted me to have a quality education.

I was never the smartest kid. Some of my classmates could read something and immediately get it, but I had to write everything down in order to understand it, and that's exactly what I did to get good grades. The way I approached my studies was also the way I approached hockey. Hard work and practice.

I first learned how to skate on the backyard rink my dad made. He put up plywood for the sides and watered it. To be honest, it was a pretty crappy rink. I can still remember how bumpy the ice was, but my older brother, Matt, and I didn't care. We were happy just to go back there and play hockey.

I was about eight years old and playing for the Vaughan Selects when I was the subject of a newspaper article. Right there on the front page of the sports section was a picture of me on the ice. My dad framed it and the article still hangs in his office. But the funny thing about the photo is that the way I was skating then is exactly the way I skate today. The position of my legs and body in the photo is identical to pictures taken of me skating in the NHL.

School may not have come easily to me, but skating did. I was a naturally fast skater from the beginning. When I was eleven, my team, the Vaughan Kings, would bring in a guy to work with us, but other than that, I didn't have any specific skating instruction. I never went to any summer hockey camps or power-skating schools. Even though I had this gift, I was never totally satisfied with myself. I've always been a small player compared to my teammates, and while it helped that I was quick on the ice, I made sure I worked on the rest of my game, especially my stick handling and puck control, so I could become a better player.

That said, when the hockey season was over, it was over, and I played soccer for the summer, not really thinking about hockey. In the long run, I think this mentality served me well because I didn't get caught up in the hype of being a hockey player and playing in the NHL someday. Instead, I put in the hours to become a good all-round athlete, one that was disciplined and reliable on and off the ice.

When I was fourteen, I started to realize that I was a pretty good player and stood out from some of the other kids. In 2000–01, the Vaughan Kings had a strong year and we went all the way to the Quebec International Pee Wee tournament, which is the biggest Pee Wee tournament in the world, with over 120 teams competing. A lot of the stars of the tournament go on to play in the NHL.

In the quarterfinals, we beat the LA Junior Kings, a team that was loaded with players like Bobby Ryan—it was basically an LA All-Star

Here is the picture that was on the front page of the
sports section in the Toronto Star. *I was playing in the*
North York Tournament in December 1994.

Team. The best part was that nobody knew who we were. Everyone had heard of the LA Junior Kings, but nobody had heard of the Vaughan Kings. We ended up losing to the Boston Minutemen in the semifinals, but it was a great tournament and I played well. By the end of Pee Wee, I thought I had chance of doing something in hockey, and when I turned fifteen, my family started getting approached by big agents and scouts.

In 2003, I heard my name thrown out there as a potential Ontario Hockey League prospect, but I wasn't too caught up in it. My parents were very passionate about my education, and they'd pushed me to get good grades all through school because they wanted me to have something to fall back on if hockey didn't work out. I was more focused on playing NCAA hockey than OHL. And one big reason for that was Mike Cammalieri.

When I was growing up, Mike lived next door to us, and his dad was good friends with my dad. Mike was five years older than me, but sometimes we'd skate together and work out in the summer. For a while we shared the same trainer, Matt Nichol. I really looked up to Mike. He also played in the Quebec International Pee Wee Tournament, and when he was selected in the OHL priority draft, he chose not to play so he could play at the college level. He ended up getting a full hockey scholarship to the University of Michigan.

I remember we went down to the Yost Arena in Ann Arbor to see him play. Seeing the Michigan Wolverines hockey team out on the ice was an unforgettable experience, and I knew right then and there that I wanted to follow Mike's career path and play there, too. Their yellow-and-blue helmets and jerseys were so distinctive, and they stuck in my mind long after the game was over. The uniforms, the arena, everything—that's what I thought of when I envisioned what it might be like to play college hockey in the United States. The school's hockey program has an incredible legacy—a record-setting number of championships, and dozens of their alumni played in the NHL. After that visit, my goal was to become a Michigan Wolverine. I wanted to be a student-athlete: to go to college *and* play hockey.

I was drafted by the OHL, but I chose to play a couple years of junior hockey to preserve my NCAA eligibility. When it came time to choose a school, the decision was easy. I had another offer, but when I met with Coach Red Berenson at the University of Michigan, he didn't mess around and offered me a scholarship on the spot. I immediately accepted.

But first, there was the 2005 NHL draft. Even if I was drafted, I wouldn't be going off to the NHL right away, so my family didn't attend the draft in Ottawa. We were watching it on TV like everyone else when Sidney Crosby was named the first overall pick. And then, just a little while later, they announced my name. The Edmonton Oilers had selected me twenty-fifth overall.

That moment was so surreal. The realization settled over me: I was in the NHL. It would be another two years before I'd even go to a training camp, but I was so happy to be an Oiler and I loved the idea of playing in a Canadian city. I actually had thought I'd be selected the pick before by the St. Louis Blues, so I felt lucky to get a chance to play in Canada. It was quite a celebration in my house.

That fall, I headed off to Michigan, excited for what the future had in store.

Going to the University of Michigan and being a Wolverine was everything I thought it would be. A lot of the guys on the team were older than me, which drove me to practice harder to get better. I put up good numbers in my first year, but I did even better in my second. Unfortunately, North Dakota knocked us out of the first round of the NCAA tournament both years. We were good; they were just better, with star players like Jonathan Toews and T. J. Oshie.

In 2007, I arrived at the Oilers training camp. I remember thinking, *Let's just see how this goes.* I knew a lot of new draft picks play a year or two in the minors before making the team, but Edmonton was going through a rebuild phase and they were bringing up some younger players. The Oilers always prided themselves on being hardworking and in top fitness, and I had no choice but to be in good shape just to keep up with the high standard that they set. I played really well at camp, and as it was coming to an end, I was still there. That's when I knew I had made the team. I was really proud of myself because I knew I had earned that spot.

On October 4, 2007, I played my first NHL game as a member of the Edmonton Oilers. My parents and Matt made the trip out to Edmonton to watch me as we faced off against the San Jose Sharks. That first game was so much fun—I even had an assist—and we beat the Sharks. There was too much going on to really think about anything, but I remember after the game, it hit me, *I just played in the NHL.* Then, all of a sudden, the dressing room doors opened, and I was talking to media. There was so much energy buzzing around the room.

Just a few nights later, we were up against the Detroit Red Wings and my dad was there watching. They were my favourite team growing up, so it was pretty amazing to be on the ice with them. And then, it happened. Joni Pitkänen came down the left side and gave me a pass back door, and I just put it in the net, scoring against All-Star Dominik

Hašek. My first NHL goal! To score against Detroit—and with my dad in the arena—was pretty special. Needless to say, we had a good chat after that game, as was our routine.

After you've played for a while, you can forget how much fun it was at the start of your NHL career. I was a young guy along with Sam Gagner and Tom Gilbert, and we all got to experience so many firsts together. But more than that, it was an honour being in the league and playing against guys I had been watching on TV. I remember it was such a big deal to be on the ice with Jarome Iginla when we played the Calgary Flames in the Battle of Alberta.

One of my heroes growing up was Joe Sakic, and near the end of my rookie season, we played the Avalanche in Colorado. I remember we were in a shootout and Dwayne Roloson was in net for us that night. I was standing at the far end of our bench and Joe was at the far end of the Avs' bench.

All of a sudden Joe leaned over and said to me, "Hey, kid, where should I shoot on Roloson?"

I just looked at him, shocked that he would speak to me, let alone ask me where to shoot on my own goalie to win the game. I didn't say a word.

When it was his turn in the shootout, he hopped over the boards, came down the ice, and took his patented wrist shot at Roloson's low blocker. Sure enough, it went in. And as he skated by our bench, he winked at me! I sat there, speechless that I had just witnessed a guy I idolized pull off a move like that.

When I was starting out with the Oilers, I would look around the dressing room at veterans like Shawn Horcoff, Steve Staios, and Ethan Moreau. It wasn't uncommon for them to come to the rink three hours before a game to make sure they were warmed up and ready to go. They always wanted to be the best in fitness testing, and they trained like animals. Watching them put in the time really hit home with me and began to rub off on me. I recognized their work ethic and began to pattern myself after them—that's how I got to be where I am now.

That first year was full of highlights. In March, I ended up setting an NHL record by scoring overtime goals in three consecutive games. I don't know how I did it. I think I got lucky because back then, overtime was 4-on-4 and it was tough to score. The first was against the Columbus Blue Jackets on March 7, 2008, the second against the Chicago Blackhawks on the ninth. By the time we went into our third overtime in a row against the St. Louis Blues on the eleventh, we were all pretty spent. But when Sam passed me the puck, I didn't have time to think—I chopped at it with my stick and scored upstairs, just under the crossbar. After that, my stick and gloves were sent to the Hockey Hall of Fame, which was cool. But what stays with me are the moments after the game celebrating with the team and my friends.

The Oilers came close to making the playoffs; in the end, we fell short. But that first season was the best time of my hockey career because I was young and playing in the NHL for the first time.

March 9, 2008. I had just scored my second goal against the
Chicago Blackhawks in what would be my third in three
consecutive games and am celebrating with the team.
(Bill Smith/NHLI via Getty Images)

I had also played all eighty-two games. I didn't think much of it then, but that was really just the beginning. As the seasons went by, my consecutive games streak began to add up. I barely noticed. My focus has always been the game and how I can help my team. And the Oilers were trying to find their footing. At the end of the 2009–10 season, we finished last in the NHL. So, I wasn't thinking about any streak; I just wanted to be my best for hockey.

Of all my years in the NHL, the 2010–11 season with the Oilers was the toughest. We still weren't playing well as a team, and I had a lingering injury that almost made me sit out a game.

It was November and we were playing the Carolina Hurricanes. I was going to the net when the defenceman's stick came up and caught me in the lip. I started bleeding right away, so they took me to the trainers' room, stitched me back up, then I went back out and played the rest of the game.

As the season went on, I kept getting hit in the same spot on my lip. The cut would open and I'd need stitches again. My lip was always swollen, so much so that people began to joke about it. One newspaper drew a caricature of me and my lip because nobody could believe how big it was.

Of all the injuries I could get, this was a small one, but the pain didn't go away. Whenever I touched it, I felt something hard. I had just started dating my wife, Allie, then and she joked that I never wanted to kiss her because of my lip. Two tough guys on the team, Zach Stortini and Steve MacIntyre, had both been hit in the lip plenty of times during the game, and they told me it was just scar tissue. The Oilers medical staff said the same. "You have to rub your lip and rub the scar tissue out of it," they all told me.

So I did—every day—but nothing changed. At one point, the team ended up sending me to a dermatologist to figure out what the heck was wrong with me. They cut my lip open in the exact same spot, but found nothing. So they stitched me back up.

Near the end of the season, we were playing the Detroit Red Wings when, I kid you not, I got hit with a high stick in the same exact spot where I was hit back in November. My lip stayed the same.

"Something is up here," I said to the doctors. "This isn't normal."

At the end of the year, I got plastic surgery to fix it, and when I woke up from the procedure, the doctor was standing over me holding out a small object. "This was in your lip," he said.

I peered at his hand. It was three quarters of my tooth! When I took the first high stick back in November, I had unknowingly chipped my tooth and it had gone into my lip and been there for five months. And like an idiot, I was trying to rub it out, thinking it was scar tissue. I couldn't believe it hadn't gotten infected.

For an athlete, even a minor injury like that can be distracting and take away from your performance on the ice, and that's what I was most preoccupied with—how I could play my best and support my team.

Maintaining my health was a part of that. Playing for the Oilers, I often saw guys sick with the flu or concussed, but I was fortunate to avoid major injury. Of course, I would feel tired and sore, but I was surrounded by a great support system of people who were very knowledgeable. One time I had signs of a concussion, but after an exam, it turned out that I just needed to get my neck worked on. Once I did that, I was able to return to the ice and I didn't miss a game. Whenever I had something going on, I got on it right away so it wouldn't become a problem and affect my playing.

Before the 2011–12 season began, I got some unexpected news. I was driving to the rink to go for a skate when my phone rang. It was on the dash and I could see that Steve Tambellini, our general manager, was calling me. Right away I knew something was up, so once I got to the rink, I phoned him back.

"Hey, I traded you," Steve said. He started to tell me how appreciative he was of all I had done for the past three seasons. Almost a minute went by with him talking but not telling me where I was going. Then, finally, he said, "Andrew, we traded you to Anaheim."

Those first three seasons with the Oilers had taught me so much and I had made lifelong friendships, especially with Sam Gagner, but I was happy to make the change. The Ducks had a good team—they had won their first Stanley Cup in 2007 and made it to the playoffs every year but one since then. I figured I couldn't get much better than Southern California after three Edmonton winters.

When I arrived in Anaheim, I was immediately comfortable with the team, but the first season ended up being a little rough. Out of our first twenty-four games, we only won seven. Our coach, Randy Carlyle, was fired that year and Bruce Boudreau came in. After that, things began to gel, and in my second season, we climbed through our division and were the second seed in the Western Conference for the 2013 Stanley Cup playoffs.

It was my first taste of the playoffs. We were up against Detroit and the series was tough. We won the first game, but lost the second in overtime. The score kept going back and forth and the game went into overtime three more times. My biggest memory was playing against Pavel Datsyuk and Henrik Zetterberg, two incredible scorers. By then, Datsyuk had been with Detroit for eleven seasons, ten of which were with Zetterberg, and they always seemed to know where the other one was on the ice. In the last game of the series, both of them were on the ice together, which screwed us up a bit, and we ended up losing. But it was an experience I'll never forget.

Playing for Anaheim was fun. I centred the third line, killed penalties, and basically did whatever they asked me to do. As a team, we had players who were tough both physically and mentally. We had a pack mentality and there were a couple guys who stuck up for each other. Being in the Western Conference was challenging, and to be successful and keep making the playoffs, we had to stick together as a team and play hard, which we did.

Those were the best years of my career. In the 2013–14 season, I scored twenty goals—a personal best. I also got a bit of an ankle sprain. We were playing the Arizona Coyotes and winning. The clock was running out and they pulled their goalie.

I was trying to shoot the puck into the empty net when I got clipped along the boards by Shane Doan. As he hit me, my leg caught underneath me, and I twisted my ankle. I missed the net and went back to the bench, hobbling on my one good leg. Just as I reached the bench, the puck came back at me, and I turned and shot it down the ice into the empty net.

After, I had my ankle looked at. It was a grade-one sprain and the pain level was manageable. I always took the mind-set that I was going to keep on playing until I couldn't, so I just taped it up and played through it.

I also played my five-hundredth game in a row. Not that I was counting. The odd time someone would bring up that I hadn't missed a game since 2007, but to be honest, when I thought of my first NHL season, all I could think of was how much energy I had and how healthy I was. At the time, I had taken for granted that I would always be in peak condition. Fortunately, I managed to avoid any other major injuries that might take me out of the game.

We made it to the playoffs four more times, and to the conference finals once.

In the 2016–17 season, I hit the 777-game mark, surpassing Craig Ramsay, who held the record for the fourth-longest playing streak in NHL history. We made it to the playoffs for our fifth year in a row and all the way to the conference finals again.

A new season began and my streak continued: eight hundredth and on and on. Until it stopped. But not because of an injury or an illness.

It was January 13, 2018, my 830th game. We were playing the Los Angeles Kings on their turf at the Staples Center in LA, and just a few minutes into the first period, I saw Adrian Kempe with the puck as he crossed the blue line into our zone. I positioned myself to body check him, but made contact as he let the puck go. The ref blew the whistle and gave me a two-minute penalty for interference.

I accepted the penalty and served my time, then was back out on the ice with Kempe for the rest of the game, not thinking twice about the hit. No one talked about it during the game.

We ended up winning 4–2, and after, when we were rehashing the high moments of the night, nothing was said by my teammates or the media about my penalty, so I didn't think anything of it. Usually if a hit is bad, someone lets you know.

But then, after the game, I was in the dressing room and our general manager, Bob Murray, came up to me. "Cogs," he said. "George called."

George Parros is the head of the Department of Player Safety for the NHL and I knew him well. I had played with him in my first season with Anaheim. George had retired in 2014 and joined the Department of Player Safety two years later.

I could tell by the look on Bob's face that he was a little worried. Something was up with my hit, I realized, and I had the sinking feeling that things were going to go sideways.

"We're gonna have a call tomorrow," he said.

The next day, Bob and I talked with George, who told me the NHL wanted to suspend me for the hit because there was significant contact to Kempe's head. I was stunned. I felt that it was open to debate that I even hit him in the head, let alone that I had done it on *purpose*.

Bob and I had both watched the video numerous times and we didn't see significant head contact. I came through his body and his head incidentally hit me as I was hitting him. I didn't raise my elbow.

"Listen," I said. "I agree that I made contact with Kempe a little late after he passed the puck. But it wasn't malicious, and he wasn't hurt."

Bob had my back the whole time, and got a little upset defending me, which as a player, I appreciated. We don't often get to see that side of a GM, but Bob was with me every step of the way. But the league pressed the issue and gave me a two-game suspension for what I felt was a grey-area hit.

It was a hard decision to accept. I wasn't trying to injure anyone—I don't think most players are—and I hadn't injured Kempe. He played the next shift. After the suspension, I noticed other, worse hits that got penalties but no suspensions, and I asked myself what the difference was.

But that's how it goes sometimes in hockey. George had a job to do and he felt that he was carrying out his duties.

It didn't go over well with the Anaheim management or the owners. They genuinely cared about me and appreciated that I came to the rink every day to work hard for them. They were proud of me as a player and the streak I had going. One of the things I loved about playing in Anaheim was the family atmosphere. It meant a lot to me to see how much they all supported me as a player and as a person.

It didn't really hit me what the suspension meant until our next game. The guys were all suiting up in the dressing room and I was in street clothes outside talking to Kent French from *Ducks Live* about it all.

After we discussed the hit, Kent asked me how I felt about my streak ending. "I know that streak hasn't driven you, but it's meant a lot to you throughout the course of your career. How tough have the last twenty-four hours been for you?"

For so long I hadn't really cared about my streak, but now that it was over—and not because of an injury or an illness, but because of a suspension—I was disappointed and overwhelmed.

"I don't talk about my streak too much, but this decision is a tough pill to swallow." I felt myself getting choked up and paused.

Maybe I was being too dramatic, but it was an emotional moment for me. I had played hard and given my all each game for eleven straight years. Playing hockey was my job. I was a professional, and like my dad going in to work each day, that's what I did whenever I came to the arena. That was me punching a clock and putting in my time, shift after shift. I took great pride in my streak because of that. And right then, I missed the game. I missed the work.

"My streak held a lot of value to me," I told Kent. "It's something I'll hold to my heart. I wish it didn't have to end this way, but all I can do is move on and get back out there and help my team."

After the interview, I went up to the press box for the first time in my career and watched as my teammates battled it out on the ice against the Colorado Avalanche. It was such a strange feeling, almost like homesickness.

After word of my suspension got out, I started receiving kind messages from people around the NHL—former players, friends, and people in management. Hearing people I respected and had looked up to for so long say some really high-quality things meant the world to me, and that's something I'll always remember.

With hockey, it's about the experience. Scoring a goal is amazing. Winning is awesome. Playoffs, trophies, and streaks are all fantastic, but at the end of the day, it's about the experience because that's what you'll remember when you have to hang up your skates.

In January 2019, I was waking up in my hotel room in Detroit when I saw the light flash on my phone. I turned it over to keep sleeping, but after a few minutes, I decided to look. It was Bob. I knew something might be up when I saw his name on the phone. I was right. After eight seasons with the Ducks, I was being traded to the Dallas Stars.

This time it was a tougher transition. I'm a routine-oriented person and I've always been loyal to my team. Ever since I started playing hockey, I've never made the decision to change teams. In minor hockey, I played AAA for the Vaughan Kings. In the juniors, I played for my high school team, the St. Michael's Buzzers. Then for the Michigan Wolverines in college. Of course, I'd been traded to different teams in the NHL—the Oilers, the Ducks, and now the Stars. But I've stayed true to each team I've played for.

After being in Anaheim for seven years, I was set in my ways. It took a while before I felt at home in Dallas, but I did. Dallas is a great family town—it has a good feel about it and my family and I love living there now. And the weather still beats Edmonton.

When the Stars traded for me, they told me that they wanted me to come in and set an example for the younger players on the team. I couldn't help but think of how Horcoff, Staios, and Moreau had done that very same thing for me when I was a rookie playing for the Oilers. The Stars knew my history, and knew that I'd played 830 consecutive games and that I approached playing hockey as my job and worked hard to give it my all.

I was excited by the opportunity to take on a new role, and I quickly learned that there isn't a nicer and more respectful person in hockey than our general manager, Jim Nill. It's an honour to play for a man like that. Jamie Benn, our captain, is a great leader, and we have a good bunch of guys on the team. As a team, we're strong. For a player, you can't get much better than that.

On February 13, 2020, we played the Maple Leafs in Toronto. This wasn't any game; this was the one-thousandth game of my career. The day of, I tried to stick to my usual routine and not think about how big this night was. It was like coming back to home ice, and all my family and friends who had supported me over the years would be there. I wanted to make them proud and have the Stars win. We did and I even got an assist. It was the perfect night and a memory that I will have for the rest of my life.

Me, Allie, Lottie, and our dog, Charlie, after
the special red-carpet ceremony the Dallas Stars
held to celebrate my thousandth game.

After the game, it hit me. I sat there in the dressing room and said, "Wow, I just played one thousand games in the NHL." A lot of great players in the history of the NHL never played a thousand games, and I had just done it.

Ten days later, we were back in Dallas and the Stars created a special night for me and my family. I stood on the red carpet next to Allie, our daughter, Lottie, my parents, and even our dog, Charlie, as Jim Nill and the Stars presented me with an engraved silver stick in honour of playing one thousand games in the NHL.

As much as that night in Dallas was about me, it was for Allie and Lottie, who have always stood by me and supported me, and for my mom and dad as well, who taught me so many life lessons. If it wasn't for my family and the sacrifices they made for me, I never would have made the NHL, let alone played a thousand games. When all is said and done, my goal is to play the right way every day that I am in the NHL, and I hope I've made the Cogliano name proud during my career. It's my family that's made me who I am.

To this day, my mom continues to teach preschool and fitness at the community centre each week. She's unstoppable—I'm sure I could still learn a thing or two from her. In 2011, my dad finally retired, but even now, after every game, I call him up. We talk, he gives me his take on how I played, then I tell him what I was thinking.

Andrew Cogliano is an NHL forward for the Dallas Stars. He has been in the NHL for thirteen seasons, starting out with the Edmonton Oilers before being traded to the Anaheim Ducks. In 2006 and 2007, he represented Team Canada at the World Junior Ice Hockey Championships and won gold both times. He holds the record for the fourth-longest playing streak in the NHL, with a total of 830 consecutive games. He started Cogs for Dogs, a charity to help local dog shelters. With his wife, Allie, and their daughter, Lottie, he splits his time between his summer home in Invermere, British Columbia, and Dallas, Texas, where he lives during the hockey season.

Hockey Talk

Emilie Castonguay

People often ask me if I've met resistance as the first female NHL hockey agent in Canada. The truth is any resistance I've met comes from the job itself. Agenting is an unpredictable, fast-paced world, and people don't have time to analyze who you are and where you come from. At the end of the day, it's not about being a man or a woman, it's about speaking the language of hockey.

And that's a language I've been speaking since I was born.

I got my love of the game from my dad. He played in a beer league, and I remember watching his games at our local rink in Montreal, Quebec. He was a big hockey fan, too. As a good Montrealer, he cheered for the Canadiens, and we'd watch the games together on Saturday nights.

When I was eight, I thought I could give hockey a try, and so I asked my dad if I could play. At the time he wasn't sure I was going to stick with hockey, so he bought me some second-hand, old-man equipment to start.

I still remember how stinky that gear was when I put it on. The whole time it was like I was smelling someone else's sweat. But that wasn't enough to deter me. Nothing could, not even the spills I took out on the ice. I just got back up and pushed through. Those first few games, I had the puck a lot because the blade on my stick was really long. I don't think it was regulation, and if I had been playing in the NHL, they'd have called for a stick measurement. I immediately loved hockey—it was powerful, but required a lot of finesse and speed, too—and when my parents saw how excited I was, they gave in and bought me some nice gear.

When it came time to choose my jersey number, I decided on number eleven, after Kirk Muller of the Montreal Canadiens. I'd watched him play in the 1993 Stanley Cup playoffs with my dad. It was the LA Kings up against the Habs in the final series. My dad was so excited— the last time the Habs had won the cup was seven years ago against the Calgary Flames in 1986. My eyes were on Kirk. When he scored a goal off a face-off, I breathed, "Wow." After that, he was my guy.

For many years, I played boys' hockey. I was one of the few girls in the league and always had to change in the referees' room, but when I was on the ice, I was just another player, trying to get the puck in the net. We all talked about playing in the NHL one day, and I was no exception.

In high school, I was playing women's hockey and getting offers from NCAA schools. By then, I knew I wasn't destined for the NHL or the Olympics, but in my mind, playing NCAA Division I hockey was the next best thing. And if I could get an education at the same time, all the better. As much as I loved hockey, I was equally passionate about my academics, and while Concordia and McGill had great programs, the NCAA was offering full-ride scholarships.

After visiting a few different campuses, I decided on Niagara University. The school had a great coaching staff and they were putting as much money into women's sports as they were into men's.

Even as I headed off to Niagara, I knew that my professional playing days were numbered. But I was a hockey player at heart—and still am—and there wasn't anything that was going to stand in the way of me and hockey. I'm kind of stubborn like that. I made a promise to myself that somehow, I would have an impact on the game in the future—maybe from within the NHL organization—and a good education seemed like my ticket in.

My ultimate goal was to come back to Canada with a finance degree and go to law school. My mom was a lawyer and I figured a law degree would give me an advantage in the hockey world. While I knew that hockey was a male-dominated business, I felt I could do any job if I put my heart and soul into it; my gender was secondary. And if I was going to knock on any doors, I'd need to have all my qualifications in hand to get someone to open them.

But first, hockey. For those four years at Niagara, our women's team were treated like pros. I wasn't the star on the ice, but I found my role as a third-line checker and was even named captain in my junior and senior years. My passion for hockey also motivated me to be a good student so I could keep getting that ice time. A lot of people go into college thinking of having fun for four years, but I never had that mentality. I put everything I had into the classroom, which is where my talents really shone. I made the dean's list and ended up graduating with honours. To top it off, I won an NCAA student athlete award in 2008.

If those four years taught me anything, it was that athletes excel when they have the time to focus on their skills and the resources to improve: two things that are hard to come by for many players, especially women, once they're out of university. I didn't fully realize it at the time, but my first hand experience was leading me away from a role in NHL management and toward the job of player-agent.

It was Pierre Gauthier who helped guide me in the right direction. In my second year of law school at the University of Montreal, while all my classmates began sending out their résumés and interning at big law firms, I reached out to Pierre, who was at that time the general manager of the Montreal Canadiens. I asked if he would meet with me and give me some advice on how I could get into the hockey world. To my delight, he said yes.

Pierre is a really brilliant academic at his core, and so for him, it was always about if someone had the knowledge. He never played pro hockey himself, and yet he has been involved in hockey for over forty years. He has a good eye for the game and knows what he is talking about—and he respects those qualities in other people, regardless of their gender. And that's an approach I took myself early on.

In that meeting, he listened as I told him that I wanted to work in the NHL in some capacity, potentially as a general manager.

"If you want to work in sports," he said, "you can't just say, 'I want to be a GM.' There are steps along the way, and you may change your mind as you go."

He explained that he didn't start out as a GM himself; he got his foot in the door as a scout first. It was all about gaining experience in different roles. He emphasized that I needed to make my way through the hockey world, building up my résumé. From then on, he was an invaluable mentor to me and was always available to provide me with career advice.

We would have a lot of debates about players and contracts, specifically the Collective Bargaining Agreement (CBA), the terms and conditions for professional players that are agreed upon by the league and the NHL Players' Association. Every time we would get into a discussion about the CBA, I'd say, "Well, that doesn't seem fair."

It became clear that I was very pro-player. From salaries to a player's right to seek a second medical opinion, I always felt the CBA favoured the team, not the player.

As I learned more about the business of hockey, I realized that hockey was first and foremost a business. There's a players' union for a reason—because players are employees of the team. I had nothing against teams and management—they are great at what they do—but with a salary cap, sometimes they have to make hard decisions, and players are often the ones getting the short end of the stick. I thought that players should be taken care of. They were the ones putting their bodies on the line and dealing with the physical repercussions later.

After a couple of conversations, Pierre said to me, "I feel like you are lot more pro-player, so maybe being an agent or working for the NHL Players' Association is something that would best fit your personality and skill set."

He was right. I knew I wanted to work for the players. Those I most admired were ones like Sidney Crosby: he's the most talented player on his team; he's also the hardest worker. Even he has to put everything he has into being a pro player in the NHL. After all, there's a reason why there are only a certain number of players that make it to the NHL. As a player-agent, I felt I could advocate for players' rights but also help them with everything else that comes with a career in pro hockey.

In 2012, when I graduated with my law degree, I approached Momentum Hockey, a boutique hockey agency out of Montreal that recruits and represents players from the juniors, the NHL, the AHL, and leagues all over Europe. I met with the president, Chris Daigle, about doing an internship.

He looked over my résumé. "I love your law degree and finance degree. You could go work for a big firm with that." Then he asked me, "What are you going to do as an agent? What do you think an agent does? And what are you going to bring to the table?"

I knew the answer to the first two questions, but the last one made me realize that I couldn't just show up with my degrees.

Chris was very clear. "I'm not going to tell you what to do. You're going to tell me what you're going to do for me and how you are going to get players and manage them."

In that moment, I understood that being an agent was like running your own business. I took it upon myself to dive in and learn as much as I could and prove to Chris that I was ready to do everything an agent does.

The next two summers, I interned for Momentum, and one of the first things I learned was that there are two sides to agenting: the business side—recruiting and representing players—and the personal side. And I saw first-hand how close agents work with players and how rewarding that work can be. At Momentum Hockey, players were not just numbers; they were members of our families. Our jobs were to represent them, yes, but also to make sure they had everything they needed to succeed and that they were achieving their dreams. From the moment we sign a player, we start building a relationship with him and his family. We might sign a player as young as fourteen and it might take ten years before he plays his first NHL game. We watch him grow up and experience all his ups and downs—that's the part that nobody sees but the player, his family, and the agent. And that's what I loved most about the work because I felt I could make a real difference.

What I liked about Momentum Hockey was that we worked as a team. I learned a lot about contracts and the inner workings of pro hockey from my colleagues. Chris was a big help to me, as was Olivier Fortier, another agent at the company, and we worked together to build relationships and sign players.

From the beginning, I never saw my gender as a barrier. I never paid attention if I was the only woman in the room. If other people did, then it was their issue, but I didn't let it get in the way of my work. I'm sure some people met me and thought, *Oh, she's a girl.* But they quickly realized that I knew what I was talking about, and any thoughts about my gender disappeared in the first five minutes. For those in the world, hockey is a universal language.

I was accepted by my peers at the agency and my colleagues on the teams and in the union, which shows how much attitudes toward women have changed and how good the hockey world really is deep down.

In 2014, when I passed the bar, Momentum offered me a job as an agent. There was no question about my answer. I knew in my heart that I was meant to follow this path. And my first step was to build my client list.

It all starts with watching a player, usually in his midget or junior years, on the ice. If I thought a player had potential, I would go to his games and watch him throughout the season. Signing a player is a big investment and we want it to be a lifelong partnership, so we take the decision to recruit someone very seriously.

It's also a big decision for the player and his family. Players are often minors when they're signed, so we always meet with the family to explain how we can support them. Our job is to show them that they can count on us to help their son and them navigate the exceptional path they're embarking on.

Many people think that being an agent is a glamorous job, but what they don't realize is how many hours it takes. In the hockey world,

Here I am in my office at Momentum Hockey.

there are only a certain number of players available for representation and so competition among agencies can be cutthroat. But I'd always tell myself, *No matter what I get, I'm never going to take my foot off the gas.* I knew that as soon as I did that, someone would pass me. That mentality helped me to keep working.

Agenting is exciting and scary as hell at the same time. It requires a lot of self-discipline. I had to get myself to the rinks across Canada. We sacrificed a lot of our free time and weekends, scouting potential players. My colleagues at Momentum and I didn't have a huge corporation to fall back on and we had to manage our expenses, so we often travelled by ourselves, which could get lonely.

But the players were worth it. When we recruited a player at fifteen years old and made sure he and his family were taken care of as he developed, then watched him get drafted into the NHL—that was a win. It's those moments when I know I've had an impact that keep me going.

For me, being a successful agent isn't just about representing NHL players; it's also about giving back and helping all athletes get the compensation and recognition they deserve. And in my second year as an agent, I had my eye on someone who was in need of just that.

In 2015, Marie-Philip Poulin was graduating from Boston University, where she had played NCAA hockey for the past four years. In the 2010 and 2014 Winter Olympics, she'd represented Team Canada and scored the winning goal in the gold medal game each year. Typically, sponsors would be lining up after that, but because she was still in the NCAA, which didn't allow students to accept sponsorships, she got zero. In my view, she was the best women's hockey player to ever play the game, and she had won Canada two Olympic golds—for no money. As a former women's hockey player, I knew how hard she worked for how little. She might have two gold medals, but those didn't pay the bills.

In general, Olympic athletes don't get enough support, but it's impossible for them to work a full-time job and train. These athletes dedicate their life to their sport for a least a decade, and when they retire from the Olympics, they're left with little compensation or real work experience. I wanted Marie-Philip to avoid that fate.

In all my conversations with Pierre, it was always about the players; that's who I was in my job for. So I sat down with the partners to talk about Marie-Philip.

"I know our main job is to represent future hockey stars," I began. "But I would really like to approach Marie-Philip Poulin about working with us." I told them about her accomplishments and how she currently had no sponsors. "It will be a long time before we see anyone as good as Marie-Philip. I think we could really help her."

There was a chance that any results I got would not be worth the effort I put in to get them, mainly because of the way companies approach female athletes and female sports. They don't see them as offering a big enough payoff, but I was in it to change that attitude. I knew Marie-Philip was the real deal and it would be hard to fail with such a great player. My results would speak for themselves.

Ultimately, the partners said that it was my decision to make.

I went to Boston to meet with her. Marie-Philip's also from Quebec, so we had a lot in common, and I told her about my own time playing NCAA hockey. "I understand that the NCAA program gives you an education," I said. "But you scored those two Olympic goals for free!"

She was so humble, to a fault almost. She was the type of person who was grateful for what she got.

I got really passionate then. "What you should get in return is a lot more. And that's what I'm going to fight for," I said. "Once you graduate, I want to be your agent. I want you to make a living out of sponsorships and become the face of women's hockey."

She looked at me. "Do you think that's possible?"

I smiled. "We're going to make it possible!"

After she graduated, we started working together, and since then, we have signed with twelve different sponsors. Now that Marie-Philip doesn't have to worry about having another job, she can focus on being a professional hockey player.

For me, that is one of my proudest achievements. I wish I could do the same for every women's hockey player, but there is a certain demand for Olympians. I just hope this paves the way for more companies to go after other stars in women's hockey.

In 2016, I got my NHLPA player-agent certification. I also became the director of legal affairs and hockey operations at Momentum,

Celebrating Les Canadiennes' Clarkson Cup win in 2017 with Marie-Philip—who scored the game-winning goal—and her parents, aunt, and uncle.

which involved negotiating all the deals with the various leagues we work with, including the juniors, and any endorsement contracts. Anything to do with legal and the NHL CBA, I'm called in.

These negotiations aren't always easy. I remember my first NHL contract, with Julien BriseBois and Steve Yzerman and the Tampa Bay Lightning. My law degree and my experience as a player and as an agent helped me pull off that deal, and in the end, the player was happy and so was his family. That was my priority.

After Steve signed the contract, I called Julien to send him the final draft.

"Congrats on your first contract," Julien said. "You did a really good job."

It was nice to hear that. He didn't have to say that, and it meant a lot to me that he did, and it gave me confidence for the future.

As much as I love being a part of the NHL machine and meeting with GMs, sponsors, and players, the best part about my job is that I feel like I'm making a difference in players' lives. Over the past six years, we've slowly built a roster of players that we're really proud of, one of whom is Alexis Lafrenière, the top prospect of the 2020 NHL draft.

The first couple times I saw Alexis play, I knew he was special. He has a hockey IQ that very few players have, and when you mix in his work ethic, skill, and talent, it's a perfect combination. When the puck touches his stick, everything goes into slow motion and he's in total control. I knew that if he kept getting better at every level, he could potentially be a franchise player. In other words, a team could build their franchise around him. He's a high-impact forward and a top scorer on the ice.

Alexis is the kind of player who will never get sick of doing his job because he's so passionate about the game. He's good at staying in the moment and doesn't look too far ahead or too far back, which is one of the reasons he's able to deal with pressure so well. He genuinely loves being in the gym, on the ice, and with his teammates. In short, he is the kind of player whom I dreamed of representing one day, the kind of player who shouldn't have to worry about the little things and just focus on playing the game.

Signing Alexis was by far one of the highlights of my agenting career. Being his agent is such a privilege, and each day, I try to do something, big or small, for his career. He's worked hard and I'm proud of all he's accomplished.

Looking back, it's hard to believe my career as a player-agent all started with some sweaty old second-hand gear. But then again, it didn't. Nothing could ever keep me out of the game. Not so long ago, I was reaching out to Pierre to help me figure out how to enter the hockey world. And now I have people asking me if they can pick my brain about becoming a player-agent. I'm happy to give back and pay it forward because we all love hockey and we're all speaking the same language.

Emilie Castonguay is a player-agent with Momentum Hockey. She played four years of NCAA Division I hockey at Niagara University, where she won a National Scholar Athlete award. After graduating with a bachelor's degree in finance in 2009, she went on to earn her law degree from the Université de Montréal in 2012. A member of the Quebec Bar Association, she became the first Canadian woman to be an NHLPA certified player-agent in 2016. Emilie lives in Montreal. A fitness fanatic, she loves hockey most of all.

 *@emcastonguay007*

www.momentumhockey.com

More Than Hockey Tape

Joey Gale

It was so cold, like the *air hurts your face and lungs* sort of cold, but my dad and brother, Mike, were both oddly eager to get outside and to our neighbourhood park. I was just three years old and a little unsure of what we were doing, but I was excited to be on an adventure, so I threw on my puffy jacket with dangly mittens clipped to the sleeves and jumped into the car warming up in the driveway.

It was a sunny Saturday morning, and when we arrived at the park, my dad and Mike grabbed these funny-looking boots out of the trunk. I thought we were headed to the playground, but they led me through the snow toward a frozen-solid pond where a group of boys was flying around on the ice, chasing this little black puck around with sticks in their hands.

We sat down on a bench together just steps away from the ice and my dad pulled my snow boots off and began to slide the cold, uncomfortable shoe things he had pulled from the trunk onto my feet. My brother, who was thirteen at the time, made it very clear to me not to touch the shiny metal part on the bottom as my dad laced up what soon would become my first pair of hockey skates.

That was my earliest memory of playing hockey. While I can almost guarantee I spent more time scooting around on my butt than actually skating, it was the start of playing a sport that would change my life.

I grew up in Minnesota—the self-described "State of Hockey"—with a loving family. Now in my late twenties, I like to joke that my childhood could loosely be described as being an only child with siblings. My sister, Kelly, is thirteen years older and Mike is ten years older, so by the time I was eight, they both were already off to college. As the youngest child, I can confidently divulge that I was much more spoiled than my siblings—sorry, guys!

When it came to playing sports, Mike and Kelly were always seen as the athletic ones in the family. Mike was a three-sport athlete, playing hockey as well as wrestling and playing soccer. Kelly, while not a hockey player, was a varsity soccer player and synchronized swimmer. Then there was me, this short, little, scrawny kid. When I was younger, I always felt pressure to meet the impossible standards of my brother and sister; however, I was never better than a C- or D-level player. Regardless of my skill, or lack thereof, my parents were always looking for ways to support me both on and off the ice.

When my brother and sister left for college in the early 2000s, our

*Here I am at age five, posing for team photos
in my Wayzata hockey jersey.*

house got a bit quieter. Mike took his car with him, opening up a new stall in our garage. My dad saw this as an opportunity to give me a space to practice hockey at home. One afternoon we decided to go to Home Depot together to find a good material I could shoot pucks off of. After searching around, we found just the stuff, checked out of the store, and made our way back to the car. On the way home, I asked my dad what I could shoot at since we didn't have a net.

"You're right," he said, swerving to make the upcoming exit. "We should get you a net. Let's go find one!"

We were suddenly on a mission. I rattled off the names of some nearby stores that I thought might sell what we were so eagerly looking for.

"Don't worry," my dad said, with a calm yet suspicious tone in his voice. "I've had my eyes on one for a while now."

What had started as a simple idea to help me practice in the garage soon became an exciting project for the two of us. It was little moments like these throughout my childhood that built a foundation of trust in, and respect and love for, my parents.

Around the age of twelve, I started to recognize that something was different about me, that I wasn't like all the other boys my age. When I'd hang out with my friends, the inevitable topic of girls would come up. I remember being at a sleepover in the summer with a handful of my teammates to celebrate a birthday. As the sun set, we all crawled into a big tent in the backyard. The conversation eventually led to who we thought the prettiest girl at school was. I played along with the conversation, but as names were randomly shouted out, I remember feeling uncomfortable.

"Joey, who do you like?" a friend asked.

I froze. How come I couldn't think of any pretty girls? I ended up naming some girls I had heard mentioned earlier. For some reason, it was so much easier for me to make a mental list of the boys I thought were cute. I remember feeling ashamed, like something was wrong with me. Why don't I like girls? I thought it might be a phase at first or maybe I was just curious about what guys were all about.

Eventually, I knew my attraction to boys wasn't a phase or just my curiosity, but I thought being gay was a bad thing that I had to hide. I desperately wanted to talk to someone and get this secret off my chest. But the thought of telling even my closest friends or my parents shut me down in fear.

Late one night, I was lying on the floor of my bedroom with my dog, Bode, a white Maltese with nothing but eleven pounds of bossiness and smiles, when I had the overwhelming urge to say the words out loud to someone, even if that someone was my dog. In that moment, my eyes filled with tears.

"I'm gay," I whispered to Bode, then let out a long, deep breath that I had been holding. He looked back at me, unfazed by the news. For a fleeting moment I felt a rush of relief, like I had just crashed through this imaginary glass barrier into my real self. But then my reality set back in.

I felt like I was trapped in my own body and I couldn't let anyone know the real Joey. Like most kids in grade school, I desperately wanted to fit in with the cool kids. I tried to dress like them; I asked for the same haircut as them. All I wanted was to eat lunch with them, but my grade school days were full of bullying, and I was afraid that it would only be worse if the other students knew I was gay. I tried to convince myself that I had to be straight or I wasn't going to be successful in life. So, on the outside, I gave off the impression that I was. Yet on the inside, I lived every day worried that people would find out I was gay and would reject me. As I tried to prove my masculinity and straightness to a world I thought wouldn't love me back, I was unintentionally creating two versions of myself. One Joey was pretending to be straight, and the other was broken and fearful of what a life out of the closet would mean.

The weight of my secret pressed on me almost every day. Would today be the day that someone would learn the truth?

Hockey became my escape. I'm by no means a rock-star player, but when my skates hit the ice, I felt like I could get away from the bullying and negative thoughts in my head and, for once, just fit in. As a typical

Minnesotan, I played in a league and spent endless hours out on the pond. As a closeted gay kid, though, I felt like I was cheating the system by playing such a masculine sport. Hockey was my way to fly under the radar. How could people think I was gay if I played hockey? Here I was, a short, scrawny kid with glasses, playing a competitive sport with guys twice my size.

I've always loved hockey. Lacing up my skates and stepping onto the ice gave me a rush I couldn't find elsewhere, and I can still recall waking up at six a.m. on those subzero Saturday mornings to my dad's voice yelling at me from downstairs to get ready for a game. The feeling of fitting in on a team and playing a game I loved is what got me on the ice most days. Looking back, it also brought me so much closer to my dad.

I deeply wanted my dad's acceptance. Growing up, I was a huge fan of the Minnesota Wild and the Minnesota Golden Gophers. Every so often my dad would snag some tickets to an evening game and we'd make a night out of it. We'd go downtown together after school got out, grab some dinner near the arena, then head over to watch the game. We probably attended three dozen or so NHL and college games. My dad never overtly made any homophobic or harmful comments to me before I came out, but during these father-son adventures, I always wondered how things could change if he knew I was gay. I soaked them up regardless.

Hockey wasn't always positive for me, though. As I got older and understood my own sexuality more, the toxic language and homophobic "chirps" that got hurled around on and off the ice often made it discouraging and uncomfortable for me to play. Some of my least favorite memories occurred before or after practices in the locker room. It seems like in hockey there's really no filter, and hateful slurs go unchecked, even at the highest levels.

I remember sitting with my teammates in the locker room after a practice one night. I was taking off my skates and gathered the snow that accumulated on the blade into my hand. I balled it up and whipped it at one of my friends like a snowball—a common prank in a boys' locker room. Much to my surprise, he jolted up, threw the snowball right back into my face, and shouted, "Fuck you, faggot."

Those words cut through me so deep. No one knew I was actually gay except for me, but in that moment, it felt like the world knew. I did my best to hold it together, even though I was processing a mix of fear and pure embarrassment. I looked down and kept getting undressed, trying to ignore the chuckles from my other teammates.

When my dad picked me up out in front of the ice rink, I felt beyond defeated, like hockey wasn't a place for me and that I was an imposter trying to fit in. What had started as a way to cope and get away from my fears, was doing the exact opposite.

Over the years, the homophobic language hurled around on the ice didn't let up, and I was constantly avoiding being caught in the cross hairs of another gay joke or slur. It only made me bury my secret deeper. I felt so divided and slowly started to distance myself from hockey. Eventually, I stopped playing altogether. I told my family, friends, and teammates that I wanted to focus on school more since college applications were just around the corner. I knew deep down that wasn't the truth, but I pretended anyway,

During my junior year in high school, I started looking at colleges. I wanted to go to a school where the classroom sizes were small and the environment felt intimate—I didn't want to be just a number on a large campus. Both Mike and Kelly had attended Drake University down in Des Moines, Iowa, and were incredibly successful after graduating. Every time we were together they'd share all these fun stories from their college days at Drake. They also met their significant others while at school (whom they both eventually married). In my mind, I couldn't help but think that if I went to Drake, then I'd have to do the same.

I didn't necessarily want to follow in their footsteps (or have the pressure of finding a wife!), so I looked at several other schools. I wanted to get away from home, but not go too far. I had this vision of a Joey no one would ever question about whether or not he was straight. I'd join a fraternity, go out to the bars and flirt with girls, and give off this impression that I was *totally straight.* What could go wrong?

My parents drove me all around the Midwest to look at schools, helped me with my applications, and even committed to paying for school. They were so supportive and left the final decision up to me. As this process was taking place, though, one thing was pressing on me—would all of this change if they found out I was gay?

One by one, my college list got shorter and shorter, and then it was down to two, Creighton and Drake. Creighton had a renowned marketing program in their business school and offered me an awesome scholarship, but it was a Jesuit school, which I knew deep inside, as a closeted gay kid, was a bad idea. Drake, on the other hand, was a private unaffiliated institution with the same great program and a beautiful campus. Because of the connections that my brother and sister had already made, Drake somehow felt like the place I should be. Even though I had all these preconceived notions about who I had to be and what I needed to do, Drake felt like home.

When I got to Drake as a freshman in 2011, I assumed that my hockey days were done. Drake didn't have a hockey team and there wasn't much, if any, pond hockey to be found. It felt like a new beginning for me in more ways than one.

I quickly connected with someone who would eventually be the first person I'd come out to. His name was Tony and he was a faculty member in the office of student life at Drake. If this were a fictional storybook, Tony would be that wise older mentor who somehow knew the answers before I even figured out the question.

I could tell he was different and unapologetically gay. His very masculine figure stood about a foot and a half taller than me—I'm five five, for reference. He had big-gauge earrings, a large black beard that covered his face, and to top it off, rainbow-painted fingernails. Some days he'd even wear heels to the student union just to make a point. Tony quickly become my rock at school. Before I came out, I knew I could go to him with anything and he'd understand and accept me.

I always imagined that heading off to college would allow me this fresh new start to be the person I always wanted to be. In reality, I was doing everything I could to prove that I was straight. Like my brother and brother-in-law, I joined a fraternity, theirs in fact, and I made up stories about wild weekend adventures to try to fool everyone, but the only person I was fooling was myself.

Then, late one night during that first year at school, I realized I wasn't happy with the Joey I had created. I was in the study room of my fraternity house helping one of my brothers, Ben, write a speech. He was running for president of the fraternity in a few days and had asked for some help rehearsing what he would say.

Ben was a junior at Drake studying actuarial sciences. He was smart, athletic, tall, and dating the president of a sorority, so sadly, not gay! I'd describe Ben as one of those types of people who somehow become your friend after one conversation. He was full of charisma and could get along with anyone. As a freshman at the time, I really looked up to him.

As we discussed why people should vote for him, I started listing off all these reasons why people loved him: he was so authentic and down-to-earth, he took time to get to know everyone on a personal level, and he wasn't trying to be someone he wasn't. He was like the straight, male version of Ellen DeGeneres—you couldn't not love him! After he finished his speech, he took off for bed.

It was late, almost two in the morning, but I stayed behind, reflecting on all the qualities that made Ben this great person, and the statements I had made about him. Then I thought: *Why can't I say those same things about myself? Who does that make me?* If I wanted to live the rest of my life as a lie, that was a decision that would stick with me forever. This realization radiated through my body. I knew if I wanted to be happy in life, I had to be the authentic Joey who had been hiding all these years. I grabbed paper and pen and drew out a triangle—at the top was love, to the left was success, and to the right was belonging.

As I sat there thinking about how I would achieve those three things, a wave a clarity washed over me. At the top of the page I wrote out in big bold letters "I'M GAY." I dated the page 10/27/12 and wrote down the time, 2:52 a.m. That moment was the first time I accepted myself for who I really am.

Even now, that moment feels surreal. That secret was something I had built my whole life on, and for the first time, I acknowledged to myself that I wanted to tear it all down and live my life to make myself happy instead of fearful of what others thought about me. As RuPaul, one of the most famous drag queens and queer icons of our time, says, "If you can't love yourself, how in the hell are you going to love somebody else?"

After an anxiety-filled night, I woke up calm and excited. I'm not sure if it was from the lack of sleep, but I knew I had to tell someone. Almost like clockwork, I found myself in Tony's office that next morning. I knocked on the rainbow flag that hung on the outside of his door and peeked in to find him painting his nails—classic Tony. I sheepishly closed the door behind me and nervously sat down on the big comfy chair beside his desk. Then I broke down.

It's almost like he knew from the second I knocked why I was there that morning. He threw a big blanket around me as a sign of support as I brushed tears out of my eyes.

"Is there something you want to share?" he asked gently.

"I'm gay," I uttered through my tears.

Without pause, he came in for a hug.

We sat together as I shared how nervous I was about coming out and how it was going to change everything in my life. I told him the story about me coming out to my dog on the floor of my bedroom.

Like a line out of a movie, he said, "And look how far you've already come."

My emotions were on high. As we talked, I bounced back and forth from laughter to tears. People came by and knocked on Tony's office door several times, but he simply ignored them. At the end of our conversation, he shared something I've held on to since that day.

He said, "Regardless of how big or small, do something every day to queer the space around you."

I remember thinking how ridiculous that was; at the time, gay marriage wasn't even legal yet in the United States.

"You think I'm going to paint my nails, hang a rainbow flag from my door, and shout from the rooftops that I'm gay?" I asked. "I'm not like that!"

He explained to me that these actions didn't need to be grandiose displays of rainbows or outwardly going against societal norms. "It doesn't need to be the elephant in the room," he said. "Try starting out with something small."

As I started to come out at Drake, I quickly found myself in situations where I was the first or only queer person to do something.

In my fraternity, I was the only out member. I was so scared to come out to my fraternity brothers, a group of masculine, straight guys, but I quickly found my fears were greater than what reality had in store. I started by telling some of my closest fraternity brothers. They usually responded with downplayed shock then some lighthearted jokes and genuine questions. Eventually, word spread in the fraternity, and I was okay with it. Brothers would approach me and ask, mostly out of valid curiosity, if it were true. I'd tell them I was gay and they'd persistently follow up with words of affirmation. Instead of losing friends, I finally felt like I was making genuine and authentic connections. When my brothers would make a gay joke or drop "no-homo," it wasn't said with hate like in a hockey locker room, and I'd jokingly fire back with something like, "Oh, that's full homo and I know full homo."

The more I got involved, the more I started to see the importance in what Tony shared with me. If I wasn't queering the space around me, I wasn't making space for other queer folks to join me.

I spent most of my sophomore year at Drake coming out. What most straight, cisgender people don't understand is that coming out is a daily or weekly process for most queer individuals. For example, you get asked what you did over the weekend by a professor or new friend—someone you haven't come out to yet—and you have to respond back with, "Well, I went to the Garden [a well-known gay bar] with a guy on a date." Surprisingly, it was always fun fielding the questions that usually followed that response.

My family were the last people I told. While I didn't intentionally want it to happen that way, I think I was subconsciously trying to protect myself from what could happen if they rejected me. My mom was the first family member I came out to. We were at my family's cabin watching the news one night, and a story about a Minnesota Vikings player supporting same-sex marriage came on. My parents were quick to comment.

"I just don't understand why we need to bring politics into football," my dad said.

My mom added, "He's not even that good; he's probably gay himself."

If words could kill, those did. How could they say that? Was it really what they thought? If only they knew. So many emotions started to rush through my head and the only thing I could do was storm out of the cabin. I shouted that I was going for a walk and slammed the door behind me.

I made my way down to the water. With tears clouding my eyes, I sat down on the sand and stared out at the calm moonlit lake. The night was so still and the heat from the day lingered in the air. My mom, almost like clockwork, said my name just over my shoulder, like she had been waiting there the whole time.

"Is there something you want to tell me?" she asked as she sat down and put her arms around me.

Without pause, I started crying and said, "I'm gay."

She hugged me even tighter and we both wept. "I love you regardless of who you are," she said. "You're my son."

In this long journey of understanding who I was and what my place was in the world, I found the most solace in what my mom said to me next. She quoted a famous Dr. Seuss line: "Those who matter don't mind, and those who mind don't matter." And all the fears I had built up about being disowned or unloved washed away that night.

With the love and support from my friends and mom, I came out to my brother, sister, and dad over the next few weeks. They each had their own way of expressing their love and acceptance to me. I had been so worried about breaking the bond I had with my dad, but he said, "Having a gay son changes nothing for me. I want you to be happy and I love you just the same."

I no longer had to hide. I was free to be the Joey I was meant to be.

I had shown up at Drake my first year with the intent of starting fresh, but it wasn't until I came out as gay that my true fresh start began. In my junior and senior years, I had a new energy and confidence in myself. I could go out to the gay bars, hang out with gay friends, go on dates, and hold a boy's hand on campus, all new things that I never had the courage to do before. Tony was my champion the whole way. Any chance he had, he pushed me to better myself and to queer my space.

There was a reason why Tony specifically used the word "queer." Many people understand it as a bad word because it's historically been used as a slur. Today, LGBTQ+ individuals are coming together to reclaim the word. "Queer" is now commonly used as an umbrella term for sexual and gender minorities who don't fall into what we typically categorize as "straight." You could use it to define your own identity (like saying "I'm queer") or the community as a whole (i.e., "the queer community"). Queering my space was another way I could reclaim the word, and I had my eyes set on school politics to start making a change.

In grade school, I had run for class president and lost. In my first year at Drake, when I was still pretending to be someone I wasn't, I ran for first-year senator, a coveted position in my eyes. Guess what? I lost again.

Both losses taught me a life lesson. Sometimes you win, and sometimes you learn. Because of my failures, I became more driven, focused, creative, and personable with everyone I worked with—sort of like what I had built up Ben to be in my head. When the opportunity to run for student body president came up, I was prepared. I built a campaign from the ground up and made sure I queered everything I could. Because I never gave up, my dream came true and I won the election.

Through the course of my presidency, I used my platform to drive equality not only on campus but at a local, state, and national level, too. It was through all this work that I landed my first job out of school at an ad agency in Des Moines, Iowa. Look what had come from me being true to myself.

Campaigning for student body president and
proudly representing my community.

After graduating from Drake in 2015, I found myself with a lot of extra time on my hands. Like any twenty-something fresh out of school, I was told to find a hobby.

By then, I had started to miss the rush I got from playing hockey. I missed lacing up my skates, taping up my stick, and the feeling of fresh ice under my feet. I felt ready to return to the ice and at peace with my past experiences. It didn't matter as much anymore if someone knew I was gay; most days, I wanted people to know. After Googling around, I found that there was indeed a league in Iowa, the Des Moines Adult Hockey League.

At first, I was reluctant to join because I didn't know any of the players. It was like the first day of school all over again. Who was going to my friend? Was I even good enough to be there? I joined anyway, but then what started to worry me was that being gay would get in the way. Would it change the locker room dynamic? Would they keep letting me play? Would guys target me on the ice? I started to fall back into my old ways and tried my best not to let my sexuality slip out. I thought it would be better if they just didn't know.

When you look at sports and entertainment today, you can find more prominent queer figures than ever before. I'm sure many people can name an LGBTQ+ Olympian, soccer player, skier, or figure skater. But in men's hockey? Or the NHL? No one. We're still not in a place in society where professional athletes can be comfortable being who they truly are. I genuinely wish I had a queer hero to look up to in hockey, someone who could pave the way for a degree of acceptance in the sport.

In 2016, I was introduced to Pride Tape—a rainbow-colored roll of hockey tape. Pride Tape is a symbol of support from those who use it when they play and is used in LGBTQ+ youth initiatives like You Can Play. Around this same time, my league was nominating players for an All-Star Game later in the season. Miraculously, I was selected by my team to compete in the big game. I was familiar with most of my teammates, but I wasn't on a first-name basis by any means, so I felt honoured by the vote of confidence.

I wanted to use this opportunity to queer hockey. Since all the players on the All-Star Team were from other teams in the league, I had no idea who most of them were, which made me rethink what I was about to do. But a week before the game, I realized I would likely never have a chance to do something like this again, so I went and bought a roll of Pride Tape. That night, I ripped the black tape off my stick, the same color of tape that I had played with my whole life, opened up the new roll of Pride Tape, and started retaping my stick like I had done countless times before. However, this time, it all felt new. I watched as I twirled the tape around and around, green, blue, purple, red, orange, yellow, and then the pattern repeated. Looking at the finished tape job, I felt equal parts joy and terror. For the first time, I was really owning my place in hockey, and wow, was it scary.

Hours before the game I rehearsed in my apartment how I would respond if someone asked about the tape. "Yeah, I just thought it looked cool." Or, "Oh, I'm just showing support. I'm not gay or anything." Would I actually commit to what I was doing, or would I chicken out as soon as someone asked? It seemed so out there for me to do, like I was driving a pin into a massive balloon of toxic masculinity. I was terrified. In reality, it felt more like a protest, as if the tape on my stick was shining a light into a sport too afraid to acknowledge difference, sexuality, and hate.

Arriving at Wells Fargo Arena in Des Moines, Pride Tape and all, I made my way down to the locker room and set my stick outside the door next to my teammates'. It hit me hard when I looked down at all of the black-and-white-taped sticks—mine wasn't just different, it stood out.

I nervously walked into the locker room, a much fancier one than I was expecting, and sat down. Instead of the usual creaky half-painted bench and standard black rubber flooring, dark green carpet sprawled across the floor and our jerseys hung from hangers in individual wooden lockers. This felt like the real deal. I looked around and quickly introduced myself to others already in the locker room, trying not to make a huge scene. Most of the guys looked vaguely familiar, but I had never spoken to any of them before. I started to put my gear on, looking up every so often to sheepishly respond with a nod or laugh to acknowledge something that was said.

Moments later, a teammate shuffled in and asked the locker room of fourteen guys, "Who's got the gay tape?" His tone was sharp and dismissive.

The locker room fell silent. I could hear my heart pounding in my ears as fear pulsed through my body. I exhaled a long, deep breath through my mouth. I knew that this was likely my only chance to come out to my teammates. I could feel my hands shaking as I let go of the laces I had been tying a moment before. This was it. I had to say something. I fired back with the only thing I could think of.

"Since we're on the big stage tonight, I thought I'd be as *fabulous* as possible," I said somewhat sarcastically.

It was stupid. *What a dumb response*, I thought. *They're going to hate me. Nobody wants to play hockey with a gay guy.*

However, I was immediately greeted with warm smiles and kind-hearted laughs from my teammates around the room.

"Oh, you didn't hear?" one guy asked, grinning good-naturedly. "He's playing for the other team!"

I smiled back, relieved by the response. And the conversation moved to who had come to watch us play.

A situation that could have blown up on me and led to an extremely tense and awkward game was defused in seconds by the group. The nerves I had built up all day washed away in that instant. I felt refreshed and alive again—like I didn't need to hold anything back anymore.

While this was a defining experience for me, it was merely a baby step forward for the hockey community. I knew that if a small league in Des Moines, Iowa, could be so accepting, the sport as a whole had promise. When I heard my name announced over the arena speakers, I took a few deep breaths and stepped onto the ice, rainbow tape shining bright in the spotlight.

While the arena was nowhere close to full, many family members and friends were scattered throughout, and I saw my boyfriend, Austin, and a few other close friends cheering me on.

As I warmed up, I couldn't stop looking down at my rainbow-taped stick. It gave me a new energy and strength, something I'd tap into later. I was playing right wing on the first line and couldn't have been more excited. Had you asked me a year earlier if I'd be doing something like this, it wouldn't even have seemed within the realm of possibility.

The pace of the game started off quick. While I was used to playing with most of the guys on the ice, the level of play was exceptionally higher. The first period was fast and furious. There were several shots on net by both teams, but no goals. The second period started just as fast as the first, but on a penalty kill, the other team scored first. No more than three minutes after they had scored, I found myself on a 2-on-1 goal-scoring opportunity. My teammate had the puck and I was wide open in front of the net. He saucered the puck behind the defender right onto my waiting stick. Boom, top shelf. I scored!

There's no better feeling than bringing your team back into the game, especially with a rainbow-taped stick. The remainder of the second period was full of strong back-and-forth passing from both teams. With about fourteen seconds left in the period, we found ourselves on a power play in the offensive zone. You know sometimes when you can just feel it? Like something electric is about to happen? I focused on the puck hitting the ice during a face-off. Our centreman pulled it off his stick right back to mine as he raced to the net. After a nice move or two to get around a defender, I passed the puck perfectly to my teammate who was waiting all by himself at the corner of the net. Goal! We did it and brought the team out of a tie.

While the third period was a strong battle, we didn't end up winning the game. Before trophies were handed out, the league commissioner announced that they first had to name a player of the game. Thinking it would be a player from the winning team, I started to tune out a bit.

In the thick of the All-Star Game, I'm number twelve,
chasing the puck with my Pride Tape stick.

The next thing I heard was the commissioner saying, "And he put up two big points for his team today." I immediately tuned back in. After a long pause, the commissioner said, "Joey Gale!"

I couldn't believe it! In a day full of ups and downs, overcoming fears, and playing a great game, I had somehow proved the impossible to myself. I was on top.

Days later, Austin and I were on vacation with my parents down in the Caribbean. A video of the game had been posted online and I was more than eager to relive the highlights. I tapped Play on the video and the voices of the two amateur announcers spilled out. My mom grabbed her reading glasses off the counter and came behind my shoulder to watch. Soon Austin and my dad joined in as well. While we crowded around the small screen, I peeked up at their three faces, attentively tuned in, occasionally laughing at the unrefined color commentary. Every time they caught a glimpse of me and my rainbow tape, they pointed down at the screen.

In that moment, I couldn't help but think back to that chilly winter morning at the park, learning how to skate for the very first time. That simple feeling of a new beginning was all too apparent again. But now? Now I felt something new—a true and tangible sense of who I was, accepted by those I loved most.

Since that All-Star Game back in 2018, Pride Tape has made some pretty big steps forward in the NHL with players and organizations. Queering a space that's historically been full of homophobia takes courage from all sides, and LGBTQ+ allies across the league are helping pave the way for players like me to come out.

It's troubling that there are still so few out gay players.

My journey wasn't easy, but I recognize and acknowledge that my privilege as a white, cisgender gay man made it easier for me because the majority of hockey players and fans physically look like me. I might have faced more challenges and confrontations if I had been, for example, a person of color or trans. We need to create a space where all players feel comfortable about coming out, becoming their true selves, and championing this movement.

Austin and I in 2019. He makes me smile like no one else.
I'm so happy he's joined me on this adventure.

We aren't there yet. Hockey needs more rainbows and Pride Tape. We need to safely call out our friends, teammates, and coaches when they use language like "that's so gay," "faggot," or "tranny." We need clear nondiscrimination policies that protect queer and, especially, trans players. Being nice to those who are different from you isn't political. Queering hockey isn't going to make it "less straight." This is about making the sport a better and more accepting space for everyone to play in, especially young kids who may be too intimidated to continue. No one should feel scared of playing hockey because of who they love.

We need more open and vocal straight allies, too. I often get asked by straight allies how they can support LGBTQ+ family or friends. It starts and ends with love. Love yourself and what makes you different. Love those who come out to you. "I love you regardless of who you love" is a phrase my mom shared with me that holds immense power, and those are words I will hold on to my entire life. Show up and support pride efforts—whether it's a pride-themed hockey game or a pride parade, be present in our community. Educate yourself, understand what queer life is like for those in your neighbourhood, city, or country. What obstacles and legal challenges still exist? And then, of course, queer your space. Queering a space can be something as simple as showing a rainbow flag or pin on an outfit or your desk; introducing yourself using your pronouns; using or recommending alternative phrases for derogatory language; wearing makeup/nail polish if it's not typically associated with how you identify; or yes, even playing hockey with Pride Tape.

While I'm no pro hockey player—or more than an amateur at best!—I believe there's value in learning lessons from those who are different from you. Let this story be an example of how you can start accepting those around you, queer or not, for who they are. To any LGBTQ+ hockey players still afraid to come out, we love you and we need you. Let's queer this space together.

Joey Gale is an award-winning account executive at a full-service advertising agency based in Seattle, Washington. An avid hockey fan, he has been playing the game since he was three years old. Now a founding partner of a nonprofit called the Seattle Pride Hockey Association, he uses his platform to advocate for LGBTQ+ athletes in the Pacific Northwest. By aligning his profession with his love for playing hockey, he plans to establish an annual pride tournament for queer players and allies. He currently lives in Seattle with his partner, Austin.

 @jjgale

/joey.gale

The Grind

Danielle Grundy

If I could isolate a turning point, it was when a producer from Sportsnet called and wanted to feature me on a segment of Chevrolet's "Power of Play," which would air on *Hockey Night in Canada*. I remember I was working in my home office when my phone rang. The woman on the other end of the line introduced herself as Karen Zylak and explained why she was reaching out.

"You want to what?" I asked, not quite believing what I was hearing.

"We think what you're doing to help young female hockey players stay in the sport is incredible through the Grindstone Award Foundation. Not only are you breaking down the financial barriers, but you're inspiring young women to believe that there's space for them on the ice."

"Thank you," I replied, still in shock. At that time I was juggling the charity among my other two careers in real estate and marketing, but all the hours of hard work that went into creating the Grindstone Award Foundation immediately were worth it just to hear this producer from Sportsnet recognize the good we were doing. Our goal from the very beginning was to empower women in hockey and improve the current state of inequality. And now it was as if we'd become legit in the eyes of the hockey world.

When Karen told me that they were also doing segments on P. K. Subban, Carey Price, and Eric Lindros, I was in disbelief. "I can't believe I'm asking this," I said. "But how did you find me?"

She paused. "When we googled women giving back in hockey, yours was one of the only names that came up."

As soon as I hung up, I dropped the phone and cried. They were mostly happy tears, but part of me was overwhelmed by just how much Grindstone was needed in Canada.

• • •

Ever since I can remember, I wanted to play hockey. Some of my first memories are of watching my older brother, Shawn, play street hockey on our cul-de-sac in Port Coquitlam, British Columbia, and wanting to join in. Eventually I did, and after that, every chance I could, I was in the street, playing ball hockey with the neighbour-hood kids. It wasn't so much about seeing Shawn play hockey first—it was my natural competitiveness and curiosity that fueled my passion for the game.

I was one of those kids who picked up sports quick, and hockey was no different. The first time I stepped on the ice was when I was five. I immediately loved the feeling of being on skates, gliding across the ice. My favourite thing was seeing how fast I could go.

But I wanted nothing more than to play hockey in an organized league. My parents had some reservations, perhaps because they both worked in medicine. My father was a licenced professional nurse at a local hospital and my mother was a rehab assistant at a local retire-ment home.

"What if you get hurt?" my mom would say. Hockey was a rough sport. "You're just a little kid."

"We're not saying no forever. You have to get tougher first," my dad would say.

What I didn't realize at the time was that money was probably one of the reasons they held off on putting me in hockey. We grew up very modestly—my brothers and I always had everything we needed, but even with both my parents working, I don't think they had a ton of dis-posable money for extracurricular sports, especially ones as expensive as hockey. When I did begin to play, my parents did their best with what they could afford, but I know they always felt like they couldn't keep up with other parents in certain ways—like buying me new hockey gear versus used. Outside of hockey trips, I remember only one family vacation, to Disneyland in California. As a kid, I didn't really understand any of this. I just wanted to play hockey like any other kid in Canada.

When I was ten, my parents took me to sign up with the Westside Minor Hockey Association in West Kelowna. It was a boys' team because in 1993 there were no girls' teams in the Kelowna Minor Hockey Association. Most kids begin playing hockey when they're a lot younger. I thought I was too old to be starting out and that my chances of going far in the game were pretty slim. But, as it turns out, I was wrong. I was a natural hockey player. My dad said I made the cut because of my skating ability and my tenacity when battling for the puck. All I knew was that as soon as I hit the ice as a hockey player for my first game, I just wanted to keep getting better and better.

I devoted all my time to hockey, to the point that my parents wanted me to remember how important my schoolwork was. That first year, they told me that if my grades didn't go up, I'd have to quit hockey. This prompted me to write a letter to Wayne Gretzky to ask if this was true.

I would watch *Hockey Night in Canada* every Saturday night with my family, but I especially loved the Canadian women's hockey games. I really liked Judy Diduck, Hayley Wickenheiser, and Nancy Drolet. They were my role models and I watched all their games and their interviews. I remember seeing one of them ripping a shot. She went top corner with a great shot, and it hit me that I could do that, too. It was little things like that, things they said or did, that stayed with me and inspired me to push myself to be the best I could be—not to put limits on my abilities—and I dreamed of one day playing for Team Canada.

Early on, I was able to stick-handle well, and it wasn't unusual for me to shoot into the top corner of the net nine out of ten times in a row because of how much I practiced. The better I played and the more points I racked up, the more confident I was every time I stepped up on the ice. Some people would tell me that I made shooting look so easy. What none of them knew was how many hours of

TO Wayne Gretzky

Oct 11
(1993)

My name is Danielle and my dad
was talking to me and said if my
grades aren't up I will have to quit
hockey and soccer is that true?
When I get on the Ice I fell like
I never want to get off.
This is my first year in hockey.
I am a hockey fan too. Is I
could ask you to send me your
autograph on card: Please.

P.S Please Please write me back
you are a Great hockey playe
: Danielle Grondy 2640 Guidi RD   Kelowna   VIZ 3J9
: 769-0288

*The letter I wrote to Wayne Gretzky. I think this says
it all about how obsessed I was with hockey.*

practice I put in to make my shot better. They never saw me at home, stick-handling with a golf ball to work on my skills every day. They didn't know about the parties that I skipped or my relative lack of social life because I was committed to being a good player.

Hockey was a big commitment for my parents, too. My parents both worked long hours, but they believed in me and my potential. Because of their jobs, they weren't often able to come to my games together, but they always made sure one of them was available to drive me to those early morning practices or be there to watch my games. When they both could attend a game, they never sat next to each other. My mom was always in the stands with the other parents while my dad stood near ice level alone. My mom has a bellowing voice that easily made her the loudest parent at the rink, and she had no problem making sure that I heard what she had to say. And in case I didn't, my parents created their own hand signals to let me know that I had to skate harder or shoot the puck. My younger brother, Jordan, would often get dragged to my games, and he had to endure my mom encouraging me at the top of her lungs the entire time. My parents did everything they could to make me the best player I could be, and when the high expectations and intensity would get to me, they were always there for me.

Here is my official player card from my first year with the Westside Minor Hockey Association. I was the only girl on the team that year, but that didn't stop me.

For many years, I continued playing on boys' hockey teams, usually as the only girl, which had its own challenges off the ice. Because there were no organized girls' teams, the rinks weren't set up for female players. For example, there were no girls' dressing rooms, which meant that I often had to put on part of my gear at home and the rest when I got to the rink. For road games, I had to improvise a bit more— I changed in storage lockers, women's washrooms, janitor's rooms, and the first-aid room as my parents stood watch by the door.

But the whole experience of playing in a boys' hockey league gave me an edge. And in five short years, new opportunities began to unfold for me beyond the boys' league and I started playing women's hockey full-time. At sixteen, I was selected to join Team BC's women's hockey team for the Canada Winter Games. That's when I really started to work on my shot. Every day, I would shoot hundreds of pucks into a net against the wall of the garage at my parents'. I also took power-skating classes at six a.m. and committed to high-performance training at the gym.

In the late 1990s, women's hockey was gaining in popularity, and there was a big push in the NCAA—the National Collegiate Athletic Association—to get more women scholarships to play varsity sports. This was all due to something called Title IX, which is a US federal education law that says schools in the NCAA must provide the same number of scholarships to women that they do to men. As a result, college hockey programs in the United States were looking to expand and they were looking at Canada.

They were looking at me.

When scholarship opportunities began to trickle in, my parents studied the other female hockey players in the province to see how I stood up. They realized that I had a good chance of going to the United States on a scholarship and signed me up to work with skating coach Dave Roy, who had just come back to BC after spending a year with Roger Neilson and the Philadelphia Flyers, and was setting up a European-style hockey camp. Some of the top male and female players from western Canada, the United States, and even from as far away as

Europe took part in Dave's camp, and he went on to develop the Pursuit of Excellence Hockey Academy, one of Canada's premier hockey schools. But at that time I got to work with him 1-on-1 and he taught me tips and tricks that went well beyond skating and helped me maximize my talents as a player.

By the time I reached grade eleven, some of the American schools invited me to come and visit their campuses. My parents and I were just a family from a relatively small town up in Canada, and we had no idea how big collegiate sports were in the United States.

I was living in Vancouver, playing for the Griffiths, a new team in the inaugural season of the National Women's Hockey League, so my parents and I had many phone calls back and forth about what school might be the best. We briefly talked about playing in Canada, but all the best programs were in the United States.

One day I came home to see my parents, and my dad sat me down at the table with a huge binder. Inside, he had printed off information about all of the Division I hockey programs in the United States. That took up a lot of paper, but it helped put everything in perspective. We ended up visiting Dartmouth, Cornell, Providence, and the University of New Hampshire. Walking around some of those campuses felt like being in a movie. Up to that point, I had only seen places like this on TV. It was a lot for me and my parents to take in. After, we narrowed the list down to Dartmouth and Providence.

Providence had a good coach and I connected well with everyone there. They also had a hockey team in which I would play on the top line and get a lot of ice time. Dartmouth, on the other hand, was a fantastic academic school and one of the top women's hockey programs in America. Their team, the Big Green, boasted an extremely high level of players. That would make it tougher for me to earn a lot of playing time, but the challenge of keeping up with the best of the best would surely improve my skills. The campus was beautiful, too, with huge trees, landscaping, manicured grounds, and historic brick buildings. It looked like the kind of perfect college campus you only see in the movies.

In the end, I chose Providence, but when I called Judy Parish, the coach at Dartmouth, to let her know, she laughed. "There's no comparison between our programs. You'd be crazy to choose Providence over an Ivy League school like Dartmouth!"

My stomach plummeted as I hung up the phone. I remember I was sitting in my grandparents' house in Vancouver all alone trying to process what Judy had just said. After a fitful night's sleep, I changed my mind, and the next day, I committed to going to Dartmouth. My parents were pleased. Dartmouth is an Ivy League school and would offer me the best education possible, on top of superior hockey training.

I was only seventeen years old and I was about to move thousands of miles away, to a different coast and a different country. When I looked back at my parents in the airport, it was a surreal moment. I knew that I was starting a whole new chapter in my life.

At first, I was worried that I would be homesick, but I quickly connected with the women on my team and they became my family, my home away from home, and the next four years were a dream.

At that time Dartmouth had one of the best women's hockey teams in the nation. Half of my teammates were members of the Canadian or the US national team, and competition among ourselves was steep. I arrived as one of the best players in BC, but now I was on the same team as all the other top players from across North America. It was a huge reality check. Each day I came to the rink, my coaches and fellow players pushed me to be a better player. And off the ice, they pushed me to be a better person. The program forced me to find another level when it came to competition, and I found a way to go beyond the limits I previously had.

We gelled as a team, and in my third season, we beat Harvard 7–2 to become Ivy League champions. By the time we got to the Frozen Four in 2004, I was playing on the second line, but it was a difficult tournament because it was an Olympic recruitment year and three of our top players had gone to play for Team Canada. Team USA had different rules for their college players, which meant their Olympians were still on the college teams, and so when we faced off with the University of Minnesota, we got pounded by their Olympians, Krissy Wendell and Natalie Darwitz.

It had been my dream to be selected to represent Team Canada on the Olympic stage, but it wasn't meant to be. I felt lucky that I was able to play alongside the top women hockey players, and their talent motivated me to keep pushing myself.

In fact, the toughest thing about my time at Dartmouth was that my parents and my brothers couldn't watch me play because none of our games were on TV back in BC and they didn't have the money to fly out to Dartmouth.

As my time at Dartmouth came to a close, I knew I wasn't ready to quit playing hockey, but it wasn't as if there was a league like the NHL I could aspire to join. A couple of my teammates were already playing professional hockey in Europe, and they told me that although the level of hockey and the pay wasn't that good, the experience of playing

This was taken seconds after I scored during a game against the University of New Hampshire in 2006.

abroad was awesome, and so I decided I would do the same—after all, I'd never been to Europe.

When DHC Langenthal in Switzerland signed me as a free agent, I hopped on a plane for my next adventure. As it turned out, I loved playing hockey overseas. I was in a totally different country and most of my teammates didn't speak much English, but the sport of hockey brought us together. One time we played a game in this cool rink that was half outdoors and half indoors. As the sun went down, the lights of a castle on a hill across from the arena came on, colouring the sky in the most picturesque way. I just stood on the ice, amazed at the sight before me. I was a long way from changing inside a storage locker in a Kelowna rink.

My teammates were right—I didn't get rich playing in Switzerland—but I was able to feed myself and still have enough money left over to travel and explore the world. Then, after two years, I felt it was time to make a career shift. I returned home to Canada, completed my MBA, and began working in real estate, and then started a digital marketing agency with a friend to complement my real estate business. I found that I was able to transfer the drive, determination, and perseverance that I had needed to exhibit daily during my athletic career to my professional career. Every day, I strove for greatness, just in a different arena, but it was hard to leave the ice.

There were only a few local adult women's hockey teams in Kelowna with whom I could continue to play. It was a hard reality to accept. I missed the game, the rush of competition. I did my best to find opportunities to play, and one year I even started my own men's team with two other women to compete in the Division III men's league, just so I could play at a higher level of hockey.

The only way to change the current landscape was to start investing in girls' hockey. In the early 2000s, the Kelowna Minor Hockey Association had expanded to include female hockey, and while it had been great to see the sport include women, the caliber of the coaching and training just wasn't the same as what I got on the boys' teams. In fact, at the time, my mom had ended up helping the coaches manage the girls' teams. A decade later there were still large gaps between the resources available to boys and those that were available to girls.

For example, nobody was offering women's hockey camps in western Canada, and I knew there were girls and women out there who wanted to learn how to play hockey, but didn't grow up watching the game on TV or have parents who hired special coaches like I did. At Dartmouth, I'd had the experience of playing with and learning from some of the best players and coaches in the world. Every day we were pumped full of invaluable hockey knowledge. I realized that not to share that knowledge and experience would be a shame. And so I started my own women's hockey camp to do just that. I called it "Grundy's Grind" and invited anyone who wanted to improve their game, no matter what level they were playing at or how old they were.

We held our first camp in 2009. Every year after that, the camp sold out. Girls and women came from as far away as the Yukon and Whitehorse to take part. I believe it makes a difference to a young woman to have another woman who has achieved success in the sport coach her and mentor her. It's not just the hockey skills, but the life lessons. My role models showed me that the sky was the limit, and that fearlessness and perseverance became part of my own mind-set. These lessons are invaluable and transcend the sport.

On top of my job and the camps, I started coaching girls' teams and working with the Kelowna Minor Hockey Association, which evolved into my becoming the head development coach, the first woman in that position. My mandate was to ensure that girls had the same resources as boys, but it was an uphill battle. The girls' teams had shorter practice times and were often bumped when rink conflicts came up, and there were many other inequities, which led to many players leaving the female program. Watching these young women come into the sport, all I could think was that we should be doing anything we could to make it easier for them to stay in the game and keep playing.

I loved the work I was doing, but I couldn't make the changes that I really wanted to see in girls' hockey at that level—to give girls the same opportunities as boys to excel at the game. I wanted them to have the same opportunity I'd had.

When I was a girl, I didn't really understand the financial burden my parents took on in order for me to play hockey. Everything from playing in the regular season to competing in tournaments costs money. Financial aid from Dartmouth was a big help, but it had taken years and thousands of dollars to get me to the competitive level of the sport at which schools like Dartmouth noticed me. It was only after I was done playing competitive hockey that I learned that my parents had re-mortgaged their house so they would have enough money for me to keep playing hockey. I never knew any of this as a kid. My parents sheltered and protected me from those kinds of harsh financial realities.

In 2014, I left the KMHA, frustrated but ready for the next thing. After six years of running the camps and coaching, it was time to do something more sustainable and impactful. My friend Sasha Podolchak, who I met through hockey—she actually attended one of my first camps—and I were sitting in my kitchen area when we came up with an idea. What if we could raise money and distribute it to families who might not otherwise be able to put their daughters into hockey? I had always wanted to do something like this.

The Grindstone Award Foundation evolved from there. We envisioned it as a way of giving back to the sport by helping young female players with financial support, equipment, and coaching. And for me personally, it would allow me to take a step back from coaching at six a.m. and running hockey camps, but still stay involved in women's hockey and pursue my career. Of course, first we had to get the charity off the ground. We needed to register as a charity, fund-raise, select a board of directors, and so much more that I didn't know at the time. Luckily, the hockey community immediately supported the idea and many people jumped at the opportunity to volunteer to help the cause. It reinforced how important this movement was, not just to me and Sasha, but to the larger community around us.

I was juggling my real estate job and my marketing company, but whenever I came home, I would get to work on the charity. For three months, I met with lawyers, accountants, nonprofit experts, and other professionals to create a road map. I never counted the hours, but I probably spent at least thirty hours a week working on the charity. Sometimes, I found it all overwhelming, but whenever that happened, I reminded myself that organizations like ours existed to help support players who needed our help, that hockey could have a positive impact on the player as a person and change her life, as it had for me. It wasn't easy, but if hockey had taught me anything, it was that I could do whatever I set my mind to—and I wanted to do everything I could to make Grindstone successful. The biggest challenge was raising the money to get the girls into hockey.

Slowly but surely, the pieces all came together. A year after we came up with the idea for Grindstone, we sponsored our very first player: Johanna Hoek, a young girl from Kelowna, BC. Johanna came from a single-income household, and the cost of registration and

With Sasha Podolchak and Johanna Hoek, the first girl
to become the Grindstone Recipient in 2015.

equipment was just too much for her family to handle. I'll never forget the smile on Johanna's face when we told her that Grindstone would be paying for her to play hockey for a season.

A year later we became an official Canadian registered charity and provided two players with a grant and equipment with the help of Play It Again Sports. And in 2017, Sportsnet called, and we were featured on Chevy's "Power of Play" airing on *Hockey Night in Canada*. From there, our charity exploded: we began an annual charity tournament each summer to raise money and bring young girls and coaches together.

Thanks to people at *Hockey Night in Canada*, NHL.com, and others, we've been able to get the word out and completely change the awareness of the charity. A lot of NHLers reached out to support us. They know how important our work is. They have wives who played hockey and daughters who play hockey. They know the barriers that

At the Chevy's "Power of Play" taping with my dad, Lawrence, and my mom, Wendy. They sacrificed so much to help me realize my dreams.

are in place, and they want to help change that. Two-time Stanley Cup champion Andrew Ladd even came to one of our fund-raisers with his daughter.

In 2019, we helped fifty families financially so they could get their daughters into hockey. To do the charity's work and see how thankful the families are when we support them and help their daughters—that makes all the sacrifice, long hours, and hard work worth it. And it makes me so proud to think we achieved that kind of success.

◆　　◆　　◆

When I pulled together our first board of directors, I read them a letter outlining our vision, but also the why behind what we do. These were the whys:

Camille, who was constantly bullied and almost quit hockey, who became a role model and leader.

Austyn, who came to our Grindstone Girls Rock the Rink event for the first time and wouldn't be playing hockey if it wasn't for Grindstone. Her team went on to win Canada 150.

The mom who, when she looked around the rink at one of our charity events and saw so many women, started crying.

The young girls from the small town of Midway in BC who had never been on the ice with so many female players or coached by a female coach, who are now inspired for the rest of their lives after one night.

The professional players who continue to struggle financially because they get paid $2,000 a year.

The coaches who day in and day out sacrifice to give back to the game while barely earning a living themselves.

Makenna Burke, who was unable to play for two years, whose father's bank account hasn't been over $1,000 since she started playing. She is a 2017 recipient of the Grindstone Award and is playing now.

This is for everyone, I explained.

After five years, I made the tough decision to step down as the president of the Grindstone Award Foundation. It was time. Looking back at that letter I read out to our board, I realized that we accomplished everything we set out to do: become a household name across Canada, be promoted on every hockey website, provide aid to families and players who need it, be infectious change makers, and, most importantly, change lives. No matter what, the core values of the Grindstone Award Foundation will never change: equality, empowerment, opportunity, think big, and break barriers. And that is something I will always be very proud of.

Even though I am no longer at the helm, Grindstone continues because there is more work to do. Our charity is more than just giving out financial aid. It's also about where we are at with women's hockey in our society. It's about making sure that every girl has the opportunity to play, to make lifelong friends and learn important lessons from hockey, but it's also about equality. Women's hockey has come a long way, but the sport still struggles, most notably with compensation. Every professional player has the right to earn a liveable wage. And since hockey is Canada's game, we should be able to correct that inequality, and we haven't yet.

With more help, the Grindstone Award Foundation can keep changing the world. Because great things are never done by one person: they're done by a team, on and off the ice.

Danielle Grundy is a former Canadian hockey player who played for the Vancouver Griffins in the NWHL as one of the youngest players in the developing league, and represented Team BC in the 1999 Canada Winter Games, before joining the Big Green at Dartmouth College in 2001 and then DHC Langenthal in Switzerland in 2006. A dedicated coach, she served as the head female development coach for the Kelowna Minor Hockey Association and ran her own women's hockey development camps, Grundy's Grind, for six years before founding the Grindstone Award Foundation. After five years, she retired from the charity and took her RV on a road trip across the continent, stopping in Dartmouth, New York City, Arizona, and all the points in between before returning to BC. Danielle is an award-winning realtor who has ranked in the top 1 percent of agents across Century 21 Canada, and the CEO of her marketing company, Lifeblood Marketing. Both jobs keep her busy when she isn't playing hockey, coaching, or working to empower women. She lives in Kelowna, British Columbia.

 *@daniellegrundy3*

@grindstoneaward

www.daniellegrundy.ca

www.grindstoneaward.com

www.lifebloodmarketing.ca

@lifebloodmarketinginc

Stick Tap

Jack Jablonski

"I don't know if I can do this anymore," I said, with tears rolling down the side of my face. I was lying in the hospital in the first days after my injury and trying to come to terms with my new reality. I was just sixteen. I had dreamed my whole life of playing hockey, and in one instant on the ice, that was all over. "I don't know if I can handle living in a wheelchair."

My therapist was in the room with me, listening as I talked. It wasn't easy for me to open up, but I was in so much emotional pain, I had to get it off my chest. My therapist just stood there, in silence, letting me vent. That was extremely important for me. I cracked open something that had been bottled up since I got to the hospital.

She didn't try to tell me that she understood what I was going through; she acknowledged my feelings. Then she helped me move forward with a sense of positivity.

I saw that if I couldn't handle living in a wheelchair, I would go down a bad road. One that was pure darkness. I took a breath. "I have a choice to make. I can sit here and do nothing. Or, I can try to get back on my feet."

• • •

I was born and raised in the heart of the American Midwest in Minnesota—the State of Hockey. And hockey was everything for me. I started skating on frozen lakes and ponds at the age of two. I didn't step inside a rink until I started skating lessons and youth hockey at the age of four.

My first big NHL hockey hero, outside of guys like Wayne Gretzky and Bobby Orr, was Pavel Datsyuk from the Detroit Red Wings. I fell in love with his hands and the way he moved on the ice, and I did my best to mimic his moves. I thought he was a creative player and I wanted to play just like him. I even wore the number thirteen jersey.

I always felt like me and hockey just clicked, and by the time I was thirteen, I began to realize that I had talent. In my final year of Pee Wee A (the highest level of competition at the time), I scored 55 goals and had over 110 points in 55 games. We took fourth place in the state tournament after being ranked outside of the top twenty to start the year. I did some off-ice training, which helped me understand the game better. My skills began to peak, and again, as a Bantam, I clocked another 50 goals and had over 100 points. We took fifth place in the state tournament after yet again being ranked outside of the top twenty to start the year.

It couldn't have been done without my best friend, Zack Hale, who was also my line mate. We had been playing hockey together since we were seven years old. He put up the same numbers as me when we shared the ice. We were a great duo—if I had a goal, he would have the assist, and if he scored, I would have the assist. The two of us would be on the ice for almost half the game, so even if opposing teams tried to target us and slow us down, there was only so much they could do.

Off the ice, Zack and I were in sync, too. We finished each other's sentences and we knew what each other was thinking, without saying a word.

I understood that physicality was a part of hockey, but I was never one to seek contact. I did my best to avoid big hits and just play my game, mainly because I was one of the smaller kids on the ice. At sixteen, I was five eight and 150 pounds—I grew taller only after my injury. But there were times when I got pushed around a fair bit. The nice thing about hockey is that you can get pushed around for fifty-eight minutes and still score the winning goal in the other two.

In the fall, I was selected to play on a stacked U-16 Minnesota Blades team, where I scored a hat trick against Shattuck St. Mary's. We beat Shattuck three times that fall. That brief season before we went to play for our high schools ended when we lost in overtime in the semi-finals, and took third place at the 2011 Nike Bauer tourney in Chicago, the biggest tournament in the country annually, going 4-1-1.

My big moment came in 2011 when I went to Benilde–St. Margaret's prep school. Benilde had one of the best high school hockey teams in the entire state every year, and making their team was a huge deal. Between playing for Benilde and the numbers I was putting up, I knew I had a real shot at the NCAA, but I tried to take everything one step at a time. The best part was that Zack made the team, too.

When I joined Benilde, we were a deep, loaded team filled with seniors and juniors. That year, approximately nine of the kids on my team would go on to play Division I NCAA hockey. The way our

Zack, number nine, and I, number three,
on the ice after I scored the game-winning goal in
our divisional championship game, March 2011.

coach, Ken Pauly, did things was to work the younger players, like me, into the game. He didn't just throw us out there and expect us to be great right away. I understood that I had to earn my ice time and the right for my minutes when I did get the chance to play.

By the start of the Holiday Hockey Classic tournament in late December 2011, through sixteen games I had put up just two assists (eye roll). Now it was the final game of the tournament and we were facing our biggest rivals, Wayzata.

In the first period, we had the puck in the offensive zone. I was behind the net, battling for it. I got the puck on my stick and came around the side of the net. I was trying to jam the puck in on my forehand when I got leveled by a defenceman. There was a pile of bodies by the net and the goalie was sprawled out, and there—even after the scuffle—was the puck just sitting there. I popped back up and fired it into the net. It wasn't the prettiest goal I ever scored, but it counted. I had put us on the board.

Things got heated as the teams battled each other, but it was normal, physical hockey between two good teams. Wayzata came back with a couple goals, but we matched those. By the third period, we were tied 3–3.

When I came on the ice for my second shift of the third period, the puck was in our defensive zone. I was playing right wing and rushed toward the front of the net, covering the weak-side defenceman. The puck popped out to me and I took off on a 2-on-2 with my other winger. As I crossed the blue line, I went wide by the opposing defenceman and slid by him, but the other defenceman on the far side was coming at me, trying to cut me off instead of staying in front of the net.

I was running out of room. I did a button hook to look for someone else coming into the offensive zone that I could pass the puck to, but before I could do this, the defenceman that I had slid by checked me on my right shoulder as I neared the boards. Simultaneously, I was hit from behind by a backchecker I hadn't seen. Backcheckers are always told to take the man without the puck, but he ran me into the boards anyway.

I was hit hard and high from behind.

I don't remember hitting the boards or falling, but the moment I made contact with the ice, I was completely aware of everything around me. I was lying on my left side, staring straight into the boards. Everything was numb except for an excruciating pain like I had never felt before in my neck.

Immediately I knew something was very wrong. The referees whistled and the entire arena went deadly silent. Around me, I heard the clatter of players and officials murmuring as everyone tried to help me.

Within minutes, the EMT paramedics were there. I told them that my neck was in a lot of pain.

"I can't feel anything else," I said.

They rolled me onto my back, and I could see my assistant coach, Chris, standing over me with the refs. I tried to move, but I couldn't.

"All right," one of the EMTs said. "Let's try to get him up on three."

"No, you don't understand," I said. "I can't feel anything. I can't move anything."

The EMTs exchanged a look—I think realizing that my injury was much worse than they had thought. My own thoughts began to spiral.

"Am I paralyzed?" I blurted out, not even fully comprehending what that meant, just knowing that I couldn't move.

"No," the EMT replied, which helped stop the panic rising inside my chest. Even if she was wrong, I think she knew that was the right answer in that moment.

They took off my skates, my gloves, and my helmet, and that's when I saw my dad coming onto the ice. I could tell by his reaction that something wasn't right.

When I said, "Dad, I can't move," his face went white.

A few minutes later, my mom was beside me. "He's okay," she said. "He's okay." She kept repeating that over and over again, trying to stay positive.

The EMTs got me on the stretcher to take me to the ambulance that was waiting outside. As they wheeled me off the ice, the players began tapping their sticks on the ice and my teammates came by and patted me on the chest. My throat grew tight and at that moment I started to cry. It hit me—I was leaving the ice for the last time as a hockey player. In my head, I was trying to tell myself that I would be out of action for two weeks, but when I was loaded into the ambulance, I knew this was much worse.

I arrived at the hospital on December 30, 2011. I wouldn't go home until April 18, 2012.

It was late Saturday afternoon when I got to the hospital. The lead doctor, Thomas Bergman, who'd played hockey for Princeton University, had been due to head home for the weekend, but when he heard a hockey player was coming in, he stayed. That man spent the whole weekend taking care of me and became one of my main two neurologists.

I spent the first week in the PICU on a lot of meds for my pain, so my memory of that time is a little foggy, but I remember the conversation when the doctors gave me my diagnosis. It's one of the few things I can recall from that week.

I was surrounded by my family when the doctors told me just how severe my spinal cord injury was. When one of them started with "I'm sorry to tell you this . . ." I knew it was bad. He got straight to the point, "You broke your C5 and C6 vertebrae. You completely severed your spinal cord."

He explained that when I had been hit twice, my body couldn't take the force and those two bones in my lower neck had been completely crushed. I was facing quadriplegia and would never walk again. The doctors were waiting for the swelling to go down in order to learn more, but it looked like I would most likely never use the left side of my body; I would be lucky to even bend my right arm.

In short, I was paralyzed.

I felt like I was having an out-of-body experience. When the doctor said the word "paralysis," I had a blank stare on my face. It took a few moments to let the news sink in, and to be honest, it didn't fully sink in for another week.

I could tell my parents were crushed. My father blamed himself for getting me into hockey, but they did their best to hide their fears and do everything they could to take care of me.

My injury had been heavily covered in the news. After my doctor left my bedside in the PICU, the media was waiting outside for him. I was in my bed, watching him speak on TV when he said, "We can fix the bone, but we can't fix the spinal cord."

Oh, yeah, I thought, *screw the doctors.* I was naive at first. But then everything really began to hit me. I was immobilized there on the bed with a feeding tube. I was sixteen years old and it felt like my life was over when it should have just been starting. My future playing for the NCAA, gone, just like that. All I had done was exactly what I loved, and now I would never skate again. All the time I had put into being the best hockey player I could be had disappeared. I was only in grade ten. How was I going to get through the next few years of high school and graduate? How was I going to be a functioning individual?

Everything was bottling up inside. I'm not a very emotional person on the outside, but inside was a different story. Finally, when it got to be too much, I let it out and spoke to my therapist. That was when I decided to fight. I had always been a hard worker on the ice; I needed to be a hard worker off the ice now. With the doctor's words still ringing in my ears, I came up with a new motto: "I understand my injury, I do not accept it."

After that first week in the PICU, I moved to the recovery unit, where my feeding tube was taken out and I started physical therapy. Everything woke up inside me. Finally, I could eat food. Finally, I could start to move more. A lot of people think physical therapy is lifting weights and reactivating muscles. For me, it was working on being able to sit up. My body had been lying down for a week and a half straight and it was in pain. My muscles had to get moving before they locked up and atrophy set it. I practiced sitting up and nothing but sitting up for a week. Once I was able to handle that, it was time to grind.

That second week in the hospital, I set my goals. I had processed my new reality and I knew what I had to do physically, mentally, and emotionally, to get where I wanted to go. Step one: be back at school for day one of my junior year. Step two: graduate high school on time with my friends. Step three: be with my hockey team.

As I settled into my hospital stay, my mom shut down her PR business and my dad took time off his job at 3M, a manufacturing conglomerate in Minnesota, to focus on helping me recover. Basically, they put their lives on hold to care for me. Every day, one of them would come to the hospital and care for me and talk to the doctors about my progress and then sleep in my hospital room overnight, while the other was at home with my younger brother, Max, and the next day, they would switch.

From the very beginning, friends, family, and my teammates circled around my family. So many people stopped by to say hi that the hospital gave me a room designed to house four separate patients. The support was overwhelming and helped me see how much good life still had to offer.

Jack Blatherwick is just one example. Jack is a famous hockey coach and trainer in Minnesota who helped train six Team USA hockey teams for the Olympics and five NHL teams. When I was in the hospital, Jack slept in his van in the parking lot, then came back to my room in the morning and stayed with me. Even after my parents had gone home or gone to bed, Jack would sit up with me until three in the morning, comparing Russian hockey to North American hockey. He became one of my best friends and I think of him as a grandfather.

Zack was by my side as much as he could be, too. He was going through a tough time himself and so we leaned on each other. We didn't have to talk all the time. Whenever we saw each other, it was a chance to just exhale and not think about the outside drama. I always felt that way when I saw my teammates. They kept me going.

Meanwhile, the captain of our team had gone on Twitter and created a hashtag for me: #jabs. Within a week, my story went viral. All of a sudden athletes—hockey players, baseball players—musicians, anyone you could imagine, were tweeting at me, wishing me luck, and saying that their thoughts and prayers were with me. Both Wayne Gretzky and Bobby Orr phoned to wish me the best, which was surreal. I couldn't believe I was talking to the two best players in the history of hockey. My hero, Pavel Datsyuk, even left me a voice mail and sent me three of his jerseys.

And then NHL teams started showing up in my hospital room. Matt Majka, the president and alternate governor of the Minnesota Wild, was the first to stop by and offer his team's support. He and Craig Leipold, the team's owner, decided that they would raise funds to help with my medical expenses during Hockey Day Minnesota, which was just a couple of weeks away. To this day, the Wild have been a mainstay in supporting me.

The San Jose Sharks were set to play the Minnesota Wild on January 10, 2012, and the day before, players from both teams stopped by to see me. After that, almost every single visiting team that came to play the Wild would pop by my hospital room for a visit. Lying in that hospital bed, I didn't feel like I was just a kid talking to famous millionaire hockey players; I felt like a hockey player talking to other hockey players who were trying to support a fallen teammate.

Those were some of the lowest days of my life, but out of those visits came the most wonderful friendships, many of which I still have today.

Jeremy Roenick is a great example. I'll never forget the day he walked into my hospital room. He had been working at NBC in New York when I got injured, and instead of flying home to Phoenix after the broadcast, he came to Minnesota. The minute he entered the room, he started talking smack. I'll admit—I brought it on myself.

You see, when I heard he was coming, I found a photo of him sitting on the bench holding his water bottle up to his mouth—the thing was, the water bottle was backwards, so he was spraying the ice. I got that photo blown up and put it above my head for when he arrived.

As soon as Jeremy walked into the room, he saw the photo, then looked at me and instantly gave me flak for it. I think he knew right there and then that this visit wasn't going to be a one-off. He stayed with me for five hours and we talked and laughed. We said our good-byes, but it wasn't goodbye forever. We've been tight ever since.

Early on, Coach Pauly asked me what he and the BSM coaching staff could do to help.

"Keep me involved with the team," I answered. "I want to help us get better and win."

As the season progressed, the sectional playoffs were in February, and if we won them, we would advance to the state championship in March. Coach Pauly agreed with my proposal, and from that point on, I became a student assistant coach, working on the Xs and Os of hockey from my hospital room, which was a great distraction, but also motivated my recovery.

•   •   •

The doctors had told me that whatever gains I made in the first twelve to eighteen months after my injury were likely to be the extent of the function I'd get back. After eighteen months, recovery often plateaus, and so I was pushing as hard as I could to gain muscle movement. They had predicted I wouldn't be able to use my left arm. I wanted to prove them wrong. And I did. My brother, Max, was hanging with me after school, as he did every day. He was standing next to me on the left side of my bed. I shocked him, and myself, when I was able to lift my left arm and hit him. My mom was there, too, and she nearly fell to the floor. At that moment one of my neurologists walked into the room. Mom said, "Do that again Jack." I did! My doctor had tears in his eyes. "Keep proving us wrong," he said.

I put in long hours of physical and occupational therapy. There were tough days when I felt like quitting, but I remembered my team and never gave up, believing that I would regain more feeling and movement in my upper body in the months ahead.

Between therapy sessions, I would watch film of the team and talk to the coaches about power plays and strategy, which made me feel like I was still a part of the team as we made our run at the championship title.

But first, we had to win our section. We were ranked eighth in the state, and not many people thought we would even make it out of our section because the number two- and five-ranked teams were also in our section.

While I saw the guys when they came to visit, I had yet to go to a game since my injury two plus months before. As sectionals approached, I came up with a plan to surprise the guys in the locker room before our first playoff game.

It was a big step forward in my physical recovery to get to the point where I could be in a wheelchair and move around. And mentally, getting out of the hospital and going to the rink was the first step toward normalcy.

Right before the guys went out onto the ice, I rolled into the dressing room. The look on their faces was priceless. They all jumped up, happy to see me. I was in a wheelchair and could barely lift my right arm, but the second I entered the room, I was back home with the boys. And when they filed out to play, I raised my hand enough to give them each a fist bump.

The next two and a half hours were emotional as I watched the game. It was tough seeing my team out there without me, but at the same time it was the best thing for me. I was able to be myself and forget about everything else that was going on and just watch my team win. Step three completed. After that, I went to every section game.

Benilde won both the quarterfinal against Holy Family, 7–0, and the semifinal game against Robbinsdale Armstrong, 5–0. The boys were buzzing.

The final was against number-two-ranked Minnetonka and held at the University of Minnesota Mariucci Arena in front of eight thousand fans. I was down on the glass behind the net and close to the locker rooms. We'd been dominating so far, and we weren't going to stop now. We put up two goals in the first, and Minnetonka hit back with

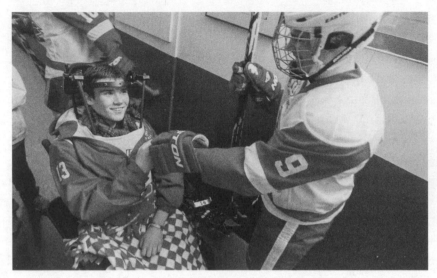

Zack giving me a fist bump at my first game back.

one, but we didn't let them get any more, and just continued to pile on the goals—one in the second, two in the third.

When it became clear that we would be the victors, Chris, the assistant coach, came up to me. "Jack, go out on the ice after they win."

"No," I replied. "I don't want to. I don't want to be in the public eye. I'm embarrassed about my appearance." I was sitting in my wheelchair with a halo screwed into my head and overwhelmed by all the cameras pointed at me even from where I was.

But Chris kept pushing me. "Jack, go on the ice. Trust me."

At the end the third period, I caved. "Fine. I'll do it."

When the game ended, the Zamboni doors opened, and I came out onto the ice in my wheelchair and joined my teammates. Immediately the entire crowd started chanting my name and gave me a standing ovation.

"Jabby! Jabby!"

I felt my eyes well up. Three different teams from the sectional tournament were sitting in the stands, and they were all shouting my name. It was a moment I'll never forget—it showed me that hockey is ger than who wins and who loses. One of my best friends, sse, wiped the tears from my face with his jersey.

were headed to the state championships, where we would face ainst the most hated team in the state, Edina.

n Minnesota, the state tournament is held at the Xcel Energy Cen- home of the Minnesota Wild, and it was about a twenty-minute rive from the hospital. My dad, Jack Blatherwick, and I headed over together. On the way there, I started not to feel well and asked if my dad could pull over for a second.

"We're about a mile away. You can handle it," my dad replied. That's just the way he is and I'm not the kind of person who complains about pain. He didn't catch the red flag.

Just as we pulled into the parking lot, I started to vomit. Jack didn't bat an eye. He was catching it and doing a great job, but his hands were tilted a little too much, so it was all funneling out onto my sweatshirt. Jack is the kind of guy who would do anything for you.

I felt so bad and apologized. I didn't know why I had gotten sick. At

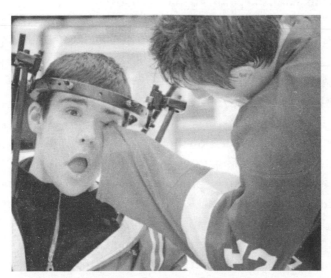

Grant Besse wiping my tears away after we won our sectional finals and I came out onto the ice.

the time I didn't realize that when you have paralysis, there [are]
signs that your body is ill, and as I would find out later, I had [a]
bladder infection.

My dad and Jack cleaned everything up and I shook off the fe[eling]
that something wasn't right. When we entered the arena, the majo[rity]
of the eighteen-thousand-plus crowd was dressed in red, our sch[ool]
colours. Typically, high school hockey fans in Minnesota don't roo[t]
for private schools, but here they were showing just what team the[y]
hoped would win.

It was a crazy, energetic match. Late in the third period we were
tied 2–2, but with less than twenty seconds left, we scored to win the
game off a neutral zone turnover. We were moving forward to the
semifinals tomorrow night against Lakeville South, who had just upset
the number one team in the state, Duluth East.

By the time I got back to the hospital for the night, I had a fever of
104. I had a hard time falling asleep, and by sunrise, I was up vomit-
ing. I was a mess. The hospital staff gave me an IV, but it only helped
a little bit.

The whole day, I kept saying that I had to go to the game. The team
needed me. The coaches needed me. I was too sick and had to settle
for watching the game on TV. After a quick 5–0 start in the first period, I went to sleep.

Even though I wasn't there to cheer them on, the boys beat Lakeville South by a landslide, 10–1.

By the day of the state final, I felt a bit better. I wasn't missing this
game for the world, so I left the hospital with an IV in my arm and a
big sweatshirt to cover it up. It was a game to remember. We were up
against Hill-Murray, but they proved to be no match for us, specifically
for our best forward, Grant Besse. He put up two goals in the first, another in the second, and two more in the third—all five goals we scored
were his, and three of them were shorthanded! It was the single greatest
performance in Minnesota high school hockey championship history.

Hill-Murray managed one goal early in the third, but that was
it. We had pounded them, 5–1, and become state champions. An

accomplishment every hockey player in Minnesota dreams of. It was surreal to watch it all. And I couldn't help but think my input on the strategy side had something to do with it.

As the game was winding down, the crowd was chanting my name and the team wanted me on the ice, so I left the suite we were in, which happened to be Craig Liepold's, the owner of the Minnesota Wild. He gave it to me and my family and friends for the tournament because it had a straight-on view of the ice. That way, I didn't have to move my neck back and forth to watch the game. My dad and I made our way down to the ice, but I couldn't get through the six bodyguards and security guards that were ordered to keep me from getting on the ice by the State High School League. They said I wasn't allowed on the ice because I wasn't on the roster. Instead, I was sent to the locker room. But the moment the guys came in and we all started to celebrate is a memory I will cherish forever.

However, the celebration didn't stop there. T. J. Moore, one of our team's captains, and his parents invited the entire team and their families to their house for an impromptu celebration. I was supposed to return to the hospital as I only had a pass to leave for the game. But my dad and Jack Blatherwick insisted that I join the team for the big celebration. We arrived in my accessible van and T.J.'s dad told us to drive up on the front lawn, where we were met by five other dads, who unloaded me from the van and hoisted me and my three-hundred-pound power wheelchair up the steps and into the house.

That night I didn't feel like I was paralyzed. I felt like part of a team that had just won the state championship. My injury was an afterthought. It was one of the best nights ever.

About that hospital pass—my mom got a call at three thirty in the morning from one of the nurses, wondering where I was. She thought I was back at the hospital with my dad, but the nurse said we weren't there. She called my dad, and soon after we returned to the hospital with the highly coveted MN State Hockey Championship Trophy on my lap. A sight not to be forgotten.

The next morning, it was back to reality. I was putting in more and more hours of therapy, and then, one day, I was ready to go home. On April 18, over a hundred days after I had been injured, I left the hospital.

By that time, my dad had gone back to work, so my mom, Max, and many close friends were there 24/7 to help me. It was good to be out of the hospital, although that was an adjustment in itself. We lived in an accessible apartment for the next six months while our home was being renovated to suit my needs, thanks to the generosity of the Benilde community, the hockey community, and beyond.

I had started doing homework during my last month in the hospital. Jack, who has a PhD, helped me with my geometry. I also read *Hamlet*, a nightmare of a book, but luckily the school gave me a pass on my science credit—they said I was dealing with enough science in my life. I agreed. Once I was home, I finished up all of my other credits, and was ready to start my junior year of high school that fall. Step one completed.

Meanwhile, I was doing five hours of physical therapy five times a week throughout the summer. I spent an hour a day on the treadmill and used electrical stimulation to help strengthen my muscles and rehabilitate my damaged nerves. This was all through a program called Activity-Based Locomotor Exercise, or ABLE, which helps retrain the spinal cord through activity-based therapies. As a part of ABLE, all my information was logged into a countrywide database to better help other people with spinal cord injuries. I still had moments when I wanted to throw in the towel, but my family and friends always helped pick me back up again.

When I made it back to school in September of 2012, I was a lot stronger and able to physically get through each day. Zack was with me every step of the way. We would always have lunch together and he'd help feed me my meal. I had therapy three times a week, but the other two weekdays, I was at team practice. I had my friends, school, and hockey. There was a growing sense of normalcy to my life.

As the one-year anniversary of my injury approached, I had made improvements beyond my own twelve-month mark and there was still time make more. I'd also become more aware of how to live with paralysis. My feeling and my function stop at my chest, right around my nipple line, so if I run into something with my chair and stub my toe, I don't feel it because the message my body sends my brain is blocked at the break in my spinal cord.

But my body compensates with something called autonomic dysreflexia. It's how my body gives me clues that something is wrong below my level of feeling. The first clue is my face will get hot and tingly, the second is goose bumps. If I don't figure out what is wrong, my blood pressure will spike. When my dysreflexia is severe, it can go up to 250 over 125 (my resting blood pressure is 100 over 50 or 60), which means I'm on the verge of having a stroke. Thankfully, I'm stroke-free.

By 2014, I was even stronger. At the time of the hit, I was five eight, 150 pounds, and now I was six two, 190 pounds. (I joked around that the one thing I gained from my injury was six inches.) I had filled out and was much healthier. I could physically move around better and the dexterity in my hands had improved. It was a great sign: the more dexterity I had, the more independence I had. Best of all, I was still making strides after that eighteen-month window. And I completed step two and graduated high school with the rest of my friends.

It had been a long journey—one that I wouldn't wish upon my worst enemy—but the support of so many made it possible. I had been so fortunate to have a network of people cheering me on and raising money for me. Everyone had been so generous, and I felt it was time to give back. I wanted to help other people with spinal cord injuries who might not have the same resources as I did be able to speed up their recovery process and get them on their feet.

On the one-year anniversary of my injury, we established the Jack Jablonski BEL13VE in Miracles Foundation to advance paralysis recovery research and benefit all people living with a spinal cord injury, and began an annual gala to raise money and awareness, which the Minnesota Wild cohost. In November of 2014, we organized a special ceremony at a Wild game to raise awareness for everyone, not just hockey players, who had suffered a spinal cord injury, and to support spinal cord research. We called it #StickTap2Hope, and our goal was to create the world's largest stick tap—we even had Dave Christian, Neal Broten, and Rob McClanahan from the 1980 USA Olympic gold medal team join us on the ice for it.

In hockey, when someone is down on the ice, the first thing players do is tap their sticks on the ice as a sign of respect. When I was being wheeled off the ice after my injury, that's what happened. In that moment, you're not just players, coaches, and fans, you're friends.

That night was extremely emotional for me because I wanted to participate, but I didn't even know if I could hold and lift the stick. Jeremy Roenick was next to me—he's the foundation's biggest spokesperson—and I turned to him. "I want to be part of this. Will you make sure I can tap my stick?"

"Of course, Jabs," he answered.

Having him by my side gave me the confidence to tap that stick.

Jeremy Roenick and I at my Jack Jablonski Foundation
"A Night to Bel13ve" Gala on November 19, 2016.

Then the whole Xcel Energy Center arena filled with the noise. *Tap. Tap. Tap.* It was music to my ears.

I was doing things I never thought I'd be able to do. When I was injured, college seemed like a fantasy, and yet, in 2015, I enrolled with a communications major and sports media minor at the University of Southern California, and it was all because of one of those hospital visits back in early 2012.

A month or so after my injury, the Anaheim Ducks had come to see me in the hospital and stayed for well over forty-five minutes. There must have been over eleven players there as well as a scout my family knew named Casey Hankinson. Casey was from Minnesota, and in our state, everyone in the hockey world knows everyone else— and he now sits on our foundation's board.

During the visit, Casey and Ryan Getzlaf pulled my dad aside. "I know college isn't something you're looking at right now," they said. "But when you do go down that road, there's this great foundation called Swim With Mike that helps physically challenged athletes. They know what happened to Jack."

Swim With Mike was founded by Mike Nyeholt, an elite swimmer who suffered a spinal cord injury in a motorcycle accident, and Ron Orr, his USC swim teammate and lifelong friend. As it turns out, Mike's former sister-in-law, Maureen Norvell, worked for the Anaheim Ducks, and when she heard the team was coming to see me, she reached out to Casey.

When I was in my senior year of high school, I visited USC, where Swim With Mike is based, and met with Ron to interview for a scholarship. It was then that I knew I wanted to go to USC. When acceptance letters went out, I was elated to learn that I'd been accepted by USC and that Swim With Mike was going to cover a large part of my tuition.

USC had everything I wanted in college and more. The flatness of the campus meant I could get around. The weather was important for my health. Because of my paralysis, I'm unable to control my body temperature. While being in Minnesota for two winters was amazing because of all the hockey, it was absolutely miserable because I was freezing the entire time. Anything below sixty degrees F or fifteen degrees C, even with sun, is like being in a Canadian winter to me. The California climate was perfect. It also meant that I could wear shorts most days, which helps me prevent any dysreflexia issues.

On top of that, USC is the top school in the country for communications, which is what I wanted to study. They also have a great disability program, helping me get all the information and notes I need to be on the same level as the rest of the class. I try to be as independent as possible, but I just can't write on my computer that fast because I use the back knuckle of my right pinkie to type. It's much easier for me to type on my phone with my right thumb, which I can do just about as fast as anyone, so I often use the Notes app on my iPhone, which is connected to my MacBook.

Going to USC was the best decision I ever made. The second best was joining the Tau Kappa Epsilon fraternity. Everyone in the fraternity accepted me with open arms and treated me as one of their equals. Early on in my injury, I was very cautious about asking for help with my needs; I was embarrassed to ask for help because it made me feel like less of a human. And even still, I maintain my independence as much as I can. I don't always want people helping me. But I've learned that having a spinal cord injury is part of who I am, and so if I need something, it's okay to ask for it. And when I did, all I had to do was post a message and I'd receive 140 offers to help. Knowing I had those friendships in my back pocket allowed me to be who I want to be—like the guy who plays beer pong.

For so long, I'd watch my fraternity brothers play beer pong and the whole time I'd be thinking, *There must be some way that I can do this, too.* I'm not a big drinker, but beer pong is a part of college life and I wanted to play just like every other college student. My right hand was my stronger one, so I figured I could make it work. And wouldn't you know, it did. As much as I loved seeing the ball go in the cup, I loved the looks on the guys' faces when I did it—it was a great sense of true normalcy.

But the unsung hero of my time at USC is my caretaker, Danny Antonio, who has allowed me to function as a human being while at school. He is the guy behind the scenes who gets things done. He's my able body. Whether it's picking up my medications, putting me to bed, or helping me shower and dress, he's there for me and I know I can trust him with my life. He and I have a great relationship and I don't know where I'd be without him.

The same goes for Zack. During my summers home from university, he took me to therapy every single day. He's the kind of guy who would do anything for you, and whenever we're together, we pick up right where we left off. To this day, we talk almost every day even though we live over four thousand kilometers apart.

Ever since I was a kid, my dream was to someday make it to the NHL. While I was at USC, I interned in the LA Kings' media department for four years. After I graduated from USC in December 2019,

January 2020, signing my contract for the LA Kings.

the LA Kings hired me as their content coordinator in the social media department. I felt like my life had come full circle. Kelly Cheeseman, the COO of the Kings, hails from Minnesota and went to Benilde–St. Margaret's, just like me, and he welcomed me to the organization. "Whatever you need, just let us know." If there's one thing about the hockey world, it's that they take care of their own.

After Ryan Straschnitzki was hurt in the Humboldt Broncos bus crash, I reached out to him to talk about the injury and about positivity, and had Jeremy Roenick reach out to him, just as he did for me. Anytime I see someone else who has suffered a similar injury, I reach out in hopes of helping them. I get in touch because it was support from others in the hockey world that helped me. And because there is hope. There is a future for people with spinal cord injuries.

The BEL13VE in Miracles Foundation—now called the Jack Jablonski Foundation—is dedicated to advancing paralysis recovery research so that it can move from the trial lab to mainstream clinics and everyone living with a spinal cord injury can access life-changing treatments. We changed the name of our foundation because science is proving that paralysis recovery is possible. It's not a miracle anymore. Our goal is to get everyone out of their chairs. That's my goal and I'm going to work every day to reach it. The way I see it, I can just sit in my chair or I can help other people. Since my injury, there have been so many advances in spinal cord research and I believe our foundation has made an impact in speeding up that process. In 2019, we took a big step forward when we hosted an event and raised over $300,000 for paralysis recovery research for both paraplegics and quadriplegics.

The quote from the doctor was, "We can fix the bone, but we can't fix the spinal cord." That has always stuck with me because I'm unwilling to believe it.

I live to prove the doctors wrong. Therapy-wise, I have accomplished many things that I was told I wasn't going to be able to do. I now have function in both of my arms. I have wrist movement in my right hand. I'm working on finger movement. On the Fourth of July in 2018, I actually wiggled my toes, something I was told would never happen.

That's why my motto is: "I understand my injury, I do not accept it."

Who knows what I'll do next. In the meantime, I'm going to keep tapping my stick. Because I am a hockey player.

Jack Jablonski is a content coordinator with the LA Kings and an integral part of All the Kings Men, *the official LA Kings podcast. He played hockey for eleven years, and in 2013, he was selected by the Chicago Steel in the USHL entry draft despite his spinal cord injury. He is the founder of the Jack Jablonski Foundation, which is dedicated to making paralysis recovery possible.*

 @Jabs_13

@jackjablonski13

www.bel13vefoundation.org

Dream Big

Katie Guay

My skates have been my passport around the globe. I've skated on Olympic rinks, NHL rinks, NCAA rinks, IIHF rinks in Europe, Scandinavia, and Asia, and rinks all across the USA. Along the way, I've met incredible friends who have enriched my life and made me laugh until I've cried more times than I can count. My skates even took me to *The Price Is Right*, where I was a contestant, one of the sillier ambitions I've had in life. As a girl growing up in the 1980s and 1990s in Westfield, Massachusetts, I could never have dreamed that my simple love of hockey would lead me down this road.

Hockey is in my DNA. I come from a very athletic family, starting with my parents. They shared the same love of sports, but they hailed from hardworking, middle-class families that didn't have the time or money for sports beyond what was offered in school. My parents were determined to give their children a better life than they had, so when it came to sports, they made sure that my siblings and I had the opportunities that they had missed out on, and we made the most of the chances we were given.

My older brother, Todd, and my older sister, Lisa, both got into hockey when they were six years old. I was only two or three at the time, but I tagged along to the rink. I still remember the smell of the arena mixed with the scent of french fries cooking at the concession stands. I would run around with the other younger kids, wishing the whole time I could be out there on the ice.

After every game, Todd would want a hockey soda or a slushy.

And since I was there, I would get one, too, either from the concession stands or from the local 7-Eleven corner store on our way home. Hockey seemed pretty fun to me and I pestered my mom and dad nonstop about letting me play.

The moment I was eligible for the mite age group, my parents signed me up. I wore my siblings' hand-me-down equipment, but I didn't mind, everything was brand-new and thrilling to me. Hand-me-downs were a part of my experience in hockey. Years later, when I started college, I had a pair of skates that had been barely used by Tara Mounsey, a two-time US Olympian. I even wore her number two jersey, which I considered to be a real honour. Looking back, that equipment was a visible symbol of support and inspiration and I felt like my heroes were skating with me as I played the game I loved.

Throughout my youth, there were no girls' teams where I lived, so I played on boys' teams. Not only was I the only girl on my team, I was the only girl in my league. Being the only girl on the ice meant I had to work hard to prove that I belonged. I was always ranked near the top of everyone in our age category, and for a few years, I was the team captain. I worked hard to earn the respect of my peers and I was honoured to wear the C.

Being the youngest of three kids also taught me how to hold my own—on and off the ice. At home, Todd, Lisa, and I were always competing, whether it was the highest jump on the trampoline, the hardest shot against a brick wall, or the biggest cannonball splash in our backyard pool. Whenever we wrestled, Lisa made sure I was working hard. She never let up on me, and because of that, I developed a natural drive to keep up with my brother and sister that served me well in hockey.

By the time I was eleven or twelve, I was in Pee Wee hockey, and it was around this time that body checking started to happen. As the lone girl on the ice, I was a bit of a target and received more than my fair share of body checks. I started tucking my hair under my helmet and serving them right back. I was a grinder and played hard to win, so checking came naturally to me.

Here I am at eight years old.

One night I checked a boy and he fell hard to the ice. He didn't re-alize that he'd been trucked by a girl until after the game. In the lobby, my mom and I overheard him say, "Mom, I got hit by a girl!" and we couldn't help but laugh.

I was working hard off the ice, too. From a young age, my dad taught me the true meaning of hard work. He put in sixty-plus hours a week as a machinist at a tool company, and as soon as I was legally old enough, I got my first job. It was on a tobacco farm, and I spent the summer tying strings around the plants and sewing the leaves. On Sundays, I had my paper route. Those mornings my dad drove me around the neighbourhood in his truck as I jumped off the tailgate and hustled to drop newspapers on doorsteps. During the hockey season, the papers were delivered well before the sun rose.

By grade nine, I made the Westfield High varsity boys' hockey team, but looking beyond high school, I realized that if I found a place to play on a girls' team, I might have more opportunity to be seen by college coaches. Luckily for me, a great opportunity popped up.

One of my youth hockey coaches, Pete "Hutch" Hutchinson, was refereeing a game at Deerfield Academy, a coed prep school that had a robust girls' hockey program. After the game, the Deerfield coach approached Hutch and asked if he knew any girls who might be a good fit for the Deerfield team. Hutch said, "As a matter of fact, I do: Katie Guay. I've coached her all the way through youth hockey. She played with the boys and she has talent."

Back then, recruiting was all about word of mouth. No one was using the Internet to promote youth players or making videos of themselves to send to various schools. Getting noticed was much harder, so it was fortunate that my youth hockey coach happened to be a referee who happened to be at Deerfield when they were actively looking for players. Without that chance encounter, who knows how long my hockey career would have lasted.

The first time my parents and I set foot on the Deerfield Academy campus for a visit, it was like entering a little utopia. Westfield High was a very large school: my ninth-grade class was larger than Deerfield's entire student body. But the facilities at Deerfield were impressive, beyond anything I had ever seen before.

While the opportunity was incredible, there were a couple of important considerations beyond hockey. One was finances. Even with the generous financial aid package Deerfield was offering, my attendance would require an additional—and significant—commitment from my parents.

The other big issue was distance. Deerfield was about an hour away from our home in Westfield, which meant I'd have to live on campus. I was only fifteen and didn't feel quite ready to live away from home, a concern my parents shared.

I also felt guilty for veering off the typical high school path and leaving my friends and siblings. But I knew that if I wanted to play hockey after high school, this was my opportunity. My parents agreed that if I was serious about pursuing the sport, Deerfield was the right choice.

I applied and was accepted. I was partnered with a mentor who was a rising junior. She gave me some much-needed guidance on what clothes to buy to comply with the dress code, what to pack for my dorm, and what to expect when I moved away from home to start grade ten. Her advice was helpful, but my first day was still daunting. As I saw the returning students reuniting after the summer, hugging each other and screaming for joy, it hit me. I knew two people in the entire school: the girl who gave me my tour and my mentor.

I jumped back into the car and said to my mom, "I want to go home."

What a moment that was for both of us. Deerfield was a prestigious school, but this move was so unfamiliar to my mom and me. Tears started to well up in her eyes and mine. "No, no," she said. "You'll enjoy it here. It's just going to take time." She gave me the confidence to get back out of the car and face my future.

And she was right. When I moved into my dorm room, I was relieved to see a familiar face. My tour guide, Jamie Hagerman, was the proctor of my dorm; she also happened to be the captain of both the soccer and hockey teams and we became fast friends. Jamie was an incredible role model for me, and she went on to play hockey with the US Olympic Team.

Deerfield was the first step in my journey to discovering the greater world beyond the borders of Westfield. And I discovered being only an hour's drive from home was a luxury compared to the students who were from farther away. I saw my parents at all my US games and the occasional Sunday when they came to visit. While the experience was a big leap outside my comfort zone, it forced me to grow as a person and as an athlete, and prepared me for a time, later in my life, when I would once again go out on a limb.

Playing girls' hockey wasn't much of an adjustment. I was a physical player and brought that style of play to the ice. Since body checking was not allowed, I got my fair share of penalties. But I was now playing hockey with top-level players from all over the United States and Canada. Many of the girls from our program went on to play college

hockey, and sharing the ice with them taught me what it took to reach that next level.

I had only been at Deerfield for a few months when the 1998 Winter Olympics started. That year was huge for women's hockey because our game was part of the Olympics for the first time in history, and for me and many other girls, it was the first time we had ever seen women's hockey on TV. It was all the more special because the players were wearing the USA jersey.

Growing up, I wore the number ninety-nine on my jersey. Wayne Gretzky was my idol, but I'd always known that I couldn't follow him because women didn't play in the NHL. Now I realized I could dream bigger than ever before. After that, Team USA's captain, Cammi Granato, became my female hockey role model, and I vowed that one day I, too, would skate on Olympic ice.

As I entered my last year of high school at Deerfield, I looked at the different colleges offering hockey programs, but wasn't sure which school would be the best choice for me. Luckily, I found a mentor in Christa Calagione, one of my assistant coaches, who had played at Harvard. I visited a few schools and talked to the coaches and the players, but remained undecided. In the back of my mind, I was considering playing both soccer and hockey, and thought I could do that at Bowdoin College in Maine. But Christa felt that Brown University in Rhode Island was the right choice. She knew the coach, Digit Murphy, and was confident it would be a good fit for me.

Brown had the first collegiate women's hockey program in the country, and the idea of following in the footsteps of those incredible women who had paved the way for girls like me to pursue hockey was thrilling.

I had to consider finances. Brown was nice and all, but Ivy League schools don't give athletic scholarships. I would have to apply for need-based financial aid, but Christa helped me through the entire application process. To my delight, I was accepted, and fortunately, received financial aid. It wasn't enough to cover all the costs, but I was determined and applied for grants and then worked every summer to

make up the difference. I knew that going to an Ivy League school was a tremendous honour and I was thrilled to have the chance to attend one.

Christa was right about Brown. My classes were full of kids from around the globe who taught me about what lay beyond my small town. And I loved Providence, Rhode Island, a city full of arts, athletics, and fine restaurants. And I was playing with and against the best of the best, including current and future Olympians, and they elevated my level of play. During my freshman year, we went all the way to the NCAA finals. It was quite a ride, and I learned lessons about hard work, conditioning, and teamwork.

My mom and dad found a way to come to every game, with their cowbells in tow. When I stepped onto the ice, they would ring those cowbells to let me know they were there. It always gave me a sense of calm. At those moments the world and I were in sync.

After my freshman year, to my utter delight, Team USA selected me to play for their Under-22 team in a national team festival and three-game summer series against Team Canada. Being on the ice alongside national-calibre players and Olympians was eye opening. I remember being behind Angela Ruggiero in a drill where we had to skate the circles. It didn't even look like she was trying, and yet with each stride, she generated so much power and speed. This inspired me to work even harder. For the games, I was placed on the fourth line, but I didn't care. I was so proud to wear my country's colors, and focused on being a strong team player, supporting my teammates, and giving it my all when my line hit the ice.

That year, we went to Montreal to play, and the following year, Lake Placid. My parents were in the stands every night, ringing those cowbells. They drove four and a half hours each way to watch me play, six times in seven days. My mom picked my dad up from work and he'd sleep in the car on the way to the game, and then on the way home, too. They'd get home at about two a.m. My dad would then sleep for two or three hours, get up at five, and go back to work until my mom would swing by to pick him up in the late afternoon. They did that over and over again, just another example of the many sacrifices they made for me. I'm forever grateful to them. Having them there to see me don the Team USA jersey was one of the greatest experiences of my life.

My two stints on the Under-22 team were the pinnacle of my playing career. While I never had another shot to play with the national team, I did continue my NCAA career at Brown, lettering all four years. But as my college days drew to a close, I knew that my playing career was also coming to an end.

I remember my final game like it was yesterday. It was 2005. We were in a three-game quarterfinal series against St. Lawrence University. We won the first game, but entered game 2 a little too confident, and lost. It came down to the last game. The winner would move on to the semifinals in the league tournament and the loser's season would end. I wanted so badly to win and play one more game in my college career. I just wasn't ready to say goodbye yet.

We played our hearts out. It was close, but we lost. As the game ended, everything hit me. This was the culmination of a lifetime of playing hockey, and it was now over. I would never play another game at that level. This was the last time I would carry my bag out of a locker room as part of a highly competitive team.

I walked into the lobby of the arena, and as soon as I saw my parents standing there, I burst into tears. I thought of all the sacrifices they made for me, how far and how often they had driven to see me play, how they were always in the stands with their cowbells, and I was overwhelmed with emotion. I just lost it. My mom hugged me tightly as the tears rolled down my face. It was the bookend to that first day when she gave me the confidence to get out of the car at Deerfield.

For an athlete, it's these moments in your career that are the hardest. And yet they force you to reflect on all that you've learned and experienced, and most of all, to understand that life goes on. And so I began facing the question all athletes must ultimately face: What now?

I graduated from Brown a few months later and moved back home with my parents so I could start paying off my student loans. I looked for a full-time job with my shiny new bachelor's degree and also joined a women's rec league with some former college players.

Up until then, my parents had generously paid my hockey expenses, but now I had to take care of the fees myself. It was an hour each way to play and gas prices spiked to an all-time high. As I tried to whittle down my college loans and make my new-car payments, thirty-six minutes of women's rec hockey was becoming rather expensive. I figured if I could officiate a couple of hockey games while at the rink, I might break even. I could never have imagined that this simple decision would change my life forever.

I got my first taste of officiating in that same women's rec league. I quickly realized that I had to relearn the game from a whole different perspective. I understood the feel and the flow of the game, but I had never really paid attention to the work of the officials, their position on the ice, or the rules of the game. To my surprise, the ice was even busier for an official than it was for a player, and officials don't even get to change on the fly.

But the biggest shock was handing out penalties. I'd received more than a few during my playing days, and now here I was, dishing out penalties to players for doing the same things I'd been guilty of myself. The first few times I refereed a game, I had a hard time putting my arm up to call a penalty.

When I did blow the whistle, all eyes were on me, and it wasn't a fun experience. The coaches and players didn't like my calls and they showed their disapproval by yelling and swearing at me. As a new official, I wasn't the best at explaining and defending my calls. To be effective, I had to know the rules cold, so I spent a lot of quality time with the rule book. Once I knew it inside and out, I was much more confident and earned the respect of the players and coaches.

In the officiating world, we consider ourselves to be the third team on the ice. Just like players, officials check the clock as it ticks down to game time and get fired up for the on-ice action. The more games I officiated, the more I enjoyed it. Those first few strides on the ice, when I would hear my skate blades underneath me and feel the wind in my face, brought me back to my playing days. It's still a thrill every time. And, having a front row seat on the goal line, in the middle of a scrum, trying to locate a loose puck, definitely gets the adrenaline flowing.

For an official, sight lines are critical. Our goal is to always be in the best position to watch the play, and that requires quick thinking, flawless footwork, and a strong knowledge of the best places to put oneself in order to see the action and make the right calls. There are times when we have to look through multiple players to see the puck, which can create real challenges. Our positioning is somewhat predictable, and smart players know that. Sometimes they try to use officials to pick off pursuing players. It takes focus to avoid those situations, keep the players in front of you, and maintain a wide field of vision. In the end, it's an interesting ballet dance between officials and players as each group pursues its own objectives.

Soon after I started officiating, I met Julie Piacentini at a women's rec league game. Julie lived in the greater Boston area, and was then working all levels of women's hockey in USA Hockey, the NCAA, and the IIHF. She also had officiated at the 2002 and 2006 Olympics.

Meeting Julie and hearing about all she had done in officiating made me realize that there was an officiating world beyond the women's rec league, and if I couldn't explore the hockey world as a player, I could do it as a referee. When I mentioned my interest to Julie, she took me under her wing.

"What's your goal?" she asked me one day.

"I'd like to officiate an international tournament," I replied.

Together, Julie and I mapped out a path for me to reach my goal. I'd need to be licensed by the International Ice Hockey Federation. To get there, I'd have to hone my skills in increasingly challenging USA Hockey games, but first, I needed to attend a USA Hockey regional development camp.

Julie and I also focused on the building blocks of good officiating. Julie taught me the basics, like when to raise my arm on a delayed offside and where I should stand in relation to the net during play. She also taught me about the two-official system, common in youth and rec hockey, the three-official system in higher-level games, and the four-official system now regularly used by USA Hockey, the NCAA, and the IIHF.

Julie invited me to work some summer leagues with high school and college players, and they provided a great opportunity to develop my skills. The games were pretty low-key and we used the various officiating systems. As the lone ref when working the three-official system, I had to skate from goal line to goal line to keep up with the play unfolding on the ice, while the linesmen had a different role, handling offsides, icings, and face-offs.

I began to work at higher levels, including college games. I was always looking for ways to do things better, and so I created a journal, and after every game, I wrote down at least one mistake I had made. One night it was my penalty selection. Another night it was my positioning on the ice. Before my next game, I would look over my list of mistakes, and make sure that I didn't repeat any of them.

Over time, I thought less about where I was supposed to be on the ice and more about the action that was unfolding before me. It was a breakthrough in my development as an official. When positioning becomes second nature, you can focus your energies on watching the game, and you put yourself in the best position to make the right calls.

In 2010, I was assigned to officiate the Under-22 camp for the USA women's national team, the very same team for which I'd played just a few years earlier. I saw the tournament from a whole different perspective, but most of all, it confirmed that I was on my way to becoming an IIHF-certified referee. I was selected for the USA-Canada game, and getting to drop the puck at the opening face-off was a tangible milestone in my journey.

That fall I received my IIHF certification. It was a great moment for both Julie and me. She helped me lay the foundation to get there. Later that season, I achieved my dream of calling an international game when I went to Caen, France, for the 2011 IIHF World Women's Championship. I was amazed at where my skates were taking me.

They were leading me to new rinks at home, too.

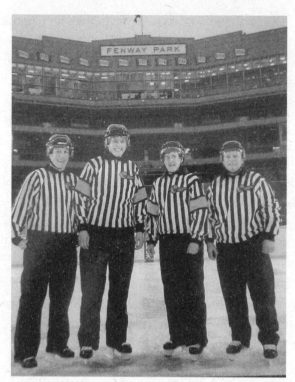

In 2010, I shared the ice with Carol Weston, Julie Piacentini, and Jean Goodwin in a women's college outdoor game at Boston's historic Fenway Park.

A year before, I was officiating NCAA women's hockey in the Eastern College Athletic Conference (ECAC) when Paul Stewart came on as the supervisor of officials. Stewy was in charge of assigning refs for NCAA Division I women's games, something he had already been doing for men's college hockey. He had a noteworthy background, having played in the NHL before becoming an official, and eventually he became the first American to referee a thousand regular-season NHL games. Coincidently, he's also a fellow Massachusetts native, and he became another mentor to me.

After I'd worked Division I women's games for a couple of seasons, Stewy told me that he thought I had enough skill to work men's college hockey. I laughed him off. Me, a woman, refereeing a men's DI game? In women's hockey, it's commonplace for men to referee, but the reverse had not been the case. And, women's hockey was comfortable for me, because it was all I had ever done. I didn't give much thought to the idea of officiating men's hockey, and the conversation came to an end.

When Stewy brought the subject up again the next season, I realized he was serious and heard him out. He told me that he believed I had the skating ability to keep up in the men's game. I understood the game well and was perfectly capable of one day working on the men's side. He encouraged me to work more junior and boys' high school hockey games to prepare me to officiate at the college level.

If Stewy had confidence in my ability to work at that level, I decided I should take the step outside my comfort zone.

The process wasn't without frustrations. Almost every time I showed up at a boys' game, I would hear, "Oh, this is the first time we've ever had a female reffing our game." I had to tune out the negativity and let my hard work on the ice speak for itself. And, as I skated more and more games, my confidence grew. I would still hear the comments, but it became easier to ignore them. While a female official reffing a boys' game was new for them, it wasn't new for me, and the players and coaches began to figure that out and eventually the comments stopped.

Working on the men's side allowed me to learn another style of hockey to use while officiating. It was exciting to be back on the ice with body checking, and it brought me back to my youth, when I played with the boys' teams and trucked that player who ran to his mother.

In 2015, a decade after I had begun officiating, Stewy called me and said, "I think you're ready to do men's college hockey." Instantly, I felt the same nerves that always accompanied new experiences. I thought back to the first time I jumped on the ice to officiate a DIII women's college game and hardly knew where to stand as a linesman, and that moment when I'd stepped onto the campus at Deerfield Academy. But I had learned from those experiences, and gained the confidence to push myself beyond what was comfortable.

Stewy assigned me to referee a men's NCAA Division I exhibition game to start. I thought it went well, and Stewy was also pleased with my performance. So, on October 9, 2015, I entered the Messa Rink at Achilles Center, home ice of Union College, to referee their regular-season game against Sacred Heart. I knew this assignment would come with a high level of scrutiny, but I also felt that I was ready for the test. After all, I had reffed a lot of hockey games, many at very high levels. I knew I could handle this one, too.

When I stepped onto the ice that night, I became the first woman to referee a men's Division I hockey game. While I was aware of that history, I just wanted to drop the puck and get the game under way. Once that happened, I was at home. It was just like any other hockey game. We worked the four-official system, and there was a lot of action that night. We ended up calling twelve penalties, six for each team. I remember wondering how the players and coaches would react. I heard a few F-bombs, which are common at that level, but I quickly found out that, from the perspective of the players and coaches, an official in stripes is an official in stripes. I was treated the same as my peers without regard to my gender, exactly as it should be.

The game ended in a 1–1 tie. But for me, and for all the female officials who came before me and who would follow me, it was a huge win. I was grateful to Stewy for opening the door and allowing me to break this glass ceiling. From the very beginning, he'd been confident in my ability, and that went a long way in helping me build my own confidence.

In the meantime, I continued to work international events. I travelled to IIHF tournaments in Norway, Sweden, Denmark, and Hungary. All told, I worked seven international championship tournaments.

Then, in the fall of 2017, I learned that I was one of four American officials chosen to work the XXIII Olympic Winter Games in Pyeong-chang, South Korea. It was an incredible honour to be selected. Ever since I watched the 1998 Games, I had dreamed of going to the Olympics. While reffing wasn't how I had originally envisioned getting onto

Olympic ice, the fact was that I was about to skate on Olympic ice, and it was just as sweet. They say that when a door closes, a window opens, and that surely was the case for me.

When I arrived in Pyeongchang, I was told that I would be refereeing the first game of the Olympic tournament. My pregame adrenaline flow was at an all-time high. The Olympic rings were plastered all over the arena and there was no hiding that I was somewhere special. As I went to skate out on the ice, I took two strides, toe-picked, and nearly fell flat on my face. I managed to catch myself and stay upright. I laughed it off, took a deep breath, and then relaxed and enjoyed a few warm-up laps on the biggest stage in the world for women's hockey.

Once the puck dropped, it was just another hockey game and I blocked out all of the Olympic hype—the rings, the press, the crowds—and focused on the action in front of me. The level of intensity for each shift was a notch up from anything I had ever seen. The hockey was fast and the skill level was impressive—and I had a front-row seat.

I was wearing a headset to announce my calls over the arena PA system, and it was fun to hear myself over the speakers. "Karaoke Katie" has been my nickname a time or two as I love to let loose on the mic, but my singing does have a way of clearing out a crowd. I wasn't too worried about that this time, though, because the fans were there to see the players, not me.

I did a number of games throughout the tournament, culminating in the semifinal between Canada and Russia, two strong teams vying for a spot in the gold medal game. Both teams were hungry to win and the fans were engaged, which made for an incredible atmosphere. It was really fun to be a part of it. In the end, Canada emerged victorious.

There were moments during those nineteen days in South Korea when I literally pinched myself to make sure I wasn't dreaming, and at one point I said out loud, "I am here. I made it to the Olympics!" I made the most of the opportunity, as I aimed to do during all of my travels with the IIHF, and watched my first live curling match and went up to the mountains to see various snowboarding, skiing, and biathlon events.

Best of all, my parents were once again in the stands. It was their first time travelling overseas and it was to watch me officiate on a different continent. I was so grateful for all the love and support they had given me over the years, and, at the end of the day, I was on Olympic ice, and they were cheering me on. It was a wonderful moment for all of us.

After the 2018 Olympics, more and more doors began to open for female officials in both women's and men's hockey. Some seemed like a long time coming. In 2010 my mentor, Julie, was the first female to referee the finals of the NCAA DI Women's Hockey Championship. After that, a couple of women had served as linesmen, but Julie was still the only woman who had worn the bands for the finals. Over the

Taking a break from the action at the 2018 Pyeongchang Olympics to snap a photo with my ever-supportive parents.

years, I had worked some NCAA quarter- and semifinal games myself, but when it came to the Frozen Four, the games were predominantly officiated by men. It became a goal of mine to follow in Julie's footsteps and be the second woman to referee the women's Frozen Four final game.

In the playoffs, crews generally stay together as they progress through the various league tournaments. In the lead-up to the 2019 Frozen Four, I was part of an all-female crew along with referee Kelly Cooke and linesmen Delaney Harrop and Amanda Tassoni. Being a part of that crew was special, as I had coached Kelly Cooke as a player during her senior year of high school, and then officiated some of her games when she was playing at Princeton. Here we were, years later, working alongside one another as officials. I reflected on the many ways Julie and Stewy had mentored me, and I vowed to pay it forward by being a good mentor to Kelly and the others.

We worked the ECAC championship, and each weekend, January through March, the four of us would load our bags into a car and venture off to an arena to work a weekend set of games. As the veteran of the group, I handled the logistics to make sure we got to our destination on time (unfortunately, that left the music selections to the youngsters). In any event, all four of us had played college hockey, and as we drove, we swapped stories and jokes. It brought me back to my college days. It wasn't the games that I remembered the most, it was the team bus trips. The four of us recaptured that team dynamic as we trekked from game to game.

Together, we moved on to the NCAA tournament. We worked the quarterfinals out at the University of Wisconsin in Madison. We returned back east and were the standby officials for the semifinals hosted by Quinnipiac University. Our fate at that point depended on the game results, because the NCAA does not typically assign tournament games to officials from the same leagues as the participating teams. That meant that if an ECAC team made the finals, our crew was done. As luck would have it, the final pitted Minnesota against Wisconsin. Our crew was tapped for the game. Not only would I reach my goal of following Julie, I would do it with Kelly, and ours would be the first-ever all-female crew to work the final game of the NCAA DI Women's Hockey Championship.

All four of us were aware that this would be a special night, and that important history was about to be made. But as we sat in the locker room before the finals, our energy shifted to the typical mental preparation. We were more than ready, and the game did not disappoint. It was very fast and showcased the extraordinary skills of the players. Our crew was solid and the game went smoothly.

Wisconsin won the game 2–0, but they weren't the only winners that day. It was an important milestone for female officials everywhere. So as the final buzzer sounded, we took a moment to share a victory that was both personal and yet also far-reaching. The crew knew how long I had been waiting to reach this goal, and sharing it with these three in particular made it so much sweeter. I thought about Julie and the many other women who had paved the way for us to be there. We proved what was possible that day, and we hoped the momentum would continue and that there would be more opportunities for other outstanding female officials. We also hoped that somewhere in the arena or watching on television, a little girl saw us working and vowed that one day she, too, would officiate a championship game.

After, we turned our attention to other barriers. For the last seven years, in August, the NHL had conducted an officials' exposure combine in Buffalo. The combine is targeted at players who have competed at a high level of hockey and are considering wearing the stripes. The camp introduces officiating at the NHL level and gives attendees a taste of the physical requirements. In 2017, I had received an invitation to attend, but the timing conflicted with an IIHF fitness testing camp in Switzerland that was part of the selection process for the Olympics. I had to turn down the invitation. But another female official attended, and the following year, three more went.

During one of our road trips that winter, Kelly was flipping through her phone and came across an officiating application for the combine. "Should we apply?" she asked.

Amanda, Kelly, Paul, myself, and Delaney following the 2019 NCAA Women's Championship game.

I quickly responded: "The more women who apply, the more women who can attend."

We both applied and were accepted, along with nine other women, six Americans and five Canadians.

At the combine, the NHL supervisors explained how they evaluate their on-ice officials, then took us to the weight room for a series of grueling off-ice tests. They had heart-rate monitors on us the whole time, tracking our recovery while we participated in various drills. Some of the tests, like the beep test, also challenged mental toughness, to see whether we were willing to push ourselves further than we thought we could go.

On the ice, we participated in skating drills that tested our forward skating, backwards skating, agility, and endurance. In one suicide drill, we skated from the top of one circle to the far blue line and then back, over and over again. The test was to complete as many laps as you could within a set period of time. One of the former NHL officials running the combine skated by and whispered: "Just keep going until you can't feel your legs. Then, keep going." And so we did. A few of the officials fell over at the end, their legs simply giving out. I managed to stay on my feet and was particularly grateful that my breakfast stayed down. But I and the women competed well.

At the start of camp, each of us was placed on a team and we took turns scrimmaging while others officiated the games. I was never known for my dangles, but when I swapped my hockey stick for a whistle, I also seemed to have traded in any signs of soft hands.

The combine was an amazing experience and all of the participants—men and women—were grateful for the chance to learn from some of the best in the game. We again felt that we were raising the bar for ourselves and the women who would follow us. But, as we left the NHL combine, we had no idea what would come of it for us.

It wasn't long before we found out. Just a few days later, Kelly and I, along with Kendall Hanley and Kirsten Welsh, received calls from the NHL asking us to officiate at the NHL Prospect Tournaments. These tournaments are for the prospective players of NHL teams to showcase their talent in hopes of making their respective team's main camp. I flew out to Anaheim, California, and had the chance to referee three games involving prospects for the Anaheim Ducks, Vegas Golden Knights, Colorado Avalanche, and LA Kings. To get that call was the most incredible feeling. It was nice to be rewarded for all the hard work I had put in over the years.

Being on NHL ice, I felt the same burst of excitement I had felt at the Olympics. The level of hockey was high. The players were competing hard, which made for intense, fast-paced games. Once the puck dropped, I adjusted to the speed of the game and made sure to be in good position to make calls. The only change was figuring out where to take my front-row seat during the handful of fights.

Of course, I'm no stranger to physical hockey—as a player, I was inclined to dish out a few choice body checks. And, when I'd offici-ated men's junior games, there was a bit of roughhousing that I'd had to break up. But at this level, the rule of thumb was to let the players have at each other until they tired themselves out, which meant I got to see the techniques that went into a good hook or uppercut. Being that close to that action was an experience I'll never forget.

An encouraging moment came after the game, when I walked by the media and heard one of the players mention to a reporter that he didn't even realize there was a female referee until the second period. I took that as a compliment, and it made me hope for the day when people will look at two refs in a game and not care if they are male or female.

During a day off in the tournament, I made my way down to the famous beaches of Orange County. As I stood on Laguna Beach with the sand between my toes, I thought of my little hometown in Massa-chusetts miles away and it hit me just how far hockey had taken me. I had to shake my head at my good fortune.

While I was in California, I used a day off to explore LA and ended up getting tickets to *The Price Is Right*. I had watched this show as a child with my grandmother, and it brought back wonderful memories to be there. To my surprise, I was selected from the audience to be a contestant! I ended up playing the Hole in One game to win a car, but missed my putt by about a centimeter. If only I had worked on my golf skills a little more, I would be driving around in a brand-new car, com-pliments of Drew Carey! But it was a fun experience, and I actually won a turntable that I gave to my parents.

All of the exposure over the last few years has gone a long way in building respect for female officials in both women's and men's hockey. Most importantly, our presence on the ice has given us the opportunity to serve as role models and spark an interest in officiating in young girls. In 2009, I was working the lines at the NCAA Frozen Four. When I was walking through the building after a game, a little girl came up to me and asked me for my autograph. I was taken aback and responded: "Wait, you realize that I'm not a player, right?" She nodded and told me that she'd seen me work some games throughout the year and she wanted my autograph. It was a great moment, and made me realize that I could be an example of what is possible. I happily signed my name on her program and wrote, "Dream big."

What a road it has been for me. Or, more accurately, what a skate. I could never have imagined that the wonder I felt at gliding on the ice as a little girl would lead to so many games on so many rinks in so many countries all around the world. While there's no question I worked hard, I also had the support of many generous and knowledgeable mentors who cared enough to spend time and energy helping me. And, of course, my family provided the backing that I needed to build my confidence on the ice and off.

I'm not done yet, and neither are female officials. We have much to accomplish and other "firsts" to achieve. For me, my new dream is to see a female referee in the NHL. Not just for whoever gets to skate that first game, but for all the little girls who are asking for autographs because they, too, are choosing to dream big.

As for me, I've reached a lot of my goals with these skates. Who knows where they'll take me next? Maybe someday I'll hear myself announcing a call over the PA system in an NHL rink. Wouldn't that just be the icing on the cake?

Katie Guay is a former American ice hockey player currently serving as a referee. In her fifteen-year career as an official, she has called games at every level of women's hockey, including the NCAA Frozen Four and the Olympics, and men's hockey at the NCAA level and preseason for the NHL. In 2019, she became the first woman to call the prestigious men's Beanpot Tournament in Boston, and in 2020, she officiated the women's 3-on-3 at the NHL All-Star Game in St. Louis. She is passionate about helping players and officials follow their dreams and is a member of the USA Hockey Foundation team.

 *@kjguay*

The Good Guys

Christian Gaudet

Wherever I go, I'm known as "Goody." It all started during my hockey-playing days. My last name's French, but when I'd score a goal, if the announcer was English, he'd pronounce my name "Goody." It only took a few times for the name to stick.

I was born and raised in the little French-Canadian village of Memramcook, New Brunswick, about thirty minutes from Moncton, the big city compared to our town of five thousand. Like most kids in Memramcook, I grew up playing hockey, but because I spoke French, I was always a little shy around my English-speaking coaches and teammates. I didn't always understand what they were saying, so I kept quiet and focused on the hockey itself.

I remember our coach, Terry, was explaining a drill in which we needed to skate from dot to dot. I was very confused because I didn't know what a dot was.

I got very good at ignoring his words and instead following his finger on the board and trying to piece together the rest.

At one point, the coach got frustrated. "Hey, come on, guys, even Christian can do these drills correctly and he doesn't even understand half the words I'm saying."

The truth was the only time I was ever really comfortable was when I was on the ice, and growing up in a small town gave me ample opportunity to lace up my skates. The guys at the arena let me go work on my game whenever the ice was not being used, and we also had an outdoor rink in our backyard where I put in hours perfecting my skating.

Nowadays, it seems like there are so many coaches and trainers and specialists available for a young hockey player, but for me, it was just the people in my community helping me out. That's how my town was. My parents were no different. We didn't have a lot of money, but my dad and mom had the biggest hearts and always found ways to give to the people around them. To this day, my dad works in construction and excavation, and he goes above and beyond to treat his clients well and give them a great price, even if they can afford more. That's just the Gaudet and Memramcook way.

Some kids are under a lot pressure to excel, and while my parents pushed me to play my best, hockey was all about having fun. Even if I didn't do that well in a game, my parents would pat me on the back

*Here I am, seven years old, at the Memramcook
arena without a care in the world.*

and tell me they were proud of me. That kept my love of the game going strong.

In middle school, I had to write out what I wanted to be when I grew up, and I scribbled down "hockey player and carpenter." Let's just say, today, I can't really build anything because hockey took over my life.

I knew that if I wanted to go far in hockey—as far as the NHL—I needed to be a reliable centre who was strong on penalty kills, good on face-offs, and most of all, a good teammate. My childhood dream was to make the Moncton Wildcats of the Quebec Major Junior Hockey League. I was a huge fan of my hometown team, and I still remember fighting for the Frisbees they would throw in the crowd between periods, and I'd go crazy for the mascot, Wild Willie.

In my second year of Bantam, I was playing AAA level in Moncton. My role on the team toward the end of that season was to shut down the opposing team's top line. I thought that was the best job for a hockey player. It wasn't about being flashy or getting recognition; it was about making a difference on the ice for the team.

That year, we won our provincial tournament and went on to the Atlantic Championship, where we were up against the best Bantam teams from Nova Scotia, PEI, and Newfoundland and Labrador. We were unstoppable. We got to the point where we were not only shutting down the top lines, but we were putting up more points than they were. We swept our way to victory, becoming the best Bantam team in the four Maritime provinces. Not bad for a French-Canadian kid from Memramcook.

And then, in 2003, at sixteen, my dream came true and I was drafted in the eleventh round to my hometown team, the Moncton Wildcats. The only thing was, my chances of actually making the team were pretty low.

The upcoming 2003–04 season was going to be a big year for the Wildcats because the team was making a push for the President's Cup, the award for the QMJHL champion. As a die-hard Wildcats fan, I knew first-hand how big a deal the President's Cup was for the team.

Since the franchise began in 1995, the Wildcats had been trying to make it to the President's Cup finals, but they always fell short in the playoffs.

The team already had Corey Crawford in net and Steve Bernier and some other big names on their roster; in total, fourteen forwards were returning from the year before. I was on the bubble and didn't know if I'd make the final cut. Our head coach, Christian LaRue, wanted someone else on the team, but our assistant coach, former NHLer Daniel Lacroix, wanted me. For some reason, he saw something in me. Thanks to him, the team kept me around and I took off from there. I was good on face-offs and penalty kills, and they realized they needed me in the lineup; I ended up on the roster as a fourth liner for the rest of the year.

We had tough competition that year, and one of the teams to beat was Rimouski Oceanic, whose star player was none other than Sid the Kid. As a sixteen-year-old, Sidney Crosby would end up leading the entire league in scoring during that regular season.

Meanwhile, I put up a handful of assists. But even if I finished a game with zero points, my dad would find a way to boost my spirits. "Hey, you really dominated Crosby on your face-offs," he'd say. "Good job. Crosby didn't score." He was always good at pointing out the positives.

I knew he was doing it out of love, but his encouragement helped me out that first year in the QMJHL. We did end up making the play-offs, and that's where everything clicked for me. I started to score goals and was bumped up to the third line. We rolled through the first round and quarterfinals, and smoked Rimouski in the semifinals, 4–1.

We had made it to the final round for the first time since the team was formed. We went up against the Gatineau Olympiques, the re-turning champions, who boasted star player Maxime Talbot. We came out strong, but we didn't have the juice and lost, 4–1.

It was a disappointment to come so close, but it made me want to win even more. I said so to the Wildcats' long-time owner, Robert Irving. "I'm going to be there when we win the President's Cup," I promised.

Despite the loss, that first year of junior hockey was incredible, and the best part was playing in front of my family and our hometown fans. It was more than hockey, too. We were only juniors ourselves, but kids would look up to us as role models. As a team, we often visited hospitals and schools and met young, aspiring hockey players. It felt good to give back to the community in this small way, and it made me feel connected to something larger than myself. I wanted to make my town proud of me, on and off the ice.

I knew I had played a part in the team's success over the year, but as I headed into the office for my end-of-season meeting with Chris and Dan, I didn't know what they were going to say.

Chris put me at ease. "You don't have to worry about being traded," he said. Then he added, "You don't have any value to other teams, but you have a lot of value to us."

I came out of that meeting really confused. I figured there was a positive in there somewhere, I just had to think about it. It's funny to me now.

In the 2005–06 season, I was named captain of the Moncton Wildcats. Just two years before, I'd been worried about making the roster at all, and here I was being given an incredible opportunity to lead the team.

That year, Ted Nolan was our coach. He'd played for the Detroit Red Wings and the Pittsburgh Penguins, and he would go on to coach the Buffalo Sabres. Ted would pull me into his office and ask my opinion about the team and how the guys were feeling. It was amazing to be included in that side of the game. The assistant captains did just as much as me, and together we had a strong leadership under Ted, who was really good at giving us authority.

A big part of our team was Brad Marchand; as captain, I had to keep a close eye on him. Every time he crossed the line or got into trouble, he'd come to me with a sad face and say, "Sorry, Goody."

All I could do was chuckle and say, "It's all right, Marchy. Just don't do it again." He was a great teammate and a true competitor. I can still picture my grandmother (a strong lady) pulling Marchy in to give

Another exciting regular season home game from my first year as captain of the Moncton Wildcats.

(Daniel St. Louis)

him a high five or a big hug after our home games. She was a big Marchand fan.

On top of Marchand, we had guys like Keith Yandle and Luc Bourdon. It was a tight team. The amount of skill everyone had was undeniable and it made a huge difference on the ice. To top it off, we all genuinely liked each other and just wanted to be part of the ride that season.

Because this was our year. Not only were we aiming for the President's Cup, we had set our sights on the Memorial Cup, the championship for the top teams from the QMJHL, WHL, and OHL. Moncton was set to host the Memorial Cup, so we knew we were going to have a shot, even if we didn't win the President's Cup. But we didn't want to get in through the back door. Our goal was to win our league tournament and show everyone that we deserved that spot.

We rolled through our league playoffs, and every home game was filled with Moncton fans. Everyone from my school bus driver growing up to my teachers asked me for tickets. It was like I had my own entourage. Because we were coming from a small town and were a long shot, I guess people identified with my journey. I was a hardworking player who played with a lot of heart, just like the people in Memramcook.

In the finals, we faced off against the Quebec Remparts, who were led by Alexander Radulov and coached by the great Patrick Roy. We were at home and the rink was sold out. It was now or never.

We dominated that game and came out victorious, beating the Remparts 4–2. People say things are unbelievable all the time, but that win, that moment, was *truly* unbelievable. We were the President's Cup champions, a historic first for the Moncton Wildcats.

And I'd kept my promise to Mr. Irving. As soon as the President's Cup was given to me, I immediately passed it to him so he could be the first person to lift it. He deserved it! After that, it was my turn.

In 2006, proudly holding the President's Cup
with my future wife, Catherine.

We had proven we were the best team in the QMJHL, but we would meet the Remparts again at the Memorial Cup. Because we were guaranteed a spot, the runner-up in our league qualified. After defeating the Peterborough Petes, for whom Jordan Staal then played, and the Vancouver Giants, who had Milan Lucic, it was once more us against them, but this time it was for the right to be called junior champions.

We felt like we were totally in charge, leading up to the final game, but there were some mind games that I didn't expect at the junior hockey level.

Patrick Roy, being Patrick Roy, started talking to reporters about how our goalie, Josh Tordjman, was playing over his head. Josh had been a rock for us all playoffs and Roy was saying he couldn't maintain that pace. Which got the media all interested. They started asking Josh if he could keep up in the final. I felt bad for him because Patrick Roy had been his childhood idol. Roy was using the media to distract us from the game at hand.

Ted wanted everyone to think we were the underdogs when we faced the Remparts. I remember him coming into the locker room and saying as much. "When you address the media, tell them that Quebec is a great team, and it's going to be a tough fight," he said. He wanted the pressure to be on them as the favourites.

In our first interview, what do you think Marchand did? The complete opposite.

"Quebec isn't that good," I heard him say to the reporters. "We're awesome and we're going to crush them."

After, he walked over to me. "Sorry, Goody. I got caught up in the moment."

At the time, I was upset, but now looking back, I can't help but laugh. That's Marchie for you.

The day of the game, Quebec knocked in two goals in the first period. We stayed strong and were outshooting them by a wide margin—we had 36 shots on goal for their 16 by the end of the second period—but nothing would go in. Not so for Quebec. By the beginning of the third period, we were down, 4–0. On a power play, Yandle slipped a goal in for us, and followed up just three minutes later with another, but it wasn't enough to turn the tide, and the Memorial Cup went to the Remparts.

It was a tough loss for all of us because the victory was there for the taking and we had done everything right up until that point.

The kicker was that most of the top guys on the team were either going pro or moving on and we knew we weren't going to get another clean shot at the Memorial Cup. This was our chance and we missed it.

I played one more season with the Wildcats and finished the year with the Springfield Falcons in the AHL. Then I had a hard decision to make: try to make a pro team right away or go off to university first, then try to make a team. I had a good talk with Danny Flynn, Dan, and Ted, who were moving on to coach the New York Islanders, and decided to take the first route. I asked Ted what I needed to work on.

"Your hands," Ted replied. "Take a chair and stick-handle with a golf ball through the legs of the chair."

I did that for a few days. As I stick-handled that stupid golf ball, I couldn't help but think, *Gee, thanks, Teddy.* It was incredibly boring.

There had to be a more fun way to improve my hands, so I reached out to a few of my buddies in the Moncton area who had played with me on the Wildcats, and we started our own ball hockey league. Our playoff MVP that year was Andrew MacDonald, who went on to play defence for the New York Islanders and Philadelphia Flyers. He completely dominated everyone and helped us win the first-ever Goody's Cup. That year, I had a little bit of extra money from charging everyone for the arena time, so I took it and bought a trophy. On the trophy, I put "Goody's Ball Hockey" as a joke more than anything, but the name stuck, and would come back sooner rather than later.

Getting called up to the NHL was harder than I expected. I was invited to two Islanders training camps and played one exhibition game against the Montreal Canadiens—in Moncton, of all places—but I mostly tooled around the East Coast Hockey League and took online classes at the same time.

In 2009, at the end of my second season in the minors, I left Ohio, where I'd been playing for the Dayton Bombers, and headed home to Moncton to spend the summer training, still wanting that shot at the NHL.

I had another motive for returning home, one that went beyond my own professional dream. Moncton had a special place in my heart. As I was coming up in the Wildcats organization, we were taught the importance of giving back. And I wanted to do that in a bigger way.

I sat down with my good friend Jean-Yves Cormier—JY—to talk about what we could do. JY and I had grown up playing hockey and we were always buddies. JY was the best man at my wedding, and I was the best man at his wedding.

"What if we expand Goody's Ball Hockey into a summer kids' program?" JY suggested.

It was an easy yes. I loved the idea. It would be a fun little project for the summer as I trained. "Yes, let's keep it small and keep the cost down," I added.

We both knew how expensive hockey can be. Neither JY nor I grew up with a lot of money, and I saw first-hand how hard my parents worked to put me through hockey. And in the years since I started playing, the programs and training required for a young player to excel seemed to double. All of those extras are pricey and not everyone can afford them, but, we said, everyone should get the opportunity to play. It wasn't about making money; it was about giving back. Our motto was: Good guys finish first.

I asked JY if we should change the name, and he said he liked it as it was. "I don't want any of the attention. You can do the training and coaching, and I'll take care of everything behind the scenes."

"Deal."

We went to work right away. One of the first things we needed to do was get support from the community. So I called up Mr. Irving and told him what we wanted to do. He loved the idea of giving back to the community and agreed to cover the costs of our T-shirts for the kids.

He was a huge help getting our program off the ground and paving the way for others to come on board.

Early on, we decided that Goody's Ball Hockey would be bilingual. The Moncton area is fifty-fifty French and English and we wanted to make sure both French and English speakers felt included.

JY and I worked really well together, and within six months' time, we were ready to host our first summer camp.

That first year, we had a hundred kids sign up, ages five to twenty-five. We split it up like minor hockey, but with two teams for each level. Every Monday to Thursday, from May to August, I'd get to the rink early and set everything up for when the kids showed up at six o'clock.

For three hours, we'd play. We couldn't afford staff, so JY and I did all the training, and our moms and sisters helped out, too. We started

This is from one of our first years putting on the ball hockey program, and I'm at the front in the ball cap explaining a ball hockey skill or a life skill, or I'm just trying to make them laugh, likely one of the three. Our program has grown so much since those early days.

off with a warm-up, then moved on to drills—a lot of passing, stick handling, and shooting—and we always finished with a game. At the end of the year, we had a tournament and a banquet.

Some kids were in hockey already; some were just trying it out for the first time. It didn't matter what level they started at; by the end of the summer, each one had improved and gained confidence. It was so rewarding to see. While we were helping kids finesse their skills, our goal wasn't to prepare them to play junior hockey or in the NHL, it was to give everyone an opportunity to play and have fun. As for JY and me, we had a lot of fun and it felt good to connect with these kids. I couldn't have asked for a better guy to go on this adventure with.

We received a lot of thank-you messages from the parents. They wouldn't say it in front of their kids, but they would e-mail us or pull us aside. One parent told us that their son cried the whole week because he wanted to go to a hockey school with his friends, but they couldn't afford it. They were so thankful to have our little camp as an option.

That fall, I headed to Texas to play for the Allen Americans in the Central Hockey League for my third season. In the playoffs, we were up 2–0 when we lost four straight games. I was devastated. Every year of professional hockey I had played was a year of Canadian university eligibility lost. Everyone starts with five years and I had two left. If I wanted to finish my accounting degree, it was now or never.

After that, I sent a message to the coach at the University of Moncton and asked about going to school and playing for his team. I decided I would go play hockey there and finish my accounting degree so I could get a new set of skills to make a life for myself outside of hockey. In those two years of hockey, I played in a national tournament, was named team captain in my last year, and made some lifelong friends.

Meanwhile, Goody's was back up and running for its second year. The template was still the same—warm-up, drills, games—but this year we added some new jerseys. In the beginning, we were focused on being efficient, so we got black-and-white jerseys. When we read the parent feedback, someone suggested we try more interesting colours, so we added blue, red, and green. JY and I looked at each other and said, "Valid point."

Over the years, we've added some other things: a mandatory anti-bullying seminar and a résumé workshop for ages thirteen to fifteen, and we've brought in police officers and local businesspeople—mostly buddies of mine—to talk to the kids. While hockey can teach many great life skills about leadership, hard work, and teamwork, hockey players can sometimes rely too much on their talent. A lot of guys think they're going to the NHL, but it doesn't always work out. I'm proof of that, and we at Goody's wanted to make sure we imparted more to our kids. I often get credit for these initiatives, but it's the people around me who do the real work. I'm just providing an avenue for them to share their expertise.

When we started in 2009, we had, as I said, about a hundred kids and charged $110 for the entire summer. Little did we know how quickly the program would grow. More and more kids started attending and we began hearing from parents, who thanked us for doing such a great job and told us what a great influence the program was on their kids. We expanded our community efforts and started hosting an annual All-Star Game and a charity run with Pro Kids, a part of the Canadian Tire Jump Start initiative to raise money for economically disadvantaged kids to join sports. Goody's isn't a big operation, but in 2019, we had five hundred kids coming out—fifty-eight teams in total—and we've raised over $12,000 for Pro Kids since 2012.

Fortunately, we've been able to keep our cost low, in large part because of our incredible volunteers and sponsors, some of whom started as attendees themselves. That was another of our main goals—finding kids with leadership skills and preparing them to be instructors themselves. Our first two volunteers, Remi "Ramrod" Robichaud and Chris Guimond, stayed on board for a long time and became our first paid staff members. In a lot of ways, everything has come full circle. Our staff used to watch me play for the Wildcats, and now our players have watched the staff when they played.

After a Pro Kids fund-raising event one year, I had just ended my speech thanking everyone when a woman came up to me and said, "It's really impressive what you do."

"Thank you," I replied.

"What's more impressive is the people that back you up." She thought it was great to see so many young people working hard to do good in the community. I always remembered that because it made me realize that JY and I had created a platform for other people to give back if they wanted to. It just goes to show that when you surround yourself with good people, good things will happen.

For example, at the end of his junior career, Philippe Myers, who hails from Moncton and is now with the Philadelphia Flyers, approached me and said he wanted to give back. I told him about the Pro Kids charity run we do, and he was immediately on board to help fund-raise. Even now, during the NHL hockey season, I'll get a text from him telling me he's got a good idea for the community. Hockey players are good people.

The planning for the camp is now year-round. Year after year, JY and I keep thinking it will get easier, but we're always trying to take the feedback and make it better. We both have full-time jobs elsewhere, but our reward is that every summer we get a chance to join the kids and play some ball hockey.

In 2015, I moved to Ottawa to work at an accounting firm. Before I even started, I told my employer about Goody's Ball Hockey and how important it was for me to be in Moncton in the summer. They were a hundred percent behind me. Each summer, I go back to Moncton for the ball hockey season, working during the day with my Ottawa accounting clients and showing up at the rink each night for my kids.

It's all about staying connected to hockey. Goody's is my summer fix. And the Gee-Gees, the University of Ottawa men's hockey team, is my winter fix. After a few years in Ottawa, I was hungry for more hockey, and when the opportunity came up to be an assistant coach with the Gee-Gees, I jumped at it. The practices are in the morning, so I can be on the ice with the players before I head to work, and the games are on the weekend.

Some people may think I'm crazy for taking on so much, but hard work is in my blood and I can't bear the thought of not being involved in the community.

When it comes to hard work, I'm not in the same league as my wife, Catherine. We started dating back in 2005, the season we won the President's Cup, and she's been with me the whole ride. Without her, I don't know if I would have made it anywhere in hockey or in life. On top of her biopharmaceutical science degree, she has a nursing and a medical degree and is now completing her internal medicine residency. Seeing how hard she works has pushed me to be better.

In 2019–20, we expanded Goody's to include a winter league for adults. We do our best to make everything as official as possible, including posting stats on our website. For a lot of guys, it's really rewarding to see their stats online for the first time. They get really into it, and if we miss an assist, we hear about it.

Patrice Cormier, a fellow New Brunswicker who played for the Winnipeg Jets, joined our league. Now, he's the kind of guy who always says, "I don't care about the stats." But when he missed one game, he sent me a message: "Hey, Goody, the website says I played an extra game, but I wasn't there. Can you fix that?"

"I thought you didn't care?" I replied.

"Yeah, but it's going to affect my points per game!"

I couldn't help but howl at that. We're talking about ball hockey here and it's great to see guys like Patrice get so involved. A lot of people lose interest in hockey when they forget why they're playing. At Goody's, we make sure that never happens.

I always tell people, I'm good, but I'm not great. It's my hard work and attitude that have made the difference. If our kids have some fun and learn our motto, "Good guys finish first," then I'm doing our job right.

Christian Gaudet is the former captain of the Moncton Wildcats and University of Moncton Aigles Bleus and the cofounder of Goody's Ball Hockey, the longest-running youth ball hockey league in the greater Moncton area. Currently, he is a chartered professional accountant for GGFL and an assistant coach with the University of Ottawa men's hockey team, and on Monday nights, he works with the kids from the Ottawa East Minor Hockey Association. Christian lives with his wife in Ottawa, then comes home to Moncton every summer to run the ball hockey program.

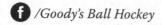 */Goody's Ball Hockey*

 *@GoodysBallHKY*

No Bad Days

Rob Facca

"He has it."

These words changed my son Louie's life forever. And mine. I was on top of the world with the perfect job and the perfect family, and in the snap of a finger, it was going to change. In that moment it would have been easy to feel sorry for ourselves and wonder why this bad thing was happening, but there was no time and there was so much to learn and do just to keep moving forward.

My story begins in my hometown of London, Ontario. London's a hockey town. Back then, when I was a kid, the OHL only had a few teams and one of them was the London Knights. They had the support of everyone in town, including me and my family. Our house was always full of hockey talk, whether the subject was whatever was happening with the London Knights or whatever the big story in the NHL was at the time—usually Wayne Gretzky and the Maple Leafs. We talked about hockey, read about it, couldn't get enough of it. This was before Netflix, so when *Hockey Night in Canada* came on, it was a big deal.

My family owns a small business, Facca Fasteners, which distributes industrial automotive parts. My dad started the company when he was twenty-seven, and the business was the reason us kids were able to enjoy all our hockey escapades. My mom, Wendy, was the die-hard hockey fan in our family. She was the brains and the CEO, so to speak, and kept everything organized in our home and our family business. My dad emigrated from Italy in 1951, and while hockey wasn't his first love, he grew to love it over time like anyone who comes to Canada. They registered all three of us kids—Joey, Lisa, and me—to play when we were young. No matter what was going on at home, work, or school, hockey was always a good distraction.

Like every other kid, hockey was everything to me, even at the tender age of five. My world revolved around going to school, hanging out with my friends, and hockey. And I loved being part of a team—it meant you had two groups of friends: one at school and one at hockey. Whether I was collecting hockey cards, watching games, or going to the rink and shooting around the puck with my friends—it was all hockey, all the time. My friends and I all just wanted to be the next Wayne Gretzky.

If I wasn't playing my own games, I was watching the Knights.

When I was growing up, my family had season tickets to all the London Knight games. It seemed like they had a home game every Friday night, and my family would pile into the car and go to the London Gardens (later the London Ice House) to cheer on our team. Those games had everything: lots of goals, big hits, and fights. For a kid obsessed with hockey, the London Knights were heroes to me and my friends.

I was a pretty good player growing up. I had a head for the game and was a goal scorer. Depending on the year, I either played AA or AAA hockey. It never really mattered to me—at the end of the day, I just loved going to the rink and playing the game with my buddies.

At the age of sixteen, I got my first real taste of junior hockey when I made the Junior B Strathroy Blades. I was still just a kid and would go to the rink without a care in the world, but a lot of the guys in the league were older—nineteen or twenty—and held down part-time jobs or went to Western University. I was still in minor hockey mode and these guys were really good. Playing against and with them was a lot of fun. They treated me well and I learned a lot from them.

In 1994, after a year with Strathroy, I got drafted into the OHL by the North Bay Centennials. I was excited by the prospect of playing in the OHL and went to training camp. Unfortunately, that path didn't pan out for me. In the fall, the NHL initiated a lockout, which meant a lot of guys who would have been in the NHL returned to their respective junior teams. North Bay asked me to stay for their Tier 2 team. I thought that if they wanted me to play Tier 2, basically Junior B, I might as well do it back at home. So I did.

Since I wasn't signed with the OHL, I started receiving letters from NCAA schools asking if I was interested in playing for their hockey teams, but because I had gone to the camp and played in a few exhibition games, I had lost my NCAA eligibility and would have to sit out a year. When the schools found that out, they quickly lost interest in me. I was running out of options if I wanted to play professionally after high school.

Luckily for me, the University of Nebraska, Omaha, was putting together a brand-new hockey program and didn't mind that I had to sit out a year of hockey. They were even offering me a scholarship. The timing was perfect. I headed down to Omaha, sat out a year, regained my NCAA eligibility, and was one of the first guys on campus. I was happy to have the chance to play somewhere, and my parents were delighted that I was going to further my education, too.

While I was excited to be playing hockey, leaving all my family and friends behind to move to a strange place filled me with so much uncertainty. I didn't know what to expect or really what I was getting myself into. Up until that point, I'd never really been away from home, and this wasn't like moving to a school a couple of hours away. Omaha was a fifteen-hour drive from London and in an entirely different country.

It was a tough adjustment at first. At home, I had my routine: I spent time with my high school buddies and played hockey Friday and Saturday nights. By then I was nineteen, and in London, I could go out to a bar with my friends, but in Omaha, the legal drinking age was twenty-one. I remember calling home and finding everyone was over for a family dinner while I was fifteen hours away, which made me miss home even more. Back then, we didn't have cellphones. When someone was gone, they were really gone.

In that first year, I was really homesick and would call my parents, sometimes twice a day.

"Listen," my mom would say. "This is a little blip."

My dad chimed in. "If you come home, you'll regret it. Your life is just starting. Enjoy the experience and give it a chance."

Hearing their voices as they reassured me that I had made the right choice helped me get through that first year in Omaha. And lo and behold, they were right, and I never ended up going home.

As I got to know my teammates, I began to feel more comfortable in my new city. The year seemed to fly. My second year, the team was busy with practices as we readied for the start of the regular season in October. Between classes, practice, and hanging out with the team, I had so many distractions I didn't have time to be homesick.

I came into college thinking I was going to be a strong player, but one of the first things I noticed about the team was that everyone was really good. I was having a great time playing with an awesome group of guys, but when it came to ice time, I didn't get much. By the end of that first season, the writing was on the wall. I knew college hockey would be as far as I would go, and made a point to enjoy it while it lasted.

Now, as a scout, I tell people, "I wouldn't have recruited me either!" But the great thing about the NCAA is it's also a chance to get an education.

By the time I was done with college, the United States felt like a second home to me, and I decided to stay in Omaha, as did many of my teammates. But it was time to find something new to do. I was lucky to get a marketing job at Budweiser right away. They're a big company in Omaha, and I was in charge of going around to venues for theme nights and fund-raising events, and setting up any promotion material. I've always been a people person, so I enjoyed meeting new people through my work.

But of course, I couldn't leave hockey behind. For fun, I started to help coach a local mite division hockey team, which is the equivalent of a novice team in Canada, never thinking it would lead anywhere beyond a hobby. I loved being back on the rink—it was a great release from the daily grind of work—and the kids were great. It was a travel team, so every weekend we would take road trips to games and tournaments in the communities surrounding Omaha.

During my first season coaching, I became friends with the dad of one of the players on my team: Jim Pflug, who was the president of the Lincoln Stars of the USJHL. One year later, he and the Stars reached out to me.

"The Stars need an assistant coach," they said. "Would you be interested? It doesn't pay a lot."

I didn't miss a beat. "Sure, I would!"

I loved coaching with the Stars. During my first year, we won the league championship and had five kids drafted into the NHL. I was young, living in the moment, and taking the opportunities as they presented themselves to me, but as I met more people, especially in the NHL and NCAA, I began to think that I was on the right path and had a shot at a career in coaching.

After two seasons, I returned my alma mater, the University of Nebraska, Omaha, to be a volunteer coach, which is a nice way of saying that I coached for little or no money. I was the director of youth hockey to help pay the bills, but I had a foot in the door. I knew I had to pay my dues and put in my time to move up in the NCAA coaching circle. This was just one step on my résumé.

It was a good fit for me because 90 percent of the kids on our team had just played in the USHL, so I had either coached them or had coached against them the previous year. And from my previous experience as a player, I could relate to new kids coming into the program, especially the Canadian kids, who composed about half our team. The other half were Americans from as far away as Chicago and Minnesota. I knew what it was like to move away from home for the first time, and I could tell if a new kid was feeling homesick. I would try my best to make them feel at home on the team. And while some kids did quit, others adapted, and playing NCAA hockey in Omaha became a way of life.

In 2007, after two seasons with Omaha, I got offered a job as an assistant coach at Northern Michigan, which I eagerly accepted. I discovered I had a knack for recruiting, which is the lifeblood of building a good team in the NCAA. It was fulfilling work. My own hockey dreams had come true when someone offered me a college scholarship, and now I was able to do that for others. My priority was always to make sure both the kids and their parents were treated as people, not prospects. I wanted them to feel comfortable and I never went in with the same pitch. I got to know the kid and his family and what they wanted from a hockey program and a school and then showed them how our university would measure up. I believed in our program, and if the player and his parents could see that, it was easy to "sell" it to them. In the end, the kid had to wake up the next morning and say, "That's where I want to go." If he didn't, that was okay. We wanted kids to follow their heart. When you play with heart, you do your best.

This new position also meant I could pay my bills solely on my coaching salary. By that time, I had met and married my beautiful wife, Nicole—Nikki—and she was six months pregnant with our first child. Nikki had never left Omaha, so I had to convince her this was a great opportunity. She was my first recruit to Northern Michigan, a place that was a thirteen-hour drive from Omaha. If I couldn't convince her to go, I wouldn't be able to convince anyone to go. She obliged and we were on our way.

Louie was born on November 9, 2007. That was the best day of my life. From that second, Louie was my little buddy and I was dreaming of him playing hockey one day and hopping in the car with me and going on trips. After one day, I was already saying to my own dad, "Louie's got big paws!" Those would serve him well as he got older and started playing hockey.

Then, once we got him home, it hit me. "Now we're in one. What do I do?" In just a week I was scheduled to go on a recruiting trip for work. I didn't want to leave Nikki and Louie so soon, but it was my job and I had to. I'm not sure Nikki was too happy with me, and I learned a lesson: never have a baby during the hockey season.

We survived that first year and I spent another two at Northern, during which we welcomed our beautiful daughter, Bella, into our family. She was born during our playoffs in March 2010. I was at the hospital for her birth at three p.m. and in the locker room by five thirty for our semifinals. After the game, I went back to the hospital and brought the staff on her floor pizza as a thank-you.

Later in 2010, Western Michigan University in Kalamazoo offered me an assistant coaching job with their hockey team, the Broncos. It was a bigger school with a bigger budget and in a better location. When I was at Northern, it was never an even playing field when we went to play schools like Michigan State and Notre Dame; we would show up and the opposing kids would look like pros with their different matching track suits for road games and home games. We were lucky to give our kids a matching sweatshirt.

The other big selling point was that the head coach at Western was Jeff Blashill, an up-and-coming coach. I accepted. I felt it was time to move on to a bigger and better challenge and work with new people. I didn't want to be on the lily pad forever, and Western would definitely be a glowing point on my growing résumé. I would be working with Jeff and Pat Ferschweiler, the other assistant coach, to revive the hockey program after it had been flailing for some time. It was a sleeping giant ready to awaken.

I felt like every decision I had made had led to this opportunity and everything in my life was falling into place: I had an amazing family, a dream job, and we were about to buy a brand-new house in Kalamazoo. Life was good.

Right as I was leaving Northern Michigan, Nikki and I had taken Louie to the doctor to look at his flat feet, which he had inherited from me. Being the proactive parents we were, we wanted to see if there were braces or arches that he could wear while he was sleeping that might help him. During the consultation, the doctor did a little blood work and took an X-ray.

"Louie's calf muscles are very tight," he observed, and recommended we take him to see a neurologist while we waited for the results from the blood tests.

At the mention of a neurologist, Nikki and I began to worry. Was Louie going to be okay? As recommended, we took him to the neurologist, thinking the worst. Duchenne muscular dystrophy had been mentioned as a possible diagnosis, and it had struck a chord of fear in us. It was a disease that gradually weakened the body's muscles, and while the doctors said there were treatments to slow the symptoms, the sad truth was that there was no cure. We pressed the doctors for their opinion.

"Let's just wait for the results and take it from there," they replied.

We waited. I began my new job at Western.

Meanwhile we started noticing that Louie was moving slower than other two-and-a-half-year-olds. Still, in my mind, this was about flat feet. Louie was so young—wouldn't this be something he would outgrow? He'd be fine, I imagined, and would play hockey and get a scholarship somewhere, like I did.

Then, one month later, I was on a plane about to take off for a weekend recruiting trip when my phone rang. It was one of Louie's doctors. She had his results.

On the PA, the flight attendant announced that everyone needed to shut off their phones.

"I'm on a plane about to take off, can I call you in two hours?"

"Well, no one will be in the office at that time," she replied.

"Can you tell me now?"

"I'm sorry. Louie has Duchenne muscular dystrophy."

As I hung up the phone, my heart sank. I wasn't prepared for the news. Anyone who knows me knows that I don't have a negative bone in my body, but that day I fought back tears as my thoughts spiraled into darkness. How could this be happening to us? Why my family? Why my son?

I tried to keep it together. I had a flight. I had a job to do.

When I got to my destination, I grabbed a rental car and drove to the hotel. Once I checked in, I headed to the rink. I needed to focus on the task in front of me. It was the only thing keeping me from falling apart. I hadn't yet called Nikki. I hadn't told anyone.

By the next morning, I couldn't take it anymore. I phoned Nikki, who was still in Nebraska because we hadn't moved into our new house yet, and I told her. She was upset, and rightfully so; we were miles apart, and she was at home with two young children, and Bella was just six months, and we'd been dealt an impossible blow. We were both devastated and struggling to understand what this meant for us, for Louie. As parents, we wanted to protect Louie from anything that would hurt him. But we couldn't protect him from this. We didn't know what to do or where to turn. We felt helpless and unable to comfort one another.

I called my dad next. At moments, I was so overcome, I couldn't even speak. On the other end of the line, my dad was falling apart. My mom got on the phone then and took over. She was a rock for us all. She called Nikki next and reassured her that everything was going to be okay.

For those first few weeks, my mom was the glue that held us all together. Meanwhile, Nikki and I threw ourselves into researching DMD. We learned that it affects one in every five thousand boys, that kids with DMD have difficulty going up stairs and jumping, that most kids need a wheelchair by the time they're twelve. The doctors assured us that there were many treatments to help Louie, but the battle we were facing hit us like a punch to the stomach.

Early on, we signed up for a support group for parents of children with DMD. Everyone shared their experience and explained how things might go for Louie and what we should do. I just kept thinking that maybe Louie's condition wasn't as severe as theirs. Or—and this thought chilled me—maybe he was worse than anyone else. I walked out of that meeting and said, "This was really depressing. How do they know? They don't know us and they don't know Louie." One meeting was enough for me.

"What are we going to do?" Nikki asked me one day.

I looked at her. "We are just going to keep doing what we can to give Louie as normal a life as possible. And we're going to do everything we can to avoid the inevitable."

I had decided not to let Louie's diagnosis change me, not to walk around with a woe-is-me attitude. That was the beginning of the No Bad Days campaign.

Every day I woke up, I always tried to say, "Somebody else has it worse." Did I still have some bad moments? Yes, for sure. When I was driving at night and alone with my thoughts, I'd start to get upset, but I never let that moment in the car outweigh the entire day.

Nikki and I leaned on each other, but we also leaned on Jeff and Pat and their families. They were also new to Kalamazoo; all we really had was each other. When I told them about Louie's diagnosis, they immediately rallied around us, and we went from being a family of four to a family of fourteen. Plus the twenty-five players on the team.

I remember Jeff breaking the news to them. He just walked into the locker room and said, "Hey, boys. Rob's family is going through a tough time. Louie has been diagnosed with Duchenne muscular dystrophy."

In an instant, Louie had twenty-five big brothers looking out for him.

The support of Jeff, Pat, their families, and the team played a huge role in helping Nikki and me through those first few months.

We were determined that Louie not end up in a wheelchair, and so we tried to be proactive and face the disease head-on. If he couldn't play hockey or football, I was fine with that, but I didn't want his condition to prevent him from having fun, going to a movie, or hanging out with his buddies at school and after school. Every kid with DMD is different. We spoke to his doctors about what medication could help mitigate his symptoms and slow the rate of muscular degeneration, and Louie was started on a special steroid. One of the potential side effects was weight gain, so we worked with a dietary specialist to come up with a diet to help him stay strong without gaining unnecessary weight. Because he lacked muscle, even something as basic as walking up the stairs was tough for him. So we got him working with a physical therapist on a stretching routine and came up with a plan to keep him moving to slow the symptoms. These three things were key to our plan of attack.

Louie was not yet three years old, and we were worried that if we told him what he had when he was so young, something would get lost in translation. We settled on telling him that he had special muscles and that's why he needed to follow his diet and do his stretches. Luckily for us, Louie loved everything we put in front of him.

That first year I was on the road a lot, recruiting players to turn our team around so we could compete for our conference championship. I felt bad leaving Nikki with so much, and I missed her, Louie, and Bella so much, but each time I walked in the door and saw my kids running toward me for hugs and kisses, everything was perfect again. The idea of never having another bad day stayed with me. If I lost a recruit, that was okay. If we lost a game, it wasn't the end of the world. There was always tomorrow. It wasn't worth dwelling on the bad moments. I decided to start a movement called "No Bad Days," and we had red rubber bracelets made with Louie's name on them and #NoBadDays, and we gave them out to coaching staff and players.

Until Louie's diagnosis, Nikki and I didn't know about muscular dystrophy. That told us that not a lot of other people knew much about it either. I wanted to change that. It was important to me to raise awareness about DMD and the need for a cure. I have a big mouth and I'm in hockey, so people found out what I was all about in a hurry.

Most teams hold cancer awareness nights, so I suggested we have a DMD awareness night. With Jeff and Pat's help, we invited families dealing with muscular dystrophy to one of our games and organized a silent auction to raise money for research.

Hockey-wise, that first year at Western was a huge success. The team went all the way to the CCHA finals and then the regional semifinals of the coveted NCAA tournament, making it their most successful season in fifteen years. The program took off from there and the entire community of Kalamazoo got behind the team—and, as a result, Louie.

In 2011, we started holding DMD awareness night during regular-season games. That year, Jeff Blashill had left to coach the Detroit Red Wings under Mike Babcock, but he made a special trip to come back and drop the puck at one of the games in a ceremonial face-off. Louie and another boy who had DMD joined Jeff and the two captains at centre ice for the face-off. It was a great moment, and the best part was when Louie walked out onto the ice, the whole arena started chanting his name. "Louie! Louie!"

After that, other teams began supporting our DMD nights and would wear a decal on their helmets that said, "No Bad Days." And we met more and more families with kids affected by the disease. Ninety percent of them were in wheelchairs, which just fueled our drive to raise money for research. We got some big prizes to entice people. Danny Dekeyser, who I had coached at Western, was now with the Red Wings, and he donated fifty-five Red Wings jerseys, which he signed. Another time, we had a raffle for a trip giveaway. A few of the games were even broadcast on Fox Sports 1 in Michigan, which helped publicize our cause.

The colour associated with DMD charity events is red, so I always made sure I was wearing red dress shoes. Even before Louie's diagnosis I had been a big shoe guy, like my dad, and I liked wearing loud colours. Whenever I walked anywhere with Louie, kids would say, "Hey, there's that kid whose dad wears goofy shoes." I never wanted Louie to be singled out for his disease, so the fact that they were commenting on my shoes instead made me smile.

Andy Murray, who had taken over as head coach, was a man of routine: he wore the same tie, shoes, etc., on game day. Like a lot of guys in hockey, he's superstitious. But one day he changed up his routine. I was wearing my red shoes, as was the other coach, when Andy walked into the locker room. He looked at the players.

"We're going to do this one for Louie tonight," he said, showing off a pair of bright red dress shoes.

The team cheered and yelled, and I found myself blinking back tears. That wasn't the kind of thing that Andy would ever do, but he did it for Louie. I love hockey for moments like those.

When Louie was six years old, my dad, Bob, told me he wanted to raise money and awareness for DMD. When Louie was first diagnosed, we had learned about Jesse's Journey, a charity founded by John Davidson, a fellow London, Ontario, native, for his son, Jesse, who was diagnosed with DMD in 1986. In 1995, John pushed Jesse across Ontario in his wheelchair to raise money for a cure, and in 1998, he walked across Canada to further the cause. John's story resonated with my dad and he and John connected early on.

Now my dad was inspired to do something similar to what John had done. Working with Jesse's Journey, he decided to walk across Ontario. He would be the first grandpa to do so.

"That's great, Dad," I said, touched by his decision. It was such a kind thing for a grandfather to do for his grandson.

My dad told me that before coming up with this idea, he used to wake up every day thinking, *What can I do?* This walk was a way to raise some money and help Louie.

In May 2012, my dad set out from Owen Sound and walked five hundred kilometres to our hometown of London, Ontario, becoming affectionately known as Grandpa Bob along the way. I wasn't too worried about my dad—he's a tough dude and in great shape. He ended up raising $250,000 for DMD research, and as he came to the end of the walk, just over a month after he started, we had a welcoming committee ready to greet him.

Nikki, Louie, and I were there with my mom, Joey, and Lisa. By that time, we had explained to Louie that he had a disease called Duchenne muscular dystrophy, but he was still kind of young to understand what his Nonno had done. He was more excited to be there because he knew with Nonna and Nonno around, he'd get lots of treats.

After my dad finished the walk, we had a banquet to celebrate his amazing journey and all of us—my mom, my siblings, Nikki, and I—presented him with a Jostens ring that looked just like a Stanley Cup ring with a map of his route on one side, the number 500 on the front for the distance, and red rubies for the colour of Duchenne.

"After every championship, there's a winner," we said. "And you are definitely a winner."

He loved that ring.

At the time of the celebration, Nikki was pregnant with our third child, and little Clara was born later that year in September.

Fast-forward to 2014, my dad called me up again. "I want to do a bigger walk."

"What's bigger?" I asked.

"Quebec City to Winnipeg."

I couldn't believe what I was hearing. "Dad, you just did a walk."

By now he was sixty-five years old, and this trek would be four thousand kilometres and take him at least seven months, which meant a lot more organizing behind the scenes. I thanked him, then expressed my concerns.

"Nope, I've made up my mind," he said. "I'm going to walk and that's that."

My dad is a determined guy and he didn't care what I or my siblings had to say. My mom was behind him a hundred percent. Together, they organized Grandpa Bob's four-thousand-kilometre Walk

Louie and my dad crossing the finish line in November 2014.

for Louie, and they made sure every dollar raised went back to research. London City Chrysler's general manager donated two caravans and a motor home for the walk, but all the hotel bills and expenses my mom and dad incurred, they paid for out of pocket.

I followed my dad's journey through the news and updates from my mom, and my parents told us stories of people they met along the way. This walk was the ultimate example of a grandpa doing something for his grandkid, and it pulled on the heartstrings of people they met along the way. It pulled on my heartstrings, too.

Of all the things that people have done for us after Louie's diagnosis, it's hard to top what my father did. And it wasn't just him. My mom, my brother, my sister, my aunt Carol, and other family members all made sacrifices to help him pull the event off. I don't have the words to express how much that meant to our family.

Thanks to those two walks, my dad, with a big assist from my mom, raised $1 million for DMD. I think my dad was a little pissed we didn't get him another championship ring after that.

That same year, I was hired as an amateur scout for the Chicago Blackhawks. It was a dream to work in the NHL, and I felt that all my coaching jobs, and my work recruiting, up until that point had led me to this new opportunity. Louie was delighted. In our house, we talk a lot about sports—mostly basketball, which Louie loves, but also hockey—and Louie is a big fan of the Blackhawks.

Two weeks later, Louie received a letter from Jonathan Toews, the captain of the team. It read:

> Dear Louie,
>
> We are honoured to welcome you and your family to the Blackhawks organization. We are excited to gain such a strong and dedicated fan like yourself. You are an inspiration to our organization.
>
> It takes a strong person to go through these types of events. There are so many people behind you, wishing you

well. The strength you have shown throughout your very own journey speaks volumes.

We can't wait to see you and your family around the rink next season.

All the best,

Jonathan Toews and the Chicago Blackhawks

Louie was blown away when he read that letter, which quickly became a keepsake of our entire family. It was, by far, the most touching thing we have received from someone in the NHL.

Hockey is a tight-knit group. We all come from competitive backgrounds, but when someone is in need, we know how to help each other out. Whenever Louie visits the Blackhawks locker room, Jonathan Toews or Patrick Kane will take him around the room and snap photos with him. And for Louie's part, he lives and breathes the Blackhawks. Every time they win, he is excited, and every time they lose, he's really pissed off. But he was really happy when they won the Stanley Cup in 2015—and so was I.

Six months before the 2019 NHL entry draft, the Blackhawks management pulled me aside. "Would Louie like to be our draft runner?" they asked.

When someone has DMD, the word "runner" isn't the first thing that comes to mind when you think of them. Every team in the NHL has a runner on draft day and they get coffee, water, and snacks for members of the team at the draft table, but the best part is that they get to go onstage with the team before they select their first-round pick, carrying a team hat and jersey to give to the player. It meant a lot to me that the team didn't look at Louie and see limitations. They just wanted him to be a part of the day.

I thanked them and said he'd love to. Louie was over the moon when I told him. The day of the draft, we were in Vancouver, and Louie couldn't stop smiling from the moment he got on the team bus to the moment we returned to the hotel later that day—everything in between was exciting. And to see his enjoyment was priceless. He was so excited to get onstage in front of everyone and give the Blackhawks jersey and hat to the number three pick. He got along great with everyone and was a real trooper during a long day.

It was a special night for me, too. During my coaching days, I had met a lot of people in the NHL and many of them were at the draft. Everyone knew Louie's story, or a version of his story, through me; all wanted to meet him. Mike Babcock and Steve Yzerman came over to say hi. Jeff Blashill, now the head coach for the Detroit Red Wings, stopped by. My favourite memory from that day is the look of joy on Louie's face as he posed for a photo with Scotty Bowman.

Even though I work for the Blackhawks, I'm constantly amazed at the kindness and generosity of everyone in the hockey world.

One day Danny Dekeyser called me up. "Rob, I'm in a slump and I can't score," he said. "Can you send some of Louie's bracelets?"

Here is Louie onstage with Kirby Dach, the Blackhawk's first-round pick (third overall), and John McDonough, Mark Kelley, and Stan Bowman. (Courtesy of the Chicago Blackhawks)

One of the highlights of the Draft Day
was Louie meeting Scotty Bowman.

"Of course," I said. I put some in the mail for him, and the night after they arrived, he had a goal and two assists.

I texted Danny right after the game and said, "You should have got those bracelets a long time ago!"

He shot back, "No doubt!" with a laughing emoji.

Since then, a few guys around the league have reached out to get bracelets.

In 2010, our lives changed in the blink of an eye, but ten years later, here we are, still going strong. Nikki's the rock of our family and we're all lucky to have her keeping us positive and keeping us in line. Louie's two sisters, Bella and Clara, are his angels, always watching out for him. Every six months, we take him to the specialists for a checkup. They never tell us that there might be a cure, but they have done a great job helping Louie maintain the muscle he has as he gets older. We continue to take each day as it comes.

As Louie has gotten older, he's come to understand his disease and knows why he needs to take his medication and do his stretches. In school, he excels. He's a good student and has a lot of friends. I see a lot of myself in him, not just in our looks, but our mannerisms, too— he's witty and quick with one-liners, always looking to put others at ease and make them laugh.

Of course, he has moments of frustration over his physical limitations. The problem is that Louie's brain is more advanced than his legs. All of his friends play on the same soccer team and he can't be a part of it. He just can't run as fast or kick the ball as hard or jump as high as they can. But when they are done playing, they all want to hang out with King Louie—that's what they call him. The odd time, he'll fall down and he doesn't want anyone to help him get up. I know that he gets a little embarrassed, but Louie being who he is, he gets over it and moves on quickly.

But while he may not be able to play soccer, he can play basketball. Despite his love of hockey, basketball remains his favourite sport and I have to do my research to keep up with all his conversations about the NBA.

At the beginning of the year, he found the basket too high, but he worked on his game, and by the end of the season, he made two baskets in practice. When he made the first basket, everyone on the team went bananas. He can't run up and down the floor more than three times, but his coach does an amazing job working around his physical limitations and puts him into the game as much as he can, which I appreciate because it gives Louie a chance to compete. In one game, Louie made a shot that nearly went in. That was a huge milestone for him. The other team had no idea that he has DMD and they weren't letting him have any freebies out on the court.

I try to go to as many of his games as I can. Sometimes, when we are driving home after, Louie will say, "I can't believe the coach didn't have me in at the end of the game."

Here we are in 2019, Bella, Nikki, Clara, me, and Louie.

And I say, "Listen, you're smart and you have a good sports IQ. Just keep working on that."

He's had a couple turnovers and he always gets so mad at himself. I love to see that in him because it shows me he wants to make the right play. The only reason he doesn't is because of his limitations. But he's fiery and competitive and doesn't give up.

Louie is twelve now. We were told that by now, he would likely need a walker or a wheelchair to get around, but he doesn't. His favourite school is the University of Michigan. Like me and my London Knights, he loves his hometown Michigan Wolverines, and it's his goal to go to school there.

But no matter what happens, we've all decided that there will be no bad days. Yes, our son has DMD, which means Nikki and I are always thinking about his next doctor's appointment and making sure he's taking his medicine, sticking to his diet, and doing his stretches every day.

We don't know how to live any other way. But, like we always say, it's okay to have a bad moment now and then, but we'll never have a bad day. The way I see it, every day with Louie is a good day. He's my hero.

Rob Facca is an amateur scout for the Chicago Blackhawks. Prior to being hired by the Blackhawks, he spent eight years working as an assistant coach for three different NCAA programs. Rob lives with his wife, Nikki, and their three children in Omaha, Nebraska.

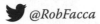 *@RobFacca*

Jesse's Journey: www.jessesjourney.com

Duchene Muscular Dystrophy: www.parentprojectmd.org

#NoBadDays

Simply a Hockey Player

Jessica Platt

Most people only know me as a transgender hockey player, but I'm an all-around athlete: I play hockey and Ultimate Frisbee, and compete in duathlons, among many other sports. I'm also a fiancée, a sister, a daughter, and a pet owner. I was a high school band geek and a sorority sister. I'm caring, compassionate, funny, and empathetic, to name a few things. As an athlete who also happens to be trans, I'm often labelled and defined by that one aspect of my identity, but I am so much more than that. This is my story.

I grew up in Brights Grove, Ontario, a little community just outside of Sarnia, the youngest of three children. My brother, the oldest, played hockey until his early teens, while my sister competed in figure skating, so every winter, I lived at the rink. My mom or dad would pick us up after school and bring us to the rink where my sister had her skating lessons, and later in the evening, I had hockey practice. From an early age, hockey was a major part of my life. It was something I loved to do more than anything else. When I wasn't at the arena, I was out on the neighbour's backyard rink, playing hockey and other games with the neighbourhood kids for hours and hours. When it got too late, I'd trudge home to a mug of hot chocolate made by my loving mom.

One of my earliest childhood memories is skating on that backyard rink with Amy, one of my best friends. Wobbling at first, but slowly and steadily getting better. I remember the first time I was able to raise the puck off the ice, I was on the rink one Saturday afternoon all alone trying over and over again. When I finally succeeded, it was all of one foot high and five feet long, but I was so proud.

But perhaps the most vivid memory would be from when I was seven years old. I was in my second year of hockey, playing minor novice, when my dad was approached by one of the travel team's coaches, who asked if I had considered playing rep hockey. My dad explained that the competition would be tough and the players better, but it was a vote of confidence for the coach to suggest it and so we decided to give it a try.

That first game, I was warming up on the ice with my team when the opposing team came on. Their goalie led the way, bragging, "Watch out, shutout goalie coming through."

I took his words as a challenge. Playing defence, I didn't always get many opportunities to score, but in the first period, I skated down the ice end to end, around the other team's defence, and shot the puck in the top left corner. That quieted the goalie down quickly. On another end-to-end rush, I scored a second goal, and by the end of the game, I had put up two more, leading my team to the win. I had never scored four goals in a game and couldn't stop talking about it for the rest of the night.

Playing hockey came easy to me. My dad always said, "You somehow just know where everyone is on the ice." On the ice, I didn't think about anything other than the game and where I needed to be and what I needed to make my body do to help my team win. If that was playing offensive and contributing to help my team score, I did it. If that was standing tall at the blue line and shutting down the opposing team with a few body checks, I did that. And when we did win, I felt that not only had we accomplished something, but also that I fit in. I was Platt, or Platty, one of the team, just happy to celebrate the win; it was a positive atmosphere. That was when everything made sense.

Off the ice, it was a different story. The body that obeyed me on the ice was becoming something I resented more and more, no longer recognizing it as I hit my puberty. I saw what was happening to my body, as opposed to my closer female friends, and it just didn't feel right. The guys I played sports with were happy, even excited, about how their bodies were changing, but that's not how I felt. I didn't talk to anyone about what I was feeling—I didn't know how to voice what I was going through. All I knew was that I was different, and I thought if I pushed my feelings down deep enough, they would go away and I could be like everyone else, what I thought was "normal."

It was in the hockey world that my ideas of what a boy should be—how I needed to act—took shape. I often heard my male teammates demeaning or making fun of women—coaches, parents, other players and schoolmates—that I knew and admired. They called people "gay" when they didn't fight or when they did anything remotely effeminate, like showing any kind of sensitivity. And if someone actually *was* gay? They were ridiculed. Early on, I realized that to fit in, I needed to be tough and shut my mouth. There were always one or two alpha males per team that would make life worse for anyone who challenged the status quo. Everyone wanted to be on their good side, or else they risked being the loner on the team, open to constant pranks and teasing. Including me. I still regret sitting by and doing nothing when the boys used the term "gay" to label anyone they thought was "weak," when the few gay people I knew were made fun of behind their backs, and when women I knew were objectified and disparaged. I said nothing because I didn't want to draw attention to myself.

Everyone saw me as a calm, confident hockey player, but I just didn't want to participate in the toxic atmosphere, so while my teammates were loud and cocky, I was quiet. At practice, I was always up front listening to the drill instructions, nodding along and taking in everything I could to improve my game. I never asked questions, just did as I was told. I once had a coach exclaim halfway through the year, "Platty! That's the first time I've heard you talk all season!" I hadn't really said anything of note, though; I was just pumped up for the game and had been chatting with one of my few hockey friends sitting next to me. After every game, I rushed to get out of my equipment and begrudgingly shower and change so I didn't have to spend a minute longer than was necessary in the locker room. This, of course, delighted my parents because we could be on our way home right away, which was especially nice after away games, when the drive could be up to two hours.

To the outside viewer, my childhood looked average, but most people didn't know the real me, not even my family. I put on a façade of being happy and pretended to be the boy that people expected me to be, but inside, I was a girl, and I felt shamed into hiding that. I hid everything I actually felt and pretended to be someone else, so much so that my friends joked that I was a robot. Hockey was the one place where I could ignore all the thoughts, questions, and confusion going on in my life, and I could just exist. I wasn't a boy, I wasn't a girl, I was simply a hockey player. But I was hiding the person I knew I was, and as I was getting older, it was harder and harder to do. I wanted so badly to fit in that I was sacrificing my happiness.

Brights Grove was a small town, and so I wasn't exposed to a lot of diversity and I didn't know much about the LGBTQ+ community. The only trans characters I saw were on TV, and often they were made fun of and called a "man in a dress." The most common joke was when a main character (always a man) kissed a trans woman; everyone would laugh and make jokes about the man's sexuality, which sent the damaging message that the trans woman was a man and that she was tricking the man into kissing her. Meanwhile the man took no accountability for something he willingly did and would get defensive and often confrontational. Later in life, I realized that these types of ideas are part of what leads to violence toward trans women. But at the time, these depictions meant I had no positive role model to identify with.

It was in high school that I discovered what it was to be transgender. I instantly knew that this was me. As I did more research online, I learned that it was possible to transition from male to female and saw the positive difference it made on people's lives. Up until that point, I had felt like I was living my life for others instead of myself—this was something I needed to do for me. As much as being transgender resonated with me, it also scared me to the core. I had no idea where to begin, let alone how to find the courage to come out.

In my conservative town, I still desperately cared what others thought of me, including my friends. So I started bringing up the subject subtly and gauging my close friends' reactions; none of us knew much about being transgender and I had no idea how they felt about it. I quickly learned who I could talk to and began to come out to a few friends. It was never easy. Each time, I trembled with the fear of rejection, but I always felt a weight lift when someone accepted the real me. My small group of friends became my safety net, my chosen family, and words can't do justice to how much I appreciate them.

I couldn't yet bring myself to tell my parents. I wanted to, but the fear was paralyzing. While the Internet had provided me with the tools to express myself, on the flip side, I had read all sorts of negative stories, of people being discriminated against, rejected by their families, beaten, or murdered just for living as their authentic self.

When I wasn't with my close, trusted friends, I found solace on the ice. I continued playing hockey all through high school, that feeling of freedom fueling me a little bit longer. I only had a couple more years of competitive hockey left, and soon I would have to choose between playing junior or beer league. After I finished my major midget season, I played one year of beer league, and then I decided to hang up my skates. I had never felt comfortable in locker rooms, and now that I knew who I was, I didn't feel safe either. The talk I heard was all too dangerous. I didn't know if someone would turn a switch and harass me verbally or physically—I was always on high alert and it was exhausting.

"I'm done," I told my parents.

They accepted this, understood that I was at the usual age when people stopped playing, but every few months, my dad would tell me it was such a shame I didn't play anymore.

"I miss going to the rink and watching you play," he would lament, then suggest a beer league I could join.

"I'm done, Dad," I'd respond.

I think both my parents knew I was struggling and wanted me to be happy again. They knew how important hockey had been to me and the joy it had brought me, but my mind was made up. I needed to figure out who I was without hockey.

Over the next two years, I worked full-time at Canadian Tire, drinking way too much, way too often. That time of my life was a haze of alcohol-fueled nights with my work friends. Drinking wasn't a healthy coping mechanism, but it did lower my inhibitions and I allowed my true self to come out more publicly at the bar. If things went poorly, I just blamed it on the alcohol. In time, though, I began to truly accept myself and tell more of my friends who I really was. They, in turn, accepted me and we became quite close. This marked the first time I told a male friend, which I had been nervous to do. Because of my previous experience with hockey players, I had it stuck in my head that no male would accept the true me, but my friend treated me with nothing but respect and asked how to address me, and, when I told him, he did so appropriately.

While things might have seemed like they were getting better, I was in a very dark place. I knew I couldn't get out of the hole I was in alone, and I relied heavily, sometimes too heavily, on my friends for support. They were incredibly empathetic and patient, but I had no drive, and seeing the positives in life was difficult. I couldn't see a future for myself. Friends suggested I go to see a professional for help, but I thought I could solve my problems by myself. I couldn't. I got to the point where I felt I needed to either change something in my life or end it. I couldn't keep living the way I was. And so I sought out a therapist whom I could express my feelings to. With her help, I decided to move away, go to university to further my education, and start fresh. Turns out, this was the best thing I could have done. My parents, who I had yet to come out to, saw this as a positive step toward a future career and gave me their full support.

In September 2009, I moved to Waterloo to attend Wilfrid Laurier University. That first year, I learned a lot about myself and found a great support system to surround me in friends that I still have to this day. While I did feel some more freedom to express myself in this new place, I wasn't ready to transition until my second year. I plotted out what I needed to do, legally, socially, and physically. The end seemed very far off, even unattainable, so I set myself smaller goals. I started by socially transitioning with my friends—Alyssa, Jen, and Natalie—and even began living part-time as my true self. By the end of the year, I decided to physically transition. But before I began the process, I knew I needed to tell my parents.

I told my mom first, in person. I sat her down as I paced around the room, shaking horribly in front of her until I just blurted it out. She responded in the most mom way and said, "I love you. No matter what, you'll still be my child."

Later, with her support, I told my dad. I wrote him an e-mail because I was terrified at the thought of disappointing him. While he didn't quite understand at first, he tried his best and was willing to learn. When he found out that I had been scared to disappoint him,

My mom has always been one of my biggest
supporters. I'm so grateful for her love and support.

he replied, "That's the silliest thing I've ever heard. How could I ever be disappointed in her?" When I heard him say this, it brought tears to my eyes. It still does. My sister reacted similarly to my mom, and my brother more like my dad. I was happy with that and happy to have my family's support.

I found the right doctors, and in August 2012, the beginning of my third year at university, with my family and friends in my corner, I was ready to start my hormone replacement therapy (HRT), and the rest of my life. There were days when I doubted I would ever get to the end of my journey, but looking back and seeing how far I'd already come kept me going. I was shedding the old layers of myself that had built up over years of pretending and letting my true self shine through.

I had left many of the sports from my youth behind, but at university, I began playing Ultimate Frisbee. When I started, it wasn't as popular as it is today, though it does remain one of the most accepting of sports, mainly because it relies on good sportsmanship. Everyone comes to play, and while the games can get very competitive, many leagues have teams with players of all different levels on them so players guard someone of a similar skill level, not necessarily following gender lines. Nobody questioned my appearance; they treated me with respect just like any other player. While I didn't play very competitively, as an athlete, I always wanted to be at my best. I got used to a certain level of play, knew what I was physically capable of, and strove to be better. The summer before I started my physical transition, I was among the quickest in the league. I played smart and rarely let people run away from me.

As I began HRT, I noticed my physical abilities begin to change when I was out on the field. The same people I could catch the previous summer were running away from me. I ran and ran, bearing down as hard as I could, but I just couldn't catch up. In my mind, I thought I should be able to run faster and jump higher, but I couldn't. That realization hit me hard as an athlete. Having to get used to a new normal was frustrating at first, but in every other area of my life, my transition brought so much happiness that I hadn't dreamed I would feel. As my body changed, I could wear the clothes I wanted. I didn't have to pretend to be someone I wasn't—I could just be me. I began to see myself when I looked in the mirror, not every day, but more and more as days went by. I might not have been as fast as I'd been on the field, but that didn't matter because I was looking at my body in a new way. I no longer saw my body as something that just served a purpose. It was me, I liked it, and I wanted to take care of it—of me.

I started going to the gym and ran often, all in an effort to get into shape. I was slightly overweight at the time, so my main goal was to get healthy, and for extra motivation, I signed up for the annual Father's Day ten-kilometre race in Brights Grove. My dad had always taken us to watch the racers when we were young, so the 10K race was a fitting one to choose. I did it for my dad, and so I could be one of the people he was watching go by. I do it every year now. I got hooked on running and wanted to keep it up.

I didn't think of returning to hockey until I graduated university in 2014. I was working full-time, but I needed a second job to make ends meet, so I got a part-time position at a training facility where, in the evenings, I helped teach kids how to skate and play hockey.

It had been more than five years since I'd been on an actual hockey rink, and I was nervous, but it only took a few steps before I was moving well around the ice. I've always loved being on the ice and I just felt great every time I went into work. I loved the job, and being able to pass on my knowledge to young kids reignited my passion for hockey, something I had left behind to pursue my transition and happiness. This experience made me realize that I really did want to play the game again. I didn't care what level—I just wanted to be on the ice in the thick of a game, competing again. I began to literally dream about the moment I could play again.

There was something holding me back, though, a barrier that's tough for trans people to get past: a locker room setting. I knew I didn't belong in a men's locker room anymore, but I didn't feel comfortable in the women's locker room. Being transgender, especially pretransition and during transition, I was constantly preparing for the moment when someone would call me out and harass me. I wasn't ready to put myself in that situation.

In 2015, I finished the last stage of where I wanted to be in my transition. Not all trans people undergo surgery, as everyone's journey is different, but for me it was the last step. It was one of the scariest decisions I've ever made, but it was something I needed to do to save my life. If I hadn't done it, I wouldn't be here today. When I woke up in the recovery room, my mom was right at my side, smiling in that way moms do; this told me she loved me and everything was going to be all right. It was like a light had switched on in my life; I felt like all was right in my world. I had achieved everything I fought for. I was no longer worried I wasn't "enough" and was finally able to just be.

My physical recovery, though, was, in a word, intense. Presurgery I had been in the best shape of my life; postsurgery, I got winded from walking up a flight of stairs. It was six months before I walked normally, but shortly after passing that milestone, I was back to running. To keep myself moving, I signed up for the next Father's Day ten-kilometre race. It was a slow run, but it was a first step in my road back to my presurgery fitness level.

Two months after I started running again, the desire to play hockey was overwhelming. I felt ready to try to navigate the feared locker room, and found a local women's summer league to join.

When I got to the arena, I was nervous. I hadn't played in so long, hadn't shared a locker room yet, and hadn't met anyone on my team. When I opened the door, everyone was welcoming and we got to know each other as we readied for our first game. We went around the room introducing ourselves, learning everyone's position, deciding who would play what, and that was it. There was no judgement. All that fear I had of being questioned or called out was pointless. We just wanted to get out there and have fun.

I stepped on the ice and started to skate around, a bit wobbly at first—like my first attempts when I was a kid on that neighbourhood rink—but to my amazement, it all started to come back. That first game was everything I had hoped it would be. For the first time, I really felt like I belonged on the ice and off it.

I wanted to play competitively again, I wanted to push myself, and I wanted to see what I could do now that I actually cared about my body and had the drive and the desire to train as an elite athlete should—something I had never had the motivation to do before. Outside of hockey, I trained, and when other teams were short players, I jumped into the fray, playing multiple games in a row. Week by week, I progressed quickly. Practice makes perfect.

I didn't know much about the world of women's hockey, apart from the Olympic team, so I searched for leagues to join and found the Canadian Women's Hockey League as well as senior-level hockey teams. I wasn't sure what the rules were for a trans woman to play hockey at the CWHL level, or the senior A level, so I sent e-mails to the CWHL and the Ontario Women's Hockey Association to learn more. I discovered that there were new guidelines, created in association with You Can Play, and older, stricter International Olympic Committee guidelines, but under both sets of criteria, I was eligible and had nothing to worry about.

Why not see what I can do? I thought. I decided to enter the CWHL draft, which was a relatively easy process. All I had to do was fill out a form and pay a fee to register. I did that, figuring I would see what happened and go from there. That summer, I trained harder than I had ever trained in my life. Without a hockey-specific training plan and having never played in university like most of the other girls, I was at a disadvantage. Still, I did what I could. During those women's-league games, I was the first on the ice and the last to leave. I played extra games and even some pickup hockey with a men's league. Outside of the rink, I shot pucks in my parents' backyard, ran, biked, and lifted weights at the gym. It was rare if a day went by during which I didn't do anything to benefit my training.

I had moved back with my parents before undergoing surgery. I knew I was going to need help, and there was going to be a period of time when I wouldn't be able to work. When I told my parents that I was going to try to play hockey again, they were excited for me. They even came to most of those summer games, and sometimes were the only people in the stands. When I told them I wanted to try out for professional hockey, they were more skeptical. There are incredibly skilled players out there, and they didn't want me to get my hopes up only to have them crushed. Nonetheless they were supportive, and they watched as I trained harder than I had ever trained in my life to achieve my goal. The coaches wouldn't have much to go on except what I wrote about myself in my draft application, so I was crossing my fingers that a team would draft me and then I could prove myself in a training camp.

As luck would have it, I was drafted by the Toronto Furies—understandably late in the draft, as I would have been seen as an unknown. After that, I attended my first training camp.

This was my chance, but right before training camp started, I got a respiratory infection. My first week was an uphill battle—I felt exhausted, slow, and weak. I couldn't catch my breath. I was doing my best, but nothing could make up for the fact that I was sick and playing against incredible players in top form.

The next week, I felt better and was able to bring more to the ice, but it wasn't enough to crack the roster. Still, at the end, the coach told me, "We saw a completely different player from the first week to the next." It consoled me to know they saw potential. I was added to the extended roster, which meant I could get called up if there were injuries. That season I played four games, not a lot, but enough to tell me I could compete with the best. It may have been only four games, but to play again, and at the highest level, was fulfilling a goal I had long since given up on.

I set myself a new goal, another big one: next year, I would make the roster. I wasn't going to be unprepared again, so I trained all year. My life was hockey, training, and work. Not much time for a social life, but it paid off. In September 2017, I made the full roster for the 2017–18 season, one year after my first training camp, and sixteen months after returning to the sport. I felt on top of the world.

As soon as I got the news, I called my parents. They had seen first-hand how hard I worked and were the biggest supporters of my return to hockey.

When they answered the phone, I screamed, "I made it!" On the other end of the line, my mom and dad cheered and told me how proud they were. It was the culmination of a full year of tireless effort since that first training camp. I wanted to make my parents proud, and this accomplishment finally made me feel like I had. I knew I couldn't have done it without their endless love and support.

The summer before the 2017–18 season, I learned more about other trans athletes in sport. Notably, Harrison Browne, who had come out earlier that year in the National Women's Hockey League to a positive reception from their fans, and Team USA athlete Chris Mosier, who was at the time featured in a Nike Ad. They both inspired me.

Seeing these positive representations, I began to wonder if I could

Here I am in action against Boston in December 2018. When I'm playing hockey I always give my all. I always want to be the best I can be.
(Lori Bolliger)

have an impact like them if I came out. Being a professional athlete would give me a platform to show others that they can live a life they've always dreamed of, they can be their true self, and most importantly, they can be happy.

Coming out was a big decision, not one I took lightly, and I thought long and hard about whether I should do it. I reached out to Chris Mosier and he provided valuable insights, outlining what I should be prepared to face. I talked it over with my family, many of my friends, and my fiancée, Kelly, who was my then girlfriend of about three months, and they all gave me their support. If anything bad was going to happen, I knew there were people who would have my back.

All my life, all I wanted to do was fit in. Because that definition of "normal" was ingrained in me growing up, I didn't want people to know about my history. I wanted them just to know me as the happy woman I had grown into. If I came out, I knew that I would no longer be labelled as a hockey player—I would be "the trans hockey player." People would know I was born male, and some might disparage me because of it.

But I also knew that sharing my story would show others with similar experiences that life does get better and that they can have the life they've always dreamed of. I didn't want others to suffer as I had for so long. There are way too many negative portrayals of trans women in the media—most news stories are about violent beatings or murder: it was time for some good news. Ultimately, the positives outweighed the negatives and I knew that my coming out would lead to more good than bad.

Over the next few months, I came out four times, first to the league, next to my coaches, then my team, and finally, publicly. Each time I came out with the backing and support of the previous group I had told, so I knew someone was in my corner in case I was met with a negative reaction. I prepared for the worst because I didn't know what to expect, but I was pleasantly surprised with the support and acceptance I was shown by everyone in the women's hockey community.

Out of everyone, I was most scared to tell my teammates. I didn't want to go back to the way things were when I was younger and feel like I didn't belong in the locker room. The coaches called a meeting before practice for me, so there was no backing out. They came in the room, turned the meeting over to me, and then all eyes were on me.

I clutched the sheet of paper with the words I had wanted to share and began to read. I opened myself up to the team, sharing my story and my plans. As I spoke, I scanned the room and saw my teammates react with smiles on their faces. When I was done, I stepped out of the room to give them space to digest the information. Shortly after, many of my teammates came out to give me a hug and tell me how proud they were of me.

Nothing changed in the locker room after that. My teammates were so supportive that I didn't have to be on guard. And it made me a better player. Instead of devoting energy to being prepared in case someone harassed me, I could give that extra effort to my game. Being true to myself allowed me to lose myself in the game—and enjoy it that much more.

I did endure plenty of negative feedback, though. Too many times I heard that I didn't deserve to play hockey with women, I didn't belong in the CWHL, and I had an unfair advantage. Some people simply told me to "burn in hell." All of these aggressive comments came from people online, typically through anonymous accounts. I still hear such comments, unfortunately, although less frequently. They're usually made by people who aren't educated about what a trans athlete must go through and the guidelines they follow in order to participate in elite sports. They think that to compete, I simply had to identify as a female with no medical intervention and that I kept the same levels of testosterone and muscle I had before I transitioned. They hate me, simply for existing in a way that brings me happiness.

These are just a few of the many misconceptions about trans women in sports, misconceptions that I want to correct. When someone attributes a trans woman's athletic ability to her testosterone and muscle, they're saying her ability is a product of how she was born. That attitude is based in the thinking that, first, men are inherently better than women in sports, and second, that a trans woman retains the advantages that testosterone provides men. The problem with the first view is that not all men are better than all women just because they are men, and more importantly, it's insulting and wrong to consider a trans woman a man. As for the second view, trans women lose a lot of speed and muscle mass when they transition, and in my experience, they often have lower levels of testosterone than the average cisgender female—if they have any testosterone at all.

I'm proof of that. In less than a year, I went from being one of the quickest runners to struggling to keep up with average players. I've been working out and training almost nonstop for three years now, and I can only bench-press around what I could in my grade-eleven gym class. The effect transition has on the human body is staggering. To say that I have an advantage because of how I was born is an insult that ignores the countless hours I've spent training to play at an elite level.

Transgender and gender nonconforming people are often pushed out of sport because they don't feel that they belong or that they can participate safely, whether that has to do with using the shared change rooms or with being harassed by other players and even teammates. My ultimate goal is to help make the hockey culture I grew up in more inclusive and accepting to both trans people and women.

The women I play with have grown up playing a male-dominated sport where they have been ridiculed for being women; they've been forced to change in closet-sized rooms just to play the game. I witnessed it with the girls I played with when I was young and heard about it from my new teammates. And currently, women's hockey lacks the resources required to produce the best players possible. Many of us have to work full-time and play hockey on the side, which means much of our training and practicing takes a backseat because there isn't enough time in the day. We're overworked. We also use second-rate gear and have limited access to trainers, physical therapists, equipment managers, and all the other benefits afforded to professional men's hockey players without question. Many young boys dream of playing professionally and reaping the rewards the NHL provides, but young girls don't get to dream that dream. For professional women players, it's all about how much you sacrifice to play the game you love. You play it out of passion, and passion alone. Because women in hockey have had to fight these barriers their whole careers, they are more empathetic and open to others entering the sport—perhaps the first step in changing men's hockey culture is to look at women's hockey.

Hockey, and sport in general, is often seen as something that brings people together. Why, though, is it often used to divide people? Why are you only invited if you are a cisgender, white male; while anyone seen as other has to fight for their spot and "earn" their acceptance? We are all human, and it's time we started treating everyone else as human, too.

Sharing my insight on equality and equity in sport and how to foster an inclusive and positive environment at Fortune's Most Powerful Women event in 2019.

I used to feel like an outsider, like I didn't belong in my own body, let alone on the ice. I pretended that I was happy, but inside, I felt like I was missing out on the life I should have been living. I was in such a negative spot in my life. I had to make a choice: give up the sport I loved or my happiness. I chose to give up hockey. I was lucky to be surrounded by incredible, supportive people. And as it turned out, I didn't have to give up hockey entirely, though the break I took from playing did help me grow. In the end, I was more than lucky—I was able to create a new life for myself, one in which I was happy and had hockey, in which I fulfilled an old dream I thought I had to give up. I had to go through hell and back to realize that dream, to know who I was and what I stood for. No one should have to do that.

I decided to share my story so people could know someone who is trans, learn more about who we are, and see that we are more than just our transness. Yes, that is an aspect of our lives, but just like everyone else, we should be defined by our character and what we bring to the table, on and off the ice.

Jessica Platt is the first openly transgender woman to play professional hockey in North America and an outspoken advocate for transgender rights. From 2016 to 2019, she played for the Toronto Furies in the CWHL and in 2019–20 was a member of the PWHPA. A You Can Play ambassador, she was also recognized as one of Canada's top twenty-five Women of Influence in 2018. She lives in Kitchener, Ontario, with her fiancée.

 *@jplatt32*

The Numbers Game

Alexandra Mandrycky

When it comes to hockey analytics, my biggest joy isn't identifying the superstars; it's finding the hidden gems. I get excited when I break down the numbers, the data, and the analytics and discover a player who has slipped through the cracks in other organizations and gone unnoticed. That, to me, is a win.

Most people working in the NHL today grew up playing the game—or at least watching it. Not me. I was never a rink rat and never had posters of my favourite hockey players on my bedroom walls. It was later in life that I came to hockey—and that story is a love story.

I grew up in Atlanta, Georgia. The only exposure I had to hockey was from my dad, who was from Philadelphia and was a big Flyers fan, but even he didn't have the NHL TV package, or anything like it. I don't think I ever saw hockey on television until high school. Only two people I knew growing up played the game, and I always wondered why they didn't play basketball, soccer, or football instead. I guess you could say I contributed to the Thrashers' doomed future in Atlanta— Winnipeg seems like a much better hockey environment, although there is certainly still a healthy contingent of hockey fans in Atlanta.

Back then, if anyone had told me that I'd one day be working in the front office of an NHL team, I'd have said it was the craziest thing I'd ever heard.

It wasn't that I didn't like sports. I was a competitive rower, taking after my dad, who had been a rower in college. Both my parents rowed together as adults, so it was natural for me to get into the sport, too.

When I started high school, I actually was thinking about becoming a lawyer. I wanted to be Elle Woods from *Legally Blonde*, but I quickly realized that I had a natural aptitude for math. In my calculus, physics, and statistics courses, I was often at the top of my class. I figured I could probably have a secure career in numbers and avoid law school altogether.

So my choice to study industrial engineering at Georgia Tech was a practical one, though once I was there, I found I really enjoyed what I was doing. In high school, anyone taking a computer science class only talked about making computer games. I wasn't interested in that and so I didn't take any computer science classes. Until Georgia Tech. That's when I learned that technology powers everything and that I could use computers to do cool things far beyond games, including analyze hockey statistics—but that's where the love part of the story comes in.

In my senior year of high school, I met a guy named Christian through a competitive rowing club. Christian was the captain of the men's squad, and I was the captain of the women's squad. I guess you could say we are classic high school sweethearts because we began dating and both went to Georgia Tech together to study engineering.

One of the first things I discovered about Christian was that he was a huge Buffalo Sabres fan. Every time I went to see him, a hockey game would be on his TV, and I quickly learned that I was supposed to hate the Toronto Maple Leafs and the Boston Bruins. The first rule in watching hockey with Christian was: Go Buffalo. Boo Boston. Boo Toronto.

Partly because of Christian, but partly also because of the game itself, I got pretty into hockey. I knew all the players' names before I even went to my first NHL game when the Sabres came to Atlanta to play the Thrashers in the spring of 2010.

Buffalo was in the running for the Stanley Cup, which meant Christian and I were watching every single Sabres game. The team made it to the first round of the playoffs and faced off against Boston. I loyally booed Boston, but it wasn't enough and the Sabres lost the

Christian and I at my first NHL game, Buffalo Sabres against the Atlanta Thrashers on March 16, 2010.

series 4–2. But I was hooked. I loved watching players break away and score a goal in just a few seconds.

Meanwhile I was taking an intense course load at school, including a class called Intro to Statistics in which we did a mini-homework assignment using baseball data. That came in handy a year later when I had to make a point to Christian about why I thought a certain hockey player was good.

This player had a fair amount of goals and assists, but Christian didn't like the way that he was playing. I was still new to the game.

"I'm going to prove it to you," I said, remembering my statistics class. Maybe I could find some hockey data.

I assumed that hockey stats were available somewhere and set out to find the info I needed to win my argument. Unlike baseball, there were no official websites that collected all the player data. Instead, I stumbled upon a whole world of people online who, on their own time and on their own computers, were compiling hockey data and writing blog posts about their findings. Their research went beyond goals, assists, and penalties and used advanced stats to evaluate the total impact of the player when he was on the ice. For example, does the player cause or prevent the other team from scoring? He may score goals himself, but is he helping his teammates score more goals, too? Goals are the way that games are won, but hockey is a team sport, so it's about collaboration. Advanced metrics take into account the context of the game instead of relying on old box-score stats alone.

When I looked closer at the stats, I realized that Christian was right about that player I thought was a strong asset to the team. Turns out, he didn't have that positive of an impact on the other players, just himself.

As I said, I was still new to the game and I hadn't yet learned how to best watch hockey, but data was definitely my way in.

I had a Twitter account and followed everyone who was talking about hockey stats online. I didn't actively engage in the conversation, but I would read their posts and then do my own analysis on my computer. I was getting an entire education in hockey and players, and I soaked up the information like a sponge. I didn't consider hockey analysis as a career path; it was a passion project.

One of my favourite websites was called ExtraSkater.com and I wasn't the only one who was a fan. In August 2014, the Toronto Maple Leafs hired its creator, Darryl Metcalf, as an analyst, and after that, he had to shut the site down. Little did I know that this would set in motion a series of events that would take me to the upper echelons of the hockey world.

Not long after ExtraSkater.com went down, Sam Ventura and Andrew C. Thomas—two guys from Carnegie-Mellon University— realized the hockey data community needed a resource and they decided to launch a hockey analytics website of their own.

They had previously created a computer program—similar to what was being used elsewhere in hockey and other sports—that would allow the user to analyze stats and create charts. They wrote a code that compiled all the NHL data. All a user had to do was download the code—and the data—onto their computer and run their own statistical models. For anyone who had a passion for hockey analytics, this was big. Now they planned to expose the results of this computer program to the world via a website.

Labor Day weekend of 2014, they launched War-on-Ice.com. WAR is a baseball acronym for Wins Above Replacement, a calculation that uses math to evaluate how good a player really is. What Sam and Andrew were doing was creating a metric for hockey's version of WAR— not just the statistic but an activity that the game often resembles.

A couple of months later, another popular hockey website was shutting down. This time it was a sad story. Matthew Wuest, the founder of CapGeek.com, a website that covered player salary statistics and the NHL salary cap, was unwell. Matt's work was invaluable to the hockey community.

In January 2015, Sam and Andrew put out a call on Twitter: "If anyone wants to help us put up salary data on our website, let us know. We think it should be publicly available."

I answered immediately. As someone who hadn't grown up playing or watching hockey, I'd been drawn to the business side of the sport. I'd never be an expert in scouting players, but I knew I could become an expert in salaries and a market. By that time, I had graduated from Georgia Tech and was consulting for a few different companies. I didn't have a ton of extra time, but I saw War-on-Ice as a gateway into the hockey analytics world and a way of giving back to a community I had gained so much from.

I guess I impressed Sam and Andrew because they brought me on to spearhead the salaries and contracts section of the website, along with helping improve some of their interactive visualizations. I was excited to join the fray and engage with people I had respected and followed for a while. Andrew, Sam, and I worked really well together and we all brought different things to the table. They weren't that much older than me, but they had more experience in statistics than I had; they also came from an academic background and were used to teaching classes, so they were really good at showing me the ropes in the beginning. On the other hand, I had experience working with larger databases and in web development, and I was able to improve some of the interfaces to enhance the user experience.

Working on War-on-Ice was a real labour of love. And when I say labour, I mean it. I ended up regularly putting in at least forty extra hours a week above and beyond my regular job.

I'd wake up early in the morning and work on War-on-Ice before going to my real job. On the West Coast, the hockey games started at four p.m., so at that time, I'd shut off my work computer, fire up my War-on-Ice computer, and spend another six or seven hours working on the data and watching hockey before heading to bed.

By then, Christian and I had gotten married and moved to Seattle, where he was getting a PhD in bioengineering at the University of Washington. There were nights when he would look at me and say, "Can you not be at the computer?" Which I always found funny seeing as he was the one who'd got me into hockey in the first place.

The truth is, I never saw those hours on War-on-Ice as work. Anyone who's volunteered somewhere knows you always have the option not to. But that wasn't the case for me, I could never not do the work, and I was so happy to be part of the hockey analytics community.

In August of 2015, I'd been working on the website for about eight months during which time Andrew had been in conversation with a few different NHL teams. He felt he could add a lot of value as an analyst at a higher level. When he told me that he was talking to the Minnesota Wild, I was genuinely thrilled for him. I personally hadn't thought of my hockey analyst work as a career option, so when he came back from a meeting with the Wild and said, "I hope you don't mind, but I told them that they should talk to you as well," I thought he was kidding.

He wasn't. I was honoured that Andrew respected me and my work enough to mention my name, but I also thought he was insane for thinking I was ready for a job like that.

Andrew didn't see it that way. His pitch to the Minnesota Wild was

*How I spent my evenings—hockey on the TV, computer
code on the laptop, cat next to me.*

that he could do a lot of the statistical models, but to truly have an impact on the team, they needed someone who could work with the technology and help build the database. Basically, had they thought about how they were going to display Andrew's numbers in a way that would make people want to look at them?

The Wild hired Andrew as their lead hockey researcher. Shortly after, I was on a jobsite with a client in my consulting business when I got a call from Shep Harder, who at the time was the director of hockey administration for the Minnesota Wild. I stepped outside to answer. Shep was wondering if I might come out to the Wild's training camp and meet with him and some of his colleagues.

"Why don't you stay for a few days and we can see if there is a fit here?" he asked.

I didn't know how to respond, so I simply said, "Okay." And went back to talk to my client. On the outside, I had to pretend that everything was fine, but inside, my mind was racing. I didn't know what to expect when I got to Minnesota, but I was eager to find out.

In September, I flew out. During my meeting with the Wild, I was told a bit about their scouting operation. They were all set on that front, but I realized that they could use some help not only in hockey analysis but also with data storage and distribution—just as Andrew had suggested. It was a skill set that they didn't necessarily have in their front office. Everyone was really receptive to my feedback and they offered me a consulting job.

The first thing I did when I got back to my hotel room after the meeting was send Christian a picture of myself wearing a Minnesota Wild jacket that the people from the team had gifted me. I was in disbelief that I had just broken into the world of professional hockey analytics.

In the beginning, I worked remotely as a consultant and would send the coaches reports on players already in the organization that they were asking about. This was for a trial period, in order to make sure what I was doing was a fit on both sides. To a certain extent, I didn't know what I had gotten myself into, and the first few months were a chance for me to see if I wanted to ditch my day job and do analysis full-time, which I did.

By December of that year, I told the Wild, "If you guys want me to be here all the time, I can move to Minnesota."

I felt it was important to be around the team and the organization to familiarize myself with how the NHL worked and how analytics could serve the organization best. I think they felt the same way I did because they agreed.

I called Christian, who was still working on his PhD in Seattle. "Soooo, I might be moving to Minnesota."

He was understandably a little stunned because we hadn't really discussed the possibility, but fortunately, he ended up being okay with it. He knew how much I loved what I was doing and we were both willing to make the sacrifice. For the next four years, he stayed in Seattle with our cat and I lived in Minnesota, traveling back and forth to see him every few weeks as my schedule allowed. I didn't expect long distance to be as difficult as it was, but one of the saving graces was just how much I loved my work with the Wild.

When I first got to Minnesota, I was very self-conscious about the fact that I didn't know every hockey player who had ever played the game. But it turned out that being unaware of some hockey history actually worked in my favour. Guy Lapointe was one of the top amateur scouts for the Wild and one of the nicest people. After I met him, I called Christian and said, "I met this person named Guy. I think he is good at hockey and was a Hall of Famer or something."

"Oh my God," Christian said, shocked. "I hope you didn't say that out loud to anyone!"

Little things like that happened all the time, but as I said, it worked to my advantage because I was never intimidated working with these hockey greats. I always respected them, but I wasn't afraid to work with them and even have a little fun.

After I read Ken Dryden's *The Game*, I learned that Guy was the prank master of hockey. He ended up teaching me a few of his pranks, and I'm proud to say that I pulled off a few of them, though I think Guy played along a few times just to let me have my fun.

I also realized that I wasn't in Minnesota to be a Rolodex of hockey stats. The team had scouts for that. If the Wild just wanted someone who knew everything they already knew themselves, they wouldn't have asked me to be in the room with them. I look at hockey from a different perspective than someone who has been involved in the game for years, and as a result, I have something unique to add to the conversation.

Having different viewpoints was something that the Wild valued. In Minnesota, the analysts would take the scout reports and look for an analytical and numerical reading to help us better evaluate players. I would be involved in any scouting meeting, on both the pro and the amateur side. A scout would talk about how a certain player was playing and then I'd chime in with, "Here's what the numbers are saying." Scouts and analysts don't always agree, but I never noticed eye rolls while I was speaking. Afterwards, people always seemed to ask me more questions.

Whether you're a scout or an analyst, everyone is trying to accomplish the same goal; they just do it in different ways. I made sure I never went into a meeting saying, "The numbers say this. This is the absolute truth, and I won't hear any other opinion." I wanted to hear what the scouts and the management had to say—and learn what they were picking up on that I wasn't—then use the numbers to help them make their decisions. In this way, I felt accepted by the hockey staff in Minnesota, and over time, I earned their respect.

When Christian and I had first moved out to Seattle, we kept hearing stories that the city would be getting an NHL team. It was always in the back of our minds and I would think, *Oh, wouldn't it be crazy if things ended up working out and I got a job with Seattle?* But it was just a joke between us. I was happily working for the Wild and saw a long future of data and analytics. Who knew when that deal would even go through?

Fast-forward three years to 2018: Seattle was awarded an NHL franchise, with Jerry Bruckheimer as the principal owner and Tod Leiweke as the team president. Then in 2019, I got a call from the Seattle NHL franchise offering me a job as their director of hockey strategy and research. I sent Christian a note: "Remember that thing we always joked about? It may actually be happening."

We were both so excited because we loved the city so much, and this was a once-in-a-lifetime opportunity for me to work for an expansion team. I would've gone to the moon to do that. I jumped at the chance to be a part of a brand-new team, and of course, to live in the same city as my husband.

I knew that Jerry Bruckheimer was a successful Hollywood producer. However, I had no idea how much he loved hockey. When I met him, I quickly discovered that he is a huge hockey nerd. I remember someone took a photo of me sitting with Tod and Jerry having coffee. When I saw it, I couldn't help but think how I was just a kid from Atlanta who had never watched hockey growing up, and there I was sitting next to one of the owners of the NHL team I was working for, the guy who produced *Top Gun* and *Pirates of the Caribbean*.

While I was proud to be one of the first employees hired in Seattle, I also felt an immense amount of responsibility. When you go to an existing franchise and have to make changes, it's easy to ask,

"Why would someone set it up like this?" When you are with a new franchise, it's your job to help lay the foundation for years to come. Whatever you do at the beginning will be what other people complain about in the future! But in all seriousness, it's an incredible opportunity. Seattle is very forward thinking and we constantly ask ourselves if we're doing something a certain way because that's how it's always been done or if there's another better way. It's exciting to know my fingerprints, so to speak, will be a big part of the team.

When I first came to Seattle, the team hadn't yet chosen a general manager, which was a little nerve-racking. I didn't know whom I'd be reporting to. Fortunately, Seattle couldn't have asked for a better person to lead the franchise from the beginning than Ron Francis. Not only did he have an amazing twenty-three-season playing career with the Hartford Whalers, Pittsburgh Penguins, Carolina Hurricanes, and Toronto Maple Leafs, which included two Stanley Cups, but his career as an executive, working as director of hockey operations, then general manager, then president of hockey operations for the Hurricanes, was impressive as well. Because he's worked on different sides of the business, he has a real respect for each department and how it fits together with the others to make a winning team.

The population of Seattle is excited about the first season of its hockey team in 2021. Anywhere I go, if I'm wearing official team gear, I get stopped by people who want to talk about the arena or the team name. Everyone is either on the season-ticket waiting list or has a friend who is.

As for me, I've embraced the challenge of using my knowledge to help the team find the players who will help them become a winner. I love discovering those hidden gems, but one of the greatest things about working for the Seattle NHL team is the emphasis on hiring diversity. Over half of our VPs are women and one of our top pro scouts is a legend of women's hockey, Cammi Granato.

In Minnesota, I had gotten used to going into scouting meetings and being the only woman in the room. I was always taken seriously because I knew what I was talking about, but just as it's important

Ricky Olczyk (assistant general manager), Ron Francis
(general manager), and myself in fall 2019.
(Courtesy of NHL Seattle)

to have different viewpoints from scouts and analysts, it's important to have different viewpoints from men and women, and from people of different backgrounds.

In early 2020, I had a scouting meeting and there was Cammi. Imagine that—two women in an NHL hockey operations department, making decisions and talking about players. How many other NHL franchises can say that? It was truly something special.

What Cammi Granato is doing as a pro scout is way more impressive than my story. After all, there is such a rich history of pro scouts in the NHL: most of them are men and, on top of that, men who have played the game at the NHL level. Having analysts in the NHL is a more recent development; these departments have only been around for five or six years, so there aren't as many barriers for women. But when I look at Cammi and women like Noelle Needham and Hayley Wickenheiser with the Toronto Maple Leafs, I see progress. And the more women who are working in the NHL, the better the chance that there will be a female general manager of a team one day.

I'm a big believer in giving people a helping hand. Back when I was working on War-on-Ice, I wouldn't have believed you if you said in five years I'd be in the NHL doing a job that didn't exist at the time for a team that didn't exist at the time. While I certainly proved that I belonged in this world, I credit Andrew for seeing my potential and giving me the push that I needed. I wouldn't have gotten here on my own. To be honest, I wish it wasn't a big deal that I'm a woman in analytics, but because I know it is, I feel it's important to be an advocate for other women and to show them that they can be analysts or scouts or work in hockey operations. You don't have to grow up playing hockey either. I didn't. I fell in love with hockey because I fell in love with numbers. Everything else fell into place.

Alexandra Mandrycky is the director of hockey strategy and research for the Seattle NHL franchise. Previously she worked for four years as a hockey analyst with the Minnesota Wild. An Atlanta native, she now lives with her husband, Christian, her son, Desmond, and cat, Luna, in Seattle, Washington.

 *@AlexMandrycky*

Hockey Proud

Jeff McLean and Dean Petruk

Jeff McLean

One of the lines we always said was, "We make the tape. You make it powerful." But we had no idea how powerful it would be to see players wrapping their sticks with Pride Tape. Those are the folks making it happen. Otherwise, it's just tape.

It all started with Bill Ranford. You know him as the NHL goalie who brought the Stanley Cup to Edmonton in 1990, but I first met Bill in an elementary school on a Canadian military base in Germany years earlier. His dad was in the military and so was mine, and we quickly became best friends.

I'm a Canadian Air Force and Navy brat. I was born in Halifax, Nova Scotia, but throughout my father's twenty-eight years in the service, I lived all over Canada. Everywhere I went, I played hockey— really poorly, to be honest. I made it to juvenile hockey, and that's about it, but I loved the game.

Fast-forward to 1998; Bill put me in touch with a guy named Dean Petruk. At that time I was living in Edmonton, working in graphic design and communications. Dean and Bill were looking for someone to help them promote a few NHL alumni events. One event was in Jackson Hole, Wyoming, and the other was in Aspen, Colorado, where the NHL Alumni All-Stars faced off against the 1980 USA Olympic hockey team. Would I be interested in doing the logos and graphic event promotions?

I couldn't pass up such an amazing opportunity and jumped at the chance to connect with the hockey world.

Dean and I immediately hit it off. Dean hailed from Edmonton and learned to play hockey on the outdoor rinks of Alberta. He had just recently moved to Vancouver and got into retail sales, but he'd been involved with the NHL Alumni and the Players' Association for a number of years.

We both loved hockey, so we had lots to talk about, and chumming around with our hockey heroes at these events was a dream come true for both of us.

We would fly to Alumni events a week early and spend all day and night getting everything ready. It was a lot of work, but it was a labour of love, and the best part was that we got to be flies on the wall for some awesome hockey games played by our childhood idols, and even hang out in the dressing room and hear all their stories.

Ever since those first events, Dean and I have been friends. We both had real jobs, but whenever there was an opportunity to get involved in a hockey project, we were there.

In 2012, my love of hockey and my day job were about to intersect in a big way. I was working for Calder-Bateman Communications, an advertising and public relations company, on a very special project. With Dr. Kristopher Wells from the University of Alberta's Institute for Sexual Minority Studies and Services, the Calder-Bateman team created a website called NoHomophobes.com to track homophobic tweets in real time. The site is still active today.

As we looked at the data, we discovered that homophobic tweets spike during sporting events. That got all of us thinking that our next pro bono advertising campaign should be about homophobia in sports. With Dr. Wells, we decided we'd focus on hockey because there aren't any "out" NHL hockey players and we had lots of connections to the NHL world in Edmonton—I knew Bill, of course, and Dr. Wells knew Andrew Ference and other members of the Oilers organization, notably Tim Shipton.

But was the NHL ready for something like this? I asked Bill—he said it was time. The Oilers were on board, too.

We wanted to show that everyone is welcome on the ice, in the dressing room, and in the stands. A teammate is a teammate and the sexuality of a player shouldn't matter.

We envisioned a traditional campaign with a central image that would last a couple of months at the height of the playing season. If the idea was strong enough, somebody might pick it up beyond the Edmonton area, and if it went national, even better. At the beginning, that was the plan.

Now came the hard part: coming up with an image to convey our message. I mulled this over as I was driving to work one day. Full disclosure—all my ideas come to me while I'm in the car. In my head, I went through my mental Rolodex of all the gear that a hockey player wears. The helmet sticker had been done, the armband had been done, the special jerseys had been done. What was something else that the player could do himself? Something that would be more of an independent choice?

Tape. Bingo.

When I got to work, I pulled a stock photo of somebody taping up his stick and Photoshopped different colours. The image looked pretty cool.

The next day, I was in the car again and I thought, *What if we could actually make a tape with the Pride colours?* I knew there were repeat patterns for hockey tape that featured everything from Team Canada to Batman logos. What if the repeat patterns were different colours? We could make a rainbow. If we could pull this off, it would take our campaign to a whole other level beyond just an image.

I called up Dean.

Dean Petruk

From the minute Jeff told me about the campaign to eliminate ho-mophobia in hockey, I was behind the idea a hundred percent. I grew up playing the game—got as far as the juvenile level—and I knew the kind of things that are said in hockey. We've all been in those dressing rooms and heard homophobic language used.

Now, as a father myself, I see how open and accepting my kids' generation is of everyone. While the world has changed a lot since my day or even my parents' day, we still struggle to make hockey a safe and inclusive space, especially for the LGBTQ+ community. Even today.

When Jeff showed me his idea for Pride Tape, it was a drawing he'd made on a napkin. A napkin! But as someone in retail, I knew right away that this was going to be big and immediately started thinking of ways to produce the tape as a product.

Together, we hoped Pride Tape would help ensure that acceptance and inclusion became the norm. But first, we would need to make the tape. And to do that, we needed money.

On December 16, 2015, Calder-Bateman created a forty-five-day Kickstarter campaign to raise $50,000. That would allow us to produce ten thousand rolls of Pride Tape and other Kickstarter rewards. It was such a bright and colourful image—it would only take a small amount to stand out.

Cheryl Meger at Calder-Bateman spearheaded the entire thing. Using a prototype for the tape, she organized a traditional PR event at the University of Alberta to launch the idea of Pride Tape and the Kickstarter campaign. This caught the attention of the Edmonton Oil-ers, and they said they would promote the tape by using it during their upcoming skills competition.

Calder-Bateman put up posters and billboards with an image of Pride Tape, and Global TV shot the Kickstarter video starring Andrew Ference and an Edmonton Pee Wee hockey club and ran it on their station. Thanks to their efforts, we were able to raise a fair amount of money within the first few weeks, but we stalled just short of our target.

Who saved the day? Well, Bill Ranford, of course.

Jeff

During the campaign, I met up with Bill in Calgary. He is the goaltending coach of the LA Kings and they were in town to play the Flames. Brian Burke was the president of hockey operations at the Flames then and so was also around. Bill suggested that Brian might want to get involved in Pride Tape and offered to be the buffer.

Brian had cofounded You Can Play, an organization dedicated to the eradication of homophobia in sports. His son, Brendan Burke, was one of the first people within the hockey world to come out, but just a few years earlier, he had tragically passed away in a car accident. Given Brian's connection to Alberta and to You Can Play, it seemed only fitting to approach him about Pride Tape.

Bill spoke to Brian and let him know that we were good friends, which paved the way for me to meet with Brian and explain what we were trying to do with Pride Tape and the Kickstarter campaign.

Brian was really receptive. After our conversation, he invited us up to the suite for both the Flames and the Kings practices, which was pretty cool for a guy like me. But more importantly, Brian liked what we were all about and that meeting led to his family making a donation.

Right after that meeting, the Oilers held their skills competition and showcased the prototype of Pride Tape, which brought in many more donations.

Between the Oilers and the Burke family, we hit our goal with just two days to spare.

Pride Tape was a reality. It doesn't matter how great the idea is; at the end of the day, it's the people and the connections that make it work.

Speaking of connections, we got even more involved with You Can

Play through Dr. Wells, who knew their VP, Jillian Svensson, and I became a western Canadian ambassador for the organization.

As the project grew, everyone from the University of Alberta to the team at Calder-Bateman Communications got really excited, including my boss and mentor, Frank Calder. I'd be in a meeting or on a phone call in my office and Frank would pop in and drop a napkin on my desk that said something like "Detroit is in" or "San Jose is in."

All the teams from around the NHL were lending their support to the project. Each time they called, Frank would write it on a napkin and drop it on my desk. My biggest regret about the Pride Tape initiative is that I didn't save those napkins!

As the first rolls of Pride Tape were being produced, we reached out to Dean to leverage his expertise and ensure that Pride Tape could become a reality, not only nationally, but around the world.

Dean

In early 2016, we received our very first shipment of Pride Tape. I was so proud to send rolls to all the friends of the Kickstarter campaign—this was something that society was missing and it was incredibly humbling to be a part of it.

After that, though, I think both Jeff and I wondered if Pride Tape would, if you'll excuse the pun, stick. Would players actually use it?

The answer was yes.

I'll never forget the first time I saw a girl walk into the arena wearing Pride Tape. I was almost in tears. With shaking hands, I pulled out my phone and snapped a blurry photo to send to Jeff.

That was just the beginning. Between my kids playing hockey and my own work at hockey charity events, I'm at a rink at least six days a week, and now I see the tape at every rink I go to. These young men and women are using it for no other reason than to show support. To think that one roll of hockey tape—one piece of tape—could have such an impact is amazing to me. Pride Tape was so much bigger than all of us.

Jeff

Not long after the launch, a small-town Prairie coach and general manager asked to meet me to talk about Pride Tape. I headed to our meeting with a bunch of tape.

When I arrived, I sat down with the coach and he told me an unbelievable story. At midnight one Saturday, he got a call from one of his players. He was distressed, afraid of the caustic environment and hypermasculinity of a typical hockey dressing room. The coach went out to the railroad tracks and, thankfully, helped the player through his anxiety.

When the rest of the team found out about the incident, they told the coach that they wanted to get Pride Tape and put it on their sticks to show support for their teammate. They wanted him to know that they considered him a member of the team, a friend, and an equal.

That story was a gut punch. I happily gave the coach the tape for the team. And not only did the boys use the tape in their games, they also used it during their town's summer parade. The parade had nothing to do with hockey or LGBTQ+ pride, but the team wanted to march in it with Pride Tape on their sticks to show support for their teammate and to show the town that they believed in equality and inclusion.

In rural Canada, it was an especially brave thing to do.

We heard many more heartbreaking stories about young players who quit hockey because they felt it wasn't for them. But to see the power of others standing up for their friends and teammates by using Pride Tape was huge.

Another time, I drove, white-knuckled, through rural Alberta in the middle of winter to sell one roll of tape at a university hockey game that was happening during the school's Pride Week celebrations. I handed the tape to the student working the penalty box, but when the rest of the students found out who I was, they got excited. They asked if I would hand out the Player of the Game award, which was a couple of toques—talk about being Canadian!—and I happily did. Some of the kids were in tears meeting me because of the tape. To them, Pride Tape was a lot more than just hockey tape.

Dean

In the beginning, Jeff and I would often say, "Can you imagine if one player put this tape on their stick for a moment?" That was our goal. Little did we know that this would be one milestone of many.

Players are very particular about how they tape their stick and what color tape they use. We were thinking that a player might use some Pride Tape on the grip of their stick or on their blade during a

Here we are at the NHL offices for our first meeting with Paul LaCaruba and Jessica Berman to talk about Pride Tape. I am on the left and Jeff is on the right.

warm-up, then they could switch back to their preferred tape in time for the game. It was up to each player how they wanted to show their support, so we created a Pride Tape user manual.

With the help of You Can Play and Paul LaCaruba at the NHL, we reached out to teams in the NHL, NWHL, and CWHL and fostered relationships with potential ambassadors. On every team in every league, there were key players who wanted to help. Without their efforts, Pride Tape wouldn't exist outside Alberta.

When we rolled out Pride Tape, the NHL began sending us videos of players wrapping their sticks with it in the quiet of the dressing room. All we could hear was the sound of the tape going around the blade of the stick. It was incredible.

After that, Pride Tape became much more than just a bright and colourful accessory. The players were sending the message to the league and to the world that they were standing up for equality and inclusion, and they were doing it without even saying a single word.

And sometimes they did speak up. One time, a few trolls jumped on a social media thread on the Tampa Bay Lightning Twitter account and were extremely negative about Pride Tape and what it stood for. The Lightning responded with, "Look, if this is the way you feel, you're not welcome in our arena."

Jeff

In 2017, the NHL began hosting Pride nights for each team. Sometimes at these events, guys would put the Pride Tape on their sticks, do a couple of laps, and then they would swap it out for their game sticks. At first, only the home teams would use Pride Tape during warm-ups. The Boston Bruins sported the tape during their warm-up when they hosted the Vancouver Canucks. When the Canucks saw the Pride Tape, they told us they wanted to support the cause, too.

In February, Dean and I were in Los Angeles for the Kings' Pride Night game. Bill Ranford was there, of course, and the day before the game, we went to see the Kings practice at their multiplex facility.

*Kris and I getting the VIP treatment from the Oilers' Tim Shipton
for their "Hockey Is for Everyone" game featuring Pride Tape.*

Brent Sopel—another Calgary native—was running a fantasy camp at the rink next door. He walked up to us and said, "Boys, I see what you're doing and it's so amazing. I want to put the tape on my stick."

We gave him a roll and watched as he put the tape on right in front of us, then he stepped on the ice and ran the camp.

To have Brent search us out and embrace the tape was a special moment.

The night of the game was even more special because for the first time, every player on the ice in that arena—no matter the team, where they were from, or what they believed in—wrapped their sticks in Pride Tape and used those sticks for the entire warm-up.

I remember standing with Dean at the corner of the arena, watching the warm-up. We could hardly believe it. Between Dr. Wells and Calder-Bateman, we had all helped create this little thing and it mattered to people. It was a very humbling moment.

Dean

From there, Pride Tape went viral. In just four years we went from hand-delivering a few rolls here and there to Alberta rinks, to shipping tape to twenty-one countries throughout the world. In Canada, we've sold tape in every territory and province; in the United States, we've sold tape in all fifty states. Jeff and I have kept our day jobs and volunteer our time for Pride Tape. Any profits go to charities like You Can Play.

As the movement grew, we began getting letters, e-mails, text messages, and Instagram DMs from people all over the world telling us what the tape meant to them. And along with the messages came photos.

Every day, we receive four or five photos of Pride Tape. It could be someone out on the lake in Lake Louise, Alberta, or at an arena in the Madison Gay Hockey Association in Chicago, Illinois, or a young woman in the UK, or a team in Sweden. The photos are all over the map, and that's not even counting the photos we get from pro photographers like Kate Frese.

Everyone wants us to use the photos and promote LGBTQ+ inclusion, which just goes to show that we are all in this together. And we all believe that hockey is for everyone. The people all over the world taking photos of themselves using Pride Tape on their hockey sticks are the heroes and ambassadors for Pride Tape. Without them, we'd be nowhere.

From all the corners of the hockey world, we've connected with ambassadors: Tara Slone from *Hometown Hockey*; Harrison Browne, the first openly transgender player in professional hockey; the Calgary Pioneers, one of the first LGBTQ+ hockey teams in western Canada; the Edmonton Rage, a new LGBTQ+ team; Brynne Van Putten, who has been a member the Blades, LA's gay hockey team, for thirty years; Braden Holtby of the Washington Capitals; Mark Borowiecki of the Ottawa Senators; and legions of online ambassadors.

Including, of course, Kurtis Gabriel.

In February 2019, something really special happened. I was at home in Vancouver watching the New Jersey Devils face off against the Montreal Canadiens. It was an NHL Pride Night, and so as usual, the players wore Pride Tape on their sticks during the warm-up. When the game began, they swapped out their Pride sticks for their regular ones. But not everyone.

I phoned Jeff in Edmonton. "You've got to turn on the Devils-Canadiens game. I think there's a guy who still has Pride Tape on the end of his stick from the warm-up!"

It was Kurtis Gabriel, a forward for the New Jersey Devils. Up until then, no NHL player had used a stick with Pride Tape on it *during* a game. Jeff and I were both freaking out. Kurtis was in the penalty box and the camera zoomed in and we could see the stick leaning against the glass, the rainbow tape on the grip in all its glory.

The best part? The game was tied until Kurtis scored a goal against the Canadiens with that same stick, clinching the Devils' 2–1 win. He had made history.

Jeff

I had goose bumps watching that goal. Kurtis had single-handedly scored for acceptance, equality, and inclusion in sport.

We got in touch with Kurtis and asked if he would be willing to meet with us. We wanted to tell him in person just what a positive impact his use of Pride Tape had. He told us that he knew someone whose family wasn't supportive of her coming out and thought keeping the Pride Tape on his stick was a little gesture that might grow into something special and meaningful.

From then on, he always played with Pride Tape. The exposure that came from Kurtis's support was phenomenal.

After that, Dean and I made a pledge that we would treat ourselves to one regular game each year, and before the 2019–20 season, we told

Kurtis that this game would be wherever he was playing. That year, he was with the AHL Lehigh Phantoms in Allentown, Pennsylvania, and every game, his fans would take photos of him and his Pride stick and send them to us.

In early 2020, a young woman named Melissa reached out to us and invited us to the Lehigh Phantoms' Pride Night. It was kind of funny that we weren't being invited by Kurtis, but rather by his fans!

"My mom will pay for your flights and put you up in a hotel," she said.

The offer was so sweet; we couldn't help but smile. We assured her that we could pay our way there.

Dean and I had another event to attend just before in Buffalo, and so we flew into Hamilton and made the drive south. From there, we would make our way to Pennsylvania. As we drove through Ontario, I showed Dean all the back roads of Wainfleet, Dunnville, and Stoney Creek, where I had played midget hockey growing up. It was like old times way back when we first started doing the NHL Alumni events and reminisced about our hockey days.

When we got to the arena in Allentown, we sat with Melissa and her dad, who had season tickets. It was great to be in a smaller rink with these hard-core AHL fans.

At one point, Melissa said to me quietly, "Oh my God, if I could ever get a Kurtis Gabriel stick, that would be the greatest thing that ever happened to me."

The Phantoms were playing the following night, so that morning, I texted Kurtis and asked him if he had another stick kicking around.

He texted me back, "Absolutely! Come down and see me after the game, and I will have it all signed up for you."

It was like we were giving Melissa a new car.

What was even more special was that day after the Phantoms' Pride Night, a woman on social media came out that she was bisexual—she had been so inspired by the support.

To me, that weekend in Lehigh is what it is all about. These are people who really love the game and it doesn't matter who they are and where they come from. They love hockey and so do the players. And when they meet each other, it's magical. We are really blessed to be a part of it.

A quick snap of Kurtis Gabriel and Melissa
with his signed stick.

Dean

If we've learned anything, it's that the hockey world is one big family. When Jeff and I look back on Pride Tape, there are so many kismet moments that made it become what it has, starting with Bill Ranford, and spreading to Dr. Wells and Calder-Bateman. Out of all the projects that we've worked on in our careers, nothing comes remotely close to Pride Tape because of how much it means to people. At the end of the day, all we did was make the tape—it was everyone else who gave it power.

Jeff McLean is the senior art director at Ray Creative Agency. From Halifax, Nova Scotia, he now lives in Edmonton, Alberta. **Dean Petruk** is the founder and head of operations at CMS, a Vancouver-based retail management company. Originally from Edmonton, Alberta, he now lives in Vancouver, British Columbia. Together with Dr. Kris Wells, he created Pride Tape, an initiative to fight homophobia in hockey. In 2017, Pride Tape won gold for social good at the Clio Awards, a prestigious advertising competition, and was included in the permanent collection of the Hockey Hall of Fame.

 /PrideTape

 *@PrideTape*

Acknowledgements

Bob McKenzie

So many people to say thank you to, so here goes:

To Kevin Hanson and Simon & Schuster Canada, thank you for allowing me to be part of this *Everyday Hockey Heroes* family; it has been a personal game changer for me, a true inspiration.

Thank you to you, that is, anyone who has chosen to purchase or read this book. I know how valuable your time and money are. I hope you find these stories as interesting and uplifting as my coauthor Jim Lang, editor Sarah St. Pierre, and I did in assembling them.

Thank you to Jim and Sarah for their tireless efforts and immense contributions that, quite frankly, dwarf my own. Jim is a dynamo, who for the vast majority of these stories conducted the interviews, transcribed them, wrote, and rewrote them in conjunction with the subjects. Sarah is the heart and soul of *Everyday Hockey Heroes*. Her passion shines through as brightly as her meticulous eye for detail and unyielding desire for great storytelling. She is the best editor I've ever worked with.

Mostly, though, thank you to the seventeen individuals who so graciously, and in many cases courageously, agreed to have their stories told here. Many laid bare their souls and relived parts of their lives that weren't easy or comfortable. Yet they did it because they wanted to share their experiences, to contribute to our hockey community in the hope that the stories would help and inspire others.

And they have. Of that there is absolute no doubt in my mind. So to one and all, thank you and take care.

Jim Lang

In late August of 2019, I received a phone call from Bob McKenzie, asking me if I was interested in teaming up again to write a sequel to *Everyday Hockey Heroes*. Well, when Bob says, "Hey, pal, let's write another book," you are writing another book. Not that it took much convincing.

It is always a privilege to work with someone of Bob's pedigree. As an added bonus, Bob and I got to be teamed up again with our amazing editor, the dynamic Sarah St. Pierre.

This book was written in two very distinct stages. The stage before Covid-19, and the stage during Covid-19. What began as just another book project in September of 2019 took a turn for the surreal as Covid-19 laid waste to thousands of people around the world in March 2020.

Hockey was shut down along with everything else around the world. It is an old saying, but you don't realize how much you love something until it is taken away from you. All of a sudden I couldn't play hockey and I couldn't watch hockey. That was tough. But it also gave the three of us more time to concentrate on this collection of diverse and inspiring stories.

As always, special thanks to my wife, Patricia, and our daughters, Adriana and Cassandra, for being so patient during the writing of the book. (And our dog, Hershey, and cat, KitKat, as well.)

Thanks to my parents for instilling in me that old-school work ethic that helps you get things done.

Thank you to my radio station, 105.9 The Region, for all of their support.

A big stick tap to my devoted agent, Brian Wood, for always being there for me.

I had the honour of speaking with some amazing men and women who hail from all over North America. Special thanks to the following: Jeremy Rupke and howtohockey.com; Danielle Grundy and the Grindstone Award Foundation; Danièle Sauvageau; Rob Facca, the Chicago Blackhawks, and #NoBadDays; Katie Guay; Andrew Cogliano and the Dallas Stars; Joey Hishon and the Owen Sound Attack; Jack Jablonski, the LA Kings, and the Jack Jablonski Foundation; Christian Gaudet and Goody's Ball Hockey; Emilie Castonguay and Momentum Hockey; Alexandra Mandrycky and NHL Seattle; and last, but certainly not least, Dean Petruk and Jeff McLean from Pride Tape.

The following websites were vital in researching this book: TSN.ca, ESPN.com, Sportsnet.ca, SI.com, NBCSports.com, Hockeydb.com, Hockey-Reference.com, Eliteprospects.com, Howtohockey.com, Grindstoneaward.com, Hockeycanada.ca, Olympic.ca, NHL.com, NHL.com/Blackhawks, USAHockey.com, NHL.com/Stars, Attack hockey.com, NHL.com/Kings, Jabby13.com, Goodysballhockey.com, Moncton-Wildcats.com, CHL.ca, Momentumhockey.com, NHL.com/Seattle, and Pridetape.com.

I cannot say enough about our editor, Sarah St. Pierre. She is dedicated, professional, and accommodating, and was driven (in a nice way!) to make sure Bob and I got everything done on time. Thanks, Sarah!

Finally, a few words about Bob McKenzie. Legions of hockey fans around the world know Bob as the highly respected Hockey Insider on TSN. While he is all that, he is also a good man. No matter how swamped he was, Bob was always there to answer any question that I had or talk over any concern. Bob's steady hand and leadership were invaluable throughout. That self-deprecating sense of humour that we see on TV and hear on the radio is not an act. Bob is, and always will be, that humble kid who grew up in a working-class household in Scarborough.

With any book project that I am lucky enough to be a part of, I always learn something along the way. And this book was no different. According to Webster's, a hero is someone who is admired for achievement or someone who shows great courage. In their own way, all the people that I worked with achieved against all odds and displayed great courage to carve out their own niche in the world of hockey and make it a better sport for everyone. I have to say, being forced to sit at home and watch Netflix during the initial stages of Covid-19 is a lot easier than some of the hardships the people in this book went through to be part of the sport that they love.

I only hope that you enjoy reading this book as much as we did.

READ ABOUT MORE
EVERYDAY
HOCKEY HEROES

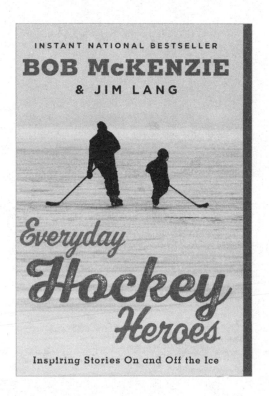

"This book is full of hockey champions who will inspire you and show you the true depth of the people in and around this game."

BRIAN BURKE,
former NHL executive